The Tranquilizing of America

RICHARD HUGHES
AND ROBERT BREWIN

THE
TRANQUILIZING
OF AMERICA

Pill Popping and
the American Way of Life

Harcourt Brace Jovanovich, New York and London

Requests for permission to make copies of any part
of the work should be mailed to:
Permissions, Harcourt Brace Jovanovich, Inc.
757 Third Avenue, New York, N.Y. 10017

Printed in the United States of America

Library of Congress Cataloging in Publication Data

Hughes, Richard, 1937–
The tranquilizing of America.

Includes index.
1. Drug abuse—United States.
I. Brewin, Robert, 1944–   joint author.
II. Title.
[DNLM: 1. Psychotropic drugs—Adverse effects.
2. Drug abuse—Occurrence—United States.
QV77 H894t]
HV5825.H84   362.2′93′0973   79-1830
ISBN 0-15-191072-3

First edition

B C D E

For our wives
Kathy Lucy-Hughes and
Sydney Shaw

Acknowledgments

We would like to thank all of the people who helped in the preparation of this book. Without their guidance, support, and assistance there would not have been a book. To name just a few:

Robert O'Connell of the Public Information Office of HEW in New York, for helping us find our way through the myriad government agencies;

Norma Swenson and Judy Norsigian of the Boston Women's Health Book Collective; Gena Corea, author of *The Hidden Malpractice*; and Doris Haire of the American Institute of Maternal and Child Health, for their insight, knowledge, and referrals to many other women for information on health issues affecting women and childbirth;

Dr. Robert Seidenberg of Syracuse, New York, and Dr. Nicholas Pace, medical director of General Motors Corporation, who helped us from the start and provided many valuable references;

Dr. Joseph A. Pursch, director of the navy's alcohol and drug rehabilitation center in Long Beach, California, for his assistance with the chapter on sedativism;

Vickie Giraldi and all the Feingold mothers, fathers, and children in Smithtown, New York; Dr. Joseph D'Agrosa, the Smithtown pediatrician; and Diane Divoky, co-author of *The Myth of the Hyperactive Child*, for sharing their time and experience with hyperactivity;

Robert Clampitt, an untiring worker in protecting the rights of children and in helping them grow, and the children of *Children's*

Express, for their help in preparation of the chapter on chemical solitary confinement;

the anonymous people at Alcoholics Anonymous world service headquarters for their help on alcoholism and dual addiction; and all the friends of Bill W. who shared their experience, strength, and hope;

Randy Wilson, an FDA information officer now with the Department of Energy, for helping obtain FDA documents and contacts in Washington;

Karst Besteman, acting director of the National Institute on Drug Abuse, and Mary Carol Kelly, NIDA's public information director, for providing statistics, documents, and tips;

Dr. Sidney Wolfe, director of the Health Research Group, for providing most valuable editing;

Frances Pastan of the Freedom of Information Office of the FDA, for expediting many requests;

officials of Hoffmann-La Roche and Ciba-Geigy for their cooperation;

Dr. Robert Butler of the National Institute on Aging, Dr. James Folsom and Kenneth Pommerenck of ICD Rehabilitation Center in New York, author Arthur Freese, and Ron Gaetano and Betsy Todd, who pioneered studies on drug use by the elderly, for their help in the chapter on the elderly;

Elizabeth McKee, our literary agent, who believed in this book from the start and made it possible;

Carol Hill, publisher of the trade division at Harcourt Brace Jovanovich, and Brian Dumaine, our editor, whose enthusiasm helped keep us going and whose skills kept us on track;

and finally our wives, who displayed patience, understanding, and love even when we did not.

Contents

The Tranquilizing of America

What Price Tranquillity?   1

The only thing that Carol, an attractive thirty-year-old stewardess for an international airline, clearly recalls about the night she was wheeled into the emergency room of St. Vincent's Hospital in the Greenwich Village section of New York City is the ambulance attendant asking a doctor—almost casually—"We've got another pillhead here. Are you going to pump her out?"

Carol remembers the next day, a bright, cheery one in July 1975, far better. It marked the end of one way of living and the beginning of a new and better way. She awakened, much to her surprise, not in the bedroom of the apartment she shared with another stewardess, but rather in a hospital bed, clad only in a hospital nightie with various tubes snaking into and around her body.

Carol was highly disoriented and very scared by the situation in which she found herself, but as she tells it:

"That day turned out to be one of the best in my life. The hospital room really shook me. I wondered what I was doing there, but it didn't take me long to find out.

"The room was crowded. My roommate, Joan, was there, along with an older stewardess I only vaguely recognized, a doctor, and a nurse. I looked at Joan and said, 'What happened?' I thought I might have been in an accident or had some dread disease that had caused me to black out and forget where I had been and how I ended up in a hospital.

"My roommate gave it to me straight; she had come home and found me passed out on the floor of the living room with a bottle of Valium next to me on the rug, empty but for one pill. She also told me it was not the first time she had come home and found me passed out on the floor or half in and half out of bed, usually with my clothes still on. But this time, when she tried to wake me, she received no response at all. In the past, Joan said, I had responded when she shook me. This time nothing happened, no response, not even a flicker of the eyes, so she called an ambulance and told them I had probably taken a drug overdose.

"I was shocked. I really could not remember the night before, let alone the other nights Joan talked about. But at the same time I felt a little guilty; I didn't want her to think I was a drug addict or anything like that. So I said, 'Oh, Joan, really you must have become too alarmed for the situation; those pills are really mild; they are just Valium I take when I get too anxious or can't get to sleep.'

"The other people in the room, the doctor, the nurse, and the woman I hardly knew at all—Peg, a supervisor I had seen in the crew room at the airport a few times—just shook their heads.

"Then Peg started talking, about herself and also, I realized, about me. She told me that she was in the hospital to talk to me because she, too, was a prescription junkie and that she understood my problems and wanted to help me.

"I told her I did not know what she was talking about, that I certainly was not a junkie, that if I took pills, they always were on doctors' orders and for my health. Without saying a word, she picked up a bag off the floor next to the bed and started taking out pill bottle after pill bottle. And she counted them, one by one, until she reached twenty-one. Peg then looked at me and said, 'I had twenty-five of these myself. I thought they would help me cope with my fears, my worries, the stress of flying all over the world, and they almost killed me. That's a very high price for a few hours of tranquillity a day, Carol. What price are you willing to pay?'

"And then I broke down and cried. I knew she was right; I knew I was hooked, and had been for several years. She told me to talk about it, to get it all out of my system, that she understood and wanted to help me with the same problem she had.

"So I talked, and I still do talk, about how I became a prescription junkie, which all started so—well, innocently. I remember my first tranquilizer prescription. I had just turned twenty-two and had just come back from my first international flight. I was tired, a little strung-out, and on edge. I had a doctor's appointment that same day, just a routine checkup, and when the checkup was over, the doctor asked me how I was feeling. And I told him I was edgy and a bit tense. I complained about how mixed up, yet still wonderful my life was and how I had a difficult time coping with the time changes, a full plane, and my lack of sleep.

"The doctor listened for about five minutes, nodded in that ever-so-wise way doctors have, reached for a prescription pad, and said, 'Take these, dear, whenever you feel a bit anxious or under stress.' 'These' turned out to be a prescription—refillable—for ten milligrams of Librium. I rushed out of his office to get the prescription filled because I was still a little nervous, walked out of the drugstore, popped a pill, and I tell you—what a wonderful feeling I had about an hour later. I thought that the world around me had turned all warm and mellow. Colors became softer and more diffuse. I felt like I had been wrapped up in a wonderfully protective coating of foam rubber that insulated me from the dirt, the grime, the madness, and the noise of New York.

"That was in 1970. I stayed on the Librium, and only the Librium, for six months. It was terrific stuff for any situation. If I were stuck in a cab on the way to the airport, worried about being late, I'd take a Librium. The randy businessman getting too close, making too many obvious suggestions, I would handle the same way. I'd walk back to the galley, take a pill out of my purse, and all of a sudden he did not seem to be that much of a bother.

"Then I started to use Librium to handle social situations. If I were nervous before a date, I'd take a Librium. Anxious during the date, I'd pop another one. Wondering whether I should go to his place after the date or not, simply take another Librium.

"My mother and father came to New York for a week from California. We have always got on each other's nerves. That week I took Librium about every other hour, and my nerves were not even bothered.

"After six months, though, Librium did not do the job it originally did. I had to take two pills to deal with the lascivious businessman. So it was time for another checkup, and by that time I had heard about Valium from some of my friends. I asked my doctor for a prescription. I told him that Librium did not work too well. He did his nodding bit again and gave me what I wanted, another prescription, this time for Valium.

"The Valium did wonders for me, at least for a while. One pill three or four times a day kept me in that mellow mood I had found and loved with my first Librium. That was at first. Then it became two Valiums, then three, and . . . I don't know how many I was taking at a time or how many times a day I was taking them toward the end. But some days, I swear, if you took a blood sample, it probably would have come out about fifty percent drug and fifty percent blood.

"Things started to go wrong with me about 1972 and got progressively worse. My mind started to develop what I called then gaps but what I know today were blackouts. I attributed it to jet lag. I started waking up with people I did not recall ever meeting, and there I was in bed with them. And by people, I mean people. Sometimes it was a man, sometimes it was a woman, and sometimes it was two or more of each.

"My sexual drive had always been strong, but I started to get a little kinky, a phenomenon that I attributed to the exotic places I traveled to and the exotic people I met. Today I realize it was due to the fact that the pills had slowed down my responses to the point where I was looking for the new, the bizarre, and the offbeat to satisfy myself.

"In 1973 I started having what I used to call accidents. Dropping full dinner trays on the plane. Nerves, I would say, and take another pill. I found myself some mornings with large strange bruises and then would vaguely remember falling down in the street the night before.

"By this time I not only was taking the Valium but had also started taking Tuinal, a barbiturate, to help me to get to sleep. That worked for a while, but then I found myself taking two

Tuinals to get even a few hours' sleep. So, I figured, I might as well take a Valium along with the sleeping pills.

"In 1974 I went to a psychiatrist. According to him, I was depressed, which I found a little bit confusing since my other doctor had told me I was anxious and needed calming down. But the shrink wrote a prescription for another pill, Tofranil, an antidepressant, and after I started taking it, I decided I must have been depressed because this one made me feel very good. My self-esteem, I thought, improved on the Tofranil, and I just added it to my daily regimen.

"At that time I started having painful menstrual cramps. I went out and got some Midol. Then I started having really fierce headaches, so I bought some Excedrin. I took those along with me on the plane and just added them to what by then had turned into the handful of pills I was taking about every three waking hours.

"I got fearful and lonely about the end of 1974. I was scared; I thought people were following me on the street. I became more reclusive, did not want to have friends over to visit me, and spent most of my nights at home just sitting and staring at the television.

"I started getting pills not just from doctors, but from friends, and I even once bought them on the street. I heard you could 'buy anything you want at the corner of Fourteenth and Third.' I had run out of Valium and really needed some. I was shaking. I hopped in a cab, went to that corner, and bought enough Valium (ten pills for ten dollars) to last me until morning. By that time, early 1975, I knew I was hooked. I knew that the pills were not doing the job they were supposed to do. I took more and more of them just to get started in the morning and a whole bunch more to get me to sleep at night. That's how I thought about pills, in bunches.

"My work deteriorated. I was always getting to the airport late or not at all. I became surly and started to neglect my appearance. My social life withered away to almost nothing, just the television set, the pills, and me.

"But then I overdosed, and that started me on the road to recovery. I left St. Vincent's and went to a rehabilitation center on Long Island. I learned I was a chemically dependent person there, that I could not live, let alone live happily, if I continued to pop pills. I learned there that pills are not a shortcut to any kind of real emotional stability, but rather a shortcut to the madhouse or the grave.

"I live pill-free today, and I am happy. How do I do it? It's not easy—I like pills so much I can feel a warm glow in my body when I look at a Dristan ad in the subway—but I have found alternative means to find the calm, the peace, and the quiet I sought in pills. For me it's the help of the loving, kind people I found in Pills Anonymous. These are people who have the same problem I do and who have learned to turn to each other rather than a pill bottle for the medication they need to live a good life."

Billions of Pills a Year

Carol, like many people in the United States, did not intend to become an addict. Rather, she was seeking chemical tranquillity because she could not find real tranquillity. According to Captain Joseph A. Pursch, USN, the man former First Lady Betty Ford credits as the guiding force behind her recovery from pill addiction and alcoholism, many people suffer from the same problem.

Dr. Pursch has treated many pillheads. He calls them sedativists and views them not as weak or immoral, but as sick people suffering from a disease he calls sedativism. Dr. Pursch calls this disease "the nation's number one health problem" and views the drug Carol took, Valium, "not as a treatment for the problems of life but a growing part of the problem itself."

Statistics compiled by the National Institute of Drug Abuse (see chart, page 10) back up Pursch's assertion and show that although Carol's trip to the emergency room may have been a uniquely horrifying experience for her, it is becoming a commonplace event in a nation that consumes tranquilizers at the rate of 120 million prescriptions (an estimated 4 billion doses) a year. The Commerce Department puts the cost of these drugs at a high dollar figure—$2 billion plus a year, or roughly 25 percent of the nation's total drug bill. Statistics compiled by NIDA's

Drug Alert Warning Network (DAWN) graphically illustrate the cost in human suffering.

Take Valium, for example, one of the drugs that brought Carol to St. Vincent's emergency room. According to the DAWN figures for the twelve-month period from May 1976 through April 1977, 54,400 people sought emergency room treatment related to the use, overuse, or abuse of Valium. That's not surprising, considering that in the same time period Valium was the largest-selling prescription drug in the country: 57.1 million prescriptions containing an estimated 3.2 billion pills.

The DAWN report indicated that in the same time period there were at least 900 deaths attributable to Valium use, plus another 200 deaths linked to its chemical predecessor, Librium, and another 100 deaths attributable to Dalmane, a drug having similar chemical properties.

Many of these deaths were caused by overdose—either accidental or intentional—according to NIDA. These drugs, as shown by Carol's case and other cases in this book, also can cause mental and emotional suffering to those who overuse or abuse them.

These three drugs, Valium, Librium, and Dalmane, together accounted for more than half of all the psychotropic (that is, drugs that act on the brain or, medically speaking, on the central nervous system) drugs prescribed in the fiscal year ending April 1977—85 million prescriptions and an estimated 5 billion doses of pills. All these drugs are manufactured by the same company, Hoffmann-La Roche, a Swiss-based multinational giant with U.S. headquarters in Nutley, New Jersey. These three drugs all belong to the same chemical class, the benzodiazepines, and since the first drug of the class, Librium, was introduced in 1960, the benzodiazepines have dominated the growing tranquilizer field.

Roche does not disclose its profits from these drugs, but industry analysts peg its U.S. profits from the benzodiazepines at about $100 million in 1978. Considering that almost half a billion Valium prescriptions have been written since the drug was introduced, it is estimated that Roche profits from Valium run in the billions, not millions, of dollars.

The benzodiazepines are not the only psychotropic drugs that are abused. Darvon, promoted as a simple and relatively safe

United States Psychoactive Drug Usage—1977

Drug Brand Name (Generic Name)	Estimated Rx's *	Estimated Pills	Estimated Deaths for Drug, Singly and in Combination	Estimated Deaths for Drug Used Alone
Minor Tranquilizers †				
Valium (diazepam)	57,084,000	3,204,062,000	900	50
Librium (chlordiazepoxide)	15,340,000	923,642,000	200	10
Equanil ⎫ Miltown ⎬ (meprobamate)	9,751,000	612,509,000	200	30
Atarax (hydroxyzine)	‡			
Serax (oxazepam)	‡			
Other benzodiazepines	‡			
Sedatives-Hypnotics				
Seconal (secobarbital)	1,507,000	67,096,000	800	250
Nembutal (pentobarbital)	1,702,000	81,869,000	600	250
Amytal (amobarbital)	375,000	34,013,000	300	30
Luminal (phenobarbital)	7,910,000	784,409,000	500	110
Dalmane (flurazepam)	12,795,000	401,709,000	100	10
Antidepressants				
Elavil (amitriptyline)	8,838,000	488,229,000	700	180
Placidyl (ethchlorvynol)	1,878,000	59,234,000	300	70
Quaalude (methaqualone)	1,352,000	50,221,000	100	10
Adapin ⎫ Sinequan ⎬ (doxepin)	4,072,000	193,830,000	200	80

* Includes refills.

† Minor tranquilizers are substances usually prescribed for complaints of anxiety, stress, and so on. Major tranquilizers are usually prescribed for use in treatment of severe mental problems. There are exceptions, though; some doctors prescribe the use of these drugs to relieve "morning sickness" in pregnant women.

‡ Figures for Atarax, Serax, and several other benzodiazepine analogs are not compiled by NIDA. NIDA estimates that Valium and Librium account for roughly 90 percent of the tranquilizer market.

United States Psychoactive Drug Usage—1977 (*continued*)

Drug Brand Name (*Generic Name*)	Estimated Rx's	Estimated Pills	Estimated Deaths for Drug, Singly and in Combination	Estimated Deaths for Drug Used Alone
Painkillers				
Darvon (*d-propoxyphene*)	30,000,000	703,409,000	1,100	320
Major Tranquilizers				
Mellaril (*thioridazine*)	7,187,000	473,398,000	200	40
Thorazine (*chlorpromazine*)	4,794,000	270,951,000	200	40

Source: National Institute of Drug Abuse

painkiller when it was introduced in 1957, had become the nation's number one legal drug killer by 1977. According to statistics compiled by NIDA, Darvon had become the third best-selling prescription drug in the United States by 1977 and had also become the second most frequently mentioned drug in coroners' reports to the DAWN network. Darvon, manufactured by Eli Lilly and Company, had sales of 30 million prescriptions, estimated at 703 million doses, that year and was linked with 1,100 deaths. Only the highly illegal heroin was the cause of more drug-related deaths.

Prescription drugs are not the only ones Americans misuse or abuse, nor are they the only ones that cause problems. The open shelves of the nation's pharmacies and supermarkets are filled with some 300,000 nonprescription over-the-counter drugs, many of which contain chemical substances that can cause pain, suffering, and even death if taken in too large a quantity or—as is more likely the case in an age of chemical escape—if mixed with other substances. Even aspirin, thought by many people to be a benign substance, can be and is a death-dealing drug. In 1977, according to the DAWN reports, aspirin was linked to 400 deaths and 17,600 emergency room visits. Acetaminophen, trade named Tylenol, which is widely promoted as a "safer" aspirin substitute, was implicated in approximately 100 deaths and 4,700 emergency room visits in the same time period.

The Easy Way Out

Medicine has a variety of names for these mind-altering drugs: psychotropics, sedatives, hypnotics, or antidepressants. They are sold by prescription and also may be found under a slightly weaker and different formulation in the over-the-counter drug section of almost any supermarket. The Food and Drug Administration classifies them by chemical class, and the manufacturers identify them by registered trade names. Yet the name *tranquilizer* seems the most apt of them all, for its Latin root signifies what so many pill takers seek in the hectic, turbulent, and confusing world of the 1970s—"quiet, calm, and stillness."

The quest for chemical calm is not new to this age or to this country. For centuries men have sought haven from the particular turbulences that have plagued them through chemical shortcuts—just as others have sought peace in monastic contemplation, meditation, or a variety of religious experiences.

Some of these shortcuts span recorded history. Alcohol, that accidental result of the fermentation of fruit, honey, or grains, is no longer accidental and is still the number one selling drug in the world. Opium, the scourge of China, still has adherents in both hemispheres. Cocaine, once used by the Andean Indians to cope with the strain of living at high altitudes, has become the vogue of many an urban cliff dweller. Betel nut, a mild narcotic, continues to stamp its brown hallmark on the teeth of millions of users in the Far East. In the Middle East, khat, the favorite drug of the nonimbibing Moslem, still makes its way from the Ethiopian highlands, where it has been harvested for centuries, to the Arabian Crescent, though today it is more likely to travel in the cargo hold of a jet than on the back of a camel.

The reasons people give for taking tranquilizers today, though, are disturbing, not only for them, but for the nation as a whole. Dr. Pursch says that people are seeking an easy way out, looking for shortcuts on a path of life that has none; in the end not only will they be disappointed but they will end up by diminishing their humanness, the essence that separates man from animals. Dr. Sidney Hook, one of the country's most respected living philosophers, is very disturbed by the wholesale tranquilization of America:

"We have abandoned our old-fashioned values. We have given up our old gods. This nation has turned to tranquilizers almost as a way of life because people want things to come easily, they no longer want to work hard, to suffer any pain, to feel any stress or anxiety. And what is life without some pain in it? It cannot be all joy.

"We are living in an age of false values, false virtues, and false philosophy where the only end seems to be pleasure and gratification.

"People who take these drugs are lazy, they do not want to take the trouble to find their own center. They are afraid to define their existence, they let a pill do it for them. That's living."

Dr. Hook, who looks upon the problems of the world from a traditional philosophical viewpoint, claims that the use of tranquilizers is a "moral problem" and a reflection of the power of another tranquilizing medium of the age: television.

"In part I blame the media—especially television—for this whole problem. People have been taught it is not necessary to experience anymore; just sit down and let television do it for you. People do not even organize their own experiences anymore. They have adopted a passive mode of living; they let all the outside forces, such as television, do it for them."

Father James Royce, SJ, terms the national turn to tranquilizers as a way of life an "example of our moral bankruptcy." Father Royce, a scholarly and thoughtful man, tries to teach his psychology students at Seattle University that "putting value in your life is far better than any of the escapist things that surround us, such as pills or television. They are both tranquilizers, for they are means of entertainment, of escape, not really the way to live a good life.

"We exist today in what many philosophers call an existential vacuum because for many people life has lost its meaning. So, if life has lost its meaning, why not take a pill, why not escape in television?

"What we should be doing is returning to the old values, the old truths, such as faith, work, friendship. Then we would have no need for pills."

Dr. Ingrid Waldron, a biologist at the University of Pennsylvania, says that to understand it, the tranquilizing of America must be examined in the social context. She says that the rise of social stress can be linked to the societal problems that strongly affect the individual's emotional life and sense of well-being, problems such as the Vietnam War, the changing male and female roles, economic uncertainty, and an increasingly competitive climate in school and work. The individual feels overwhelmed by these issues and seeks to obviate their effect on his life by the use of a pill, a methodology encouraged by the individual's peers and doctor. This approach, she says, not only attacks the wrong problem but in the end leaves the individual and the society with an even greater set of problems.

In a paper called "Prescribing Valium and Other Drugs" published in 1977, she argued that while the increasing use of Valium and other mind drugs reflects increasing stress, this method of treatment would "appear to have significant social consequences in itself. Perhaps, significantly, it focuses attention on individual malfunction and the alleviation of the symptoms of distress, rather than on seeking to understand and deal with the problems and their causes. As a consequence, social and economic problems are dealt with in the framework of a medical model for the relief of individual distress, rather than in a social and political context of co-operative efforts for societal change."

This chemical approach to the problems of the United States in the 1970s, in addition to the nation's failure to attack them, results, according to Dr. Waldron, in "new victims who keep the doctor constantly busy with a stream of distressed patients."

These victims, as Dr. Waldron terms them, sooner or later will have to pay a price for taking the chemical shortcut. As she points out, many of the tranquilizers have potent and sometimes deadly side effects.

People are already paying the price. Medical research in the 1970s has turned up alarming evidence that the tranquilizers are not the safe, benign substances that many doctors and many patients believed them to be. Probably the most pernicious effect of this class of drugs is on the mind. Although they do, to use a phrase that many former pillheads used to relish, "take the edge off" anxiety, pain, and stress, they also take the edge off life itself. All these substances act on the one organ that truly differentiates man from animals: the mind. Even the person who uses tranquilizers only in the manner his physician recommends is making a trade-off that should be questioned—these pills not only numb the pain but numb the whole mind.

The Effects of Tranquilizers

Much of the medical research done on the most widely prescribed class of tranquilizers, the benzodiazepines, has focused on the positive effects of the drugs: their proved ability to relax, to enable a person to cope with difficult and often stressful situations and to work and live through conditions that would otherwise be emotionally debilitating. In the late 1970s, though, researchers started to examine what adverse effects these drugs could have on the seat of the emotions, the mind. The results of this initial research should serve as a sobering warning to anyone considering taking even small doses of the benzodiazepines for a short period of time.

In a paper published in *Research Communications in Psychology, Psychiatry and Behavior* in 1976, Dr. Louis Gottschalk warned: "We have enough data here to indicate that certain of the benzodiazepines are capable, *after a single dose* [emphasis added], of significantly disrupting certain kinds of cognitive and/ or intellectual functions. Furthermore, this phenomenon outlasts the antianxiety effect of these drugs."

In a follow-up paper published in *Current Therapeutic Research* in February 1977, Dr. Gottschalk, who is a professor of psychiatry at the University of California—Irvine, advanced his thesis even further. Noting that his earlier studies had convinced him that the benzodiazepines had an amnesic effect, Dr. Gottschalk said:

"The implications of [my] present findings, however, in combination with previous findings of . . . amnesic effects with the benzodiazepines should not be taken lightly or ignored, for at the present time the medical or legal profession does not regard the taking of a single daily dose of these drugs as interfering with mental competency or responsibility of an individual. This idea should be questioned and examined further."

Carol, the stewardess who started her trip down the road to chemical tranquillity with one Librium and woke up in a hospital bed five years later, can relate very well to Dr. Gottschalk's research.

"I think the worst part of the whole pill experience was what it did to my mind. I had always been bright, had considered myself an intelligent, thinking person. But the last year or so I was on pills my mind literally started to go. I could not read a book all the way through. I did not have the interest, nor could I really comprehend what I was reading. I lost interest in all the things my mind—you know, the part of me that made Carol different from all those other people—really liked. I stopped going to the ballet; I switched from classical to rock, the louder the better. I believe my mind had rotted away under the influence of all those pills.

"My concentration did not snap back overnight. It has come back, but very slowly. It took me about six months before I could even concentrate on a magazine, and it took me another six months off pills before I could even read a book."

Roche Laboratories admits that Valium does have an effect on the thinking process but argues this effect is less damaging than the often debilitating effects of high levels of anxiety, stress, or strain on cognition. In an interview, Dr. Bruce Medd, Roche's medical director, asserted: "Anxiety, stress, and fear definitely interfere with the ability of people to think. The medication enables them to reduce the stress in their lives, freeing people to use their minds constructively. There is a trade-off between the reduction of stress and the effect the drug has on the thinking process, but I believe it is a valid trade-off."

But research conducted by Dr. David Knott of the University of Tennessee in Memphis raises serious questions about how valid the trade-off really is. Dr. Knott is in the midst of a long-range research project on the effects the benzodiazepines have on the brain, and he believes that the drugs cause damage to the mind.

"I still have some more work to do," Dr. Knott said, "but so far I am very convinced that Valium, Librium, and other drugs of that class cause damage to the brain. I have seen damage to the cerebral cortex that I believe is due to the use of these drugs, and I am beginning to wonder if the damage is permanent."

Dr. Knott also believes that the benzodiazepines attack the brain in another way. Instead of calming people down, they produce anger, rage, and hostility, not exactly what a person expects when he takes a pill to calm down. The medical profession refers to this as a "paradoxical rage reaction," but Dr. Knott is beginning to wonder if such a reaction is not a true one: "I am seeing so much of this, I wonder if it's not a true reaction. I think people should be aware that there are many cases of this kind of reaction being reported."

Dr. Medd of Roche dismisses the reports of rage reactions as few and scattered: "If such a thing was going on, we would certainly know about it and be concerned. There also would be more than a few papers in the medical literature dealing with the subject of rage reactions." Despite Dr. Medd's claim, there are more than a few papers in the literature. A computer search of the data bank which the National Institute of Mental Health maintains on drugs produced twenty-five reports and papers on rage reactions to the benzodiazepines.

Such reactions are commonly reported by the people who may have paid one of the higher prices for chemical tranquillity, the alcoholics who in their quest to control or curb their disease became hooked on yet another drug. Paul, a network news producer in New York, is one alcoholic who became hooked on pills and remembers his rages vividly: "I used to be quite mellow when I drank. But then I started on the Valium—it was better than a morning drink because it did not smell on my breath and worked very quickly—and I became more and more hostile. Toward the end I would fly into a rage without the slightest provocation."

Tranquilizers are prescribed for many alcoholics by doctors who do not take the time and effort to discover that the symptoms of anxiety and stress described by an alcoholic patient are actually the result of their drinking. For a time some doctors also prescribed tranquilizers for alcoholics because the drug companies promoted them as a "cure," a cure that in reality only ended up by dually addicting many people.

Adults are not the only ones to pay a stiff price for the tranquilizing of America. Some drugs were devised to treat not adults having a difficult time with a marriage, a job, or just the hassle of commuting, but children. These drugs were actively promoted not only to doctors but also to educators, PTAs, and the media.

Brian Cummings is one of those children. Brian's mother, Carol Cummings, thought that her son was a normal, active, eager, happy little boy. But when he started school, she was told something different. Carol Cummings was told her son was not a typically active young boy; rather, he was "learning disabled" and needed to take a drug called Ritalin to calm down his hyperactivity in order to learn.

Brian was only one of many schoolchildren in the late 1960s diagnosed as having a minimal brain dysfunction (MBD) and put on drugs; in fact, some school systems made drug treatment mandatory for continued enrollment. Ciba-Geigy, the manufacturer of the drug used to treat MBD, held "educational seminars" for educators, telling them, in essence, "We have a cure, a solution for the children who disrupt your classrooms. Put them on Ritalin." Consequently millions of children who, in an earlier, less chemically oriented age, would have been merely classified as rambunctious or mischievous were in the pill-popping society of the United States diagnosed as "sick" and treated with a powerful psychoactive drug.

Children even younger than Brian Cummings have paid a steep price as the United States becomes more and more of a drugged society. Douglas Cohen started life bearing the marks of his exposure in the womb to one of the routinely prescribed psychoactive drugs. Douglas's mother, Laura, had been taking an antidepressant, Tofranil, also manufactured by Ciba-Geigy, when he was conceived. She asked her doctors, a psychiatrist and an obstetrician, if she should discontinue the drug if she was pregnant. They both told her not to worry. But Laura Cohen did worry and six weeks into her pregnancy stopped taking the medication.

But for Douglas it was too late. The first six weeks of human embryonic development are vitally important. In the six weeks

Laura Cohen took the drug the damage to her child's organs had been done. He was born with a second hole in his penis and a urinary tract infection.

Laura blames her doctors for the malformation Douglas was born with, and she blames a commonplace medical practice in the 1970s: extreme reliance on medications.

"Today he is finally all right, after three operations. But that's not the point. He would have been born all right if it had not been the desire of doctors to keep me on medications, even when I asked them questions."

Laura Cohen's child is not the only one to bear the scars of the drugs his mother took. Several studies in the 1970s have raised serious questions about the adverse effects on the fetus of the most popular tranquilizers of the past quarter-century, including Miltown, Valium, and Librium. Despite the strong evidence linking these drugs with birth defects, the Food and Drug Administration was slow in warning against their use in pregnancy.

Many of the drugs routinely taken for problems of stress or strain are also used in another field that affects our most precious national asset, the health and well-being of future generations. Many of the drugs used to relieve the pains of living, such as Demerol, are also used in childbirth to relieve the pain of that experience. Medicated childbirth has been common since 1847, and until very recently it has never been questioned. In the late 1960s, though, several researchers started examining the effect these drugs had on the fetus and on the baby's development.

The elderly are not immune either. People are living longer, but as the tranquilizing of America spreads, they may not be living more happily. Many elderly people spend their last years—years that should be filled with the golden glow of contemplating life past and life present in leisure—routinely dosed daily on the most powerful of the tranquilizers, the phenothiazines. These drugs are given to these senior citizens, not to calm their minds or nerves, but rather to make them more malleable and tractable patients.

These episodes are not unique. They are but part of a growing catalog of horror stories that result from more and more Americans seeking answers to their emotional and medical problems in a pill capsule.

The Unbreakable Circle of Drug Dispensing

It would be easy to lay the blame on the drug companies or the doctors alone. But the fault does not lie entirely with them: the fault lies also with people who seek an easy way out, individuals who trust too much in a man in a white coat and who do not ask pertinent questions.

Partly, the misuse of tranquilizers is the result of the age we live in, an age in which science is a god and can do no wrong. It is the result of people's seeking to live a life without pain, whether it is on the golf course, in the office, the home, or the delivery room. It is the result of living in an era in which drugs have wiped out disease, and in which people now look to drugs to wipe out the other problems of the world.

The number of mind-altering drugs ingested in this country is also the result of a health care system that is tightly organized around what might be called an unbreakable drug-dispensing circle. This circle consists of a profit-motivated drug manufacturer that must spend heavily to develop new drugs and spend equally heavily to promote them; an often harried physician who has read drug ads and believes them; and a patient who is seeking and has come to believe it is his right to receive instant relief for whatever problem, mental or physical, plagues him. All play equal roles in this circle, and until the circle is broken, the use of psychoactive drugs—and the problems associated with them—will continue to grow.

Promotion of these drugs is necessary because development costs are high. A drug company can spend years researching hundreds of drugs; some of the research leads nowhere, and some pays off in sales potential.

Drugs that have high sales potential have to pick up the freight for all the costs. The drugs today that have the greatest potential are the tranquilizers and psychoactives. It is not surprising that once a company develops a patentable new tranquilizer (and a patent on a drug is very important because it gives the drug company exclusive rights to manufacture, and therefore profit from, a drug during the seventeen-year life of the patent), it promotes that drug with all the razzmatazz that

Madison Avenue would muster to launch a new cigarette or laundry detergent.

And drug promotion is a very expensive proposition. Although the pharmaceutical companies guard the dollar value of their advertising budgets zealously, it is estimated that $1.5 billion a year is spent promoting prescription drugs. This large sum of money does not help promote a consumer product that requires a lot of expensive television time or ads in a score of consumer magazines; rather, all is spent to reach a somewhat limited audience of doctors, hospital pharmacists, and nurses through the pages of medical magazines, professional journals, and detail men, the twentieth-century answer to the patent-medicine men who once roamed this country with horse and wagon, huckstering magic elixirs to naive audiences.

An example of this kind of selling and the success drug companies have is the campaign for Darvon, the painkiller that now tops the nation's legal drug death list. Lilly introduced Darvon in 1957 with much fanfare, promoting it via magazine advertisements and detail men as a potent painkiller without the potential for abuse and addiction shown by earlier painkillers, such as codeine. The company's ads and the detail men constantly emphasized that Darvon was a nonnarcotic and therefore nonaddicting analgesic.

But what Lilly said about Darvon in its promotional material did not fit the facts that many researchers, concerned about the increase in use of Darvon and the deaths attributable to it, had discovered. In the eyes of many medical researchers, Darvon was addictive and should have been classified as a narcotic. It has a chemical structure similar to methadone, and it did cause addiction. By 1976 the Justice Department had determined that despite what Lilly claimed, Darvon is a narcotic. The Justice Department found the drug was also being widely abused—and was sold on the streets for anywhere from 25 cents to $1.50 a capsule. So severe were the problems associated with wide-scale use of Darvon (the sales of which brought Lilly $140 million in revenues in 1977) that the Health Research Group petitioned HEW Secretary Joseph Califano to have Darvon banned as an "immediate hazard" in late 1978. The Nader-backed group also petitioned Attorney General Griffin Bell to reclassify Darvon as an extremely restricted drug. In late January 1979 the Senate Monopoly and Anticompetitive Activities Subcommittee held hearings on the drug. Meanwhile, a Lilly spokesman declared, "The pending government review of Darvon will reveal that no serious injuries or fatalities have ever resulted from the proper use of the product." With the review moving at a slow pace, Lilly continued to sell and promote this drug.

The doctor, particularly the family physician, the general practitioner, or the obstetrician/gynecologist, appreciates the help the drug companies give him. These so-called primary care physicians treat the majority of patients, and it is they, not the psychiatrists, who dispense the bulk of tranquilizers. In fact, psychiatrists account for only 25 percent of the tranquilizer prescriptions written in any given year.

The reason for this is that most Americans take not only their physical problems but also their mental problems to these primary care physicians. Many of the minor complaints a patient has today—insomnia, lower back pain, or anxiety—either are psychic in origin or can best be treated by treating that center of all bodily pain, the brain.

Also, many diseases, by their nature, are stress-producing. So quite often a patient with a legitimate physical complaint will often end up receiving a tranquilizer to treat whatever secondary minor mental problems go along with it.

The doctor can't begin to cope with keeping track of even a small number of drugs, so he often uses the advice of a detail man or an advertisement when it comes time to prescribe one or more drugs. And in the case of the tranquilizers, that advice may be the sales pitches in a Valium ad rather than any sound medical reasons.

Doctors have also learned that the easiest, not to mention often the quickest, way to treat is to prescribe. Many complaints that patients have today are for minor aches and pains that are nonspecific. Getting to the root of these problems could take thirty minutes of the doctor's time while the waiting room fills up with more patients. Writing a prescription takes only thirty seconds; a tranquilizer probably does little harm, makes the patient feel better, and gets the doctor off the hook.

The patient, for his part in the drug-dispensing circle, is relieved to get a prescription, even more relieved if it is for a tranquilizer. It tells him that the problem has been explained, been defined, analyzed, and treated. Relief is in the form of Valium, Librium, or Miltown.

The patient often puts subtle or not so subtle pressures on the doctor to get a tranquilizer prescription. These pressures include a list of complaints guaranteed to produce the right kind of reaction from the doctor, a prescription. Other patients just flat out ask their doctors for a Librium or a Valium Rx. They say they have heard that a friend or a relative has had the same problems they have, received a tranquilizer prescription, and now feels much better. The doctor, faced with this—and a limited amount of time—often gives in to his patient's demands.

Some patients are true addicts or "doctor shoppers." They visit one doctor after another, feign a set of symptoms that they know will usually secure a prescription for Valium, and are on their way to yet another doctor.

The unlimited number of doctors available to these prescription junkies, the laxness with which tranquilizers are dispensed, and the lack of a system of controls make legal, as opposed to illegal, drug addiction easy. A recent survey of tranquilizer prescriptions at a large hospital in New York turned up the fact that in a three-month period, twelve outpatients accounted for more than 10,000 doses of various kinds of tranquilizers handed out by the pharmacy. Similarly, at the Hazelden Institute, a treatment facility for prescription junkies, searches of incoming patients' luggage reveal that some of these people have Rx's from ten or more doctors. These are not isolated situations. Multiply these by the number of hospitals, doctors, and pharmacies in the country, and a true picture of the tranquilizer epidemic begins to emerge.

The lack of controls falls squarely in the lap of the one group that could begin to break the circle of drug dispensing: the regulators. The regulatory agencies, however, are ensnarled in their own red tape, understaffed, overworked, slow to stamp out drug problems once they occur, and even slower to anticipate the problems.

The consumer takes a tranquilizer with full faith that his prescription has been monitored by a regulatory system geared to his protection, health, and safety. This is true only to a certain extent. The system is actually one of poor governmental checks on an industry that has learned, and learned well, to avoid governmental influence over it. A perfect case in point is Darvon—the Justice Department flatly states that the drug is addictive, but the drug company not only ignores Justice but claims a review by the FDA will show that the drug is safe!

One official of the FDA believes something more should be done to classify the sale of the most ubiquitous tranquilizer of the age, Valium. That official is Dr. Edward Tocus, a twenty-year veteran on the staff of the FDA. He is currently serving as chief of the Drug Abuse Staff, Division of Neuropharmacological Products, Bureau of Drugs. Dr. Tocus is deeply troubled by the widespread abuse of Valium, not only about the effect it has on the individual who becomes "hooked" on the drug, but also about its societal impact.

In an interview he stated: "I am really worried about Valium. I am worried about the children my wife teaches and the kind of world they are going to grow up in. I am worried about kids who might grow up learning that 'coping' and 'Valium' are interchangeable.

"I am going to give you my unbiased but heartfelt opinion about this drug. I think the way Valium is being used almost constitutes an epidemic. We are rapidly approaching with this drug what I consider to be a large-scale national public health problem.

"We are developing a population dependent on this drug equal to the number of alcoholics in this country.

"We are in a situation now where we see at least as many people being hurt by this drug as are being helped by it. We have a lot of people being harmed by this drug, and something has to be done about it."

Dr. Tocus does not believe that further restrictions on the sale of Valium will stop the wholesale drugging of America. He and other health professionals believe that the answer to the problem lies with each and every individual, who sooner or later must come to the conclusion that life without recourse to drugs is far better than life with drugs. Government, he believes, can lead the way, but it is up to the individual to follow.

Dr. Tocus believes that man must learn to "cope" with his own resources and seek the help of his fellow man. If not, then maybe the world Orwell predicted for 1984 will come to be, with drugs ruling men, rather than men ruling their own lives.

The Tranquilizing of America is a guide to the chemicals that pervade today's life. It offers—for the interested—lessons learned by those who have suffered from the wholesale drugging of America. This book looks at the hazards of the tranquilizer age and examines the long-term effects of drugs, not only on the individual, but on the nation as well. We hope it will help those with drug problems to seek the kind of aid that Dr. Tocus recommends. We also believe it will serve as an aid to people who may unwittingly be starting down the road to chemical escape.

Our intention is to make people aware of the need for a pill-free life in what is now a pill-popping world.

Sedativism: The New Health Crisis | 2

For the first time in its history, in 1977, Alcoholics Anonymous surveyed its 1 million members to find out about their drug problems. AA was founded in Akron, Ohio, by two alcoholics, one a doctor and the other a stockbroker, to help each other. Historically, AA had limited its primary mission to helping people recover from alcoholism. However, the growing number of people coming into the self-help program in the 1970s who had problems with pills as well as booze led the fellowship's general services office to conduct the unprecedented survey.

The results are startling, not only in terms of the numbers but also regarding the implications for society. The survey confirmed what many AA members had been observing since the late 1960s: a very high percentage of persons coming into the fellowship were hooked on both alcohol and one or more psychoactive prescription drugs. Since the middle 1950s, alcoholics in AA have told of difficulties with Miltown, the first popular mass tranquilizer, but there were relatively few of those dually addicted persons compared to the numbers in the seventies who recounted their addiction to the newer tranquilizers, Librium and Valium.

While only 18 percent of all AA members responding to the survey reported drug addiction in addition to alcoholism, the numbers of people under thirty and the numbers of women of all ages were substantial. Women, who are prescribed more tranquilizers more often than men, reported a far larger prescription drug habit than men, with 29 percent of all women saying they were addicted to more than one drug. Young women showed the strongest dual addiction pattern, with 55 percent of all women under the age of thirty reporting they had been addicted to prescription tranquilizers in addition to alcohol.

If these figures hold true for even a small segment of the population outside AA, the United States has a severe and largely hidden national health problem. With roughly 1 million members, AA constitutes a small membership relative to the number of alcoholics in the nation. The generally accepted estimate is that there are 10 million alcoholics in the United States with only about 10 percent, or 1 million, in recovery programs. HEW estimates that an additional 8 to 20 million Americans have moderate to severe drinking problems but have not yet crossed the line into alcoholism. This means that up to 30 million Americans are susceptible to dual or poly addiction, or what some addiction experts now call sedativism. With the tranquilizer era barely twenty-five years old, it is too early to come up with any scientifically valid statistics on how many people suffer from sedativism, but it clearly is a growing health problem, and the AA survey is a tip-off to its wide dimensions. If one applies the AA percentages to a conservative estimate of 20 million Americans who either are alcoholic or have a severe drinking problem, the dual addiction population exceeds 3 million, and a large proportion would be young people, particularly women between the ages of twenty-five and thirty-five. As we shall show later in this chapter, nearly half of all the people entering rehabilitation centers today are addicted to alcohol plus Valium or one of the other common tranquilizers.

The problem of dual addiction in the United States became front-page news in 1978, when former First Lady Betty Ford made a public admission of her addictions. At the time she was a patient at the Alcohol Rehabilitation Center of the Long Beach, California, Naval Hospital, which she agreed to enter after a dramatic confrontation with her family about her drinking and pill taking. In a late addition to her autobiography, *The Times of My Life*, Mrs. Ford told how she unwittingly drifted from social drinking to alcoholic drinking and how she grew dependent on the painkillers and tranquilizers she was taking on the advice of her doctors for a pinched nerve and arthritis. The always forthright Mrs. Ford came forward with her personal and agonizing story to help the millions of "chemically addicted people like me, women who don't recognize they have a problem . . . but the pillbox in their purse is filled with tranquilizers and the ice tray in their hands or the coffee at their desks is laced with vodka just to keep them going."

Mrs. Ford suffered from what her doctor, Captain Joseph A. Pursch, director of the Long Beach rehabilitation center, and Dr. Stanley Gitlow, a New York physician, call sedativism. With alcohol so widely used and with tranquilizers so readily available and acceptable as a means of coping, sedativism has become "the nation's number one health problem," says Pursch. "The most prescribed sedative is Valium, and it might as well be termed solid alcohol because the brain can't tell the difference between Valium and alcohol. Sadly, but also true, many doctors treat alcoholism as a Valium deficiency. Valium is not a treatment for the problems of life. In fact, it may become part of the problem."

The problems associated with alcohol are well known. It is involved in roughly half the annual count of 47,000 traffic deaths. The National Institute on Alcohol Abuse estimates that excessive drinking on and off the job costs American industry at least $15 billion a year. Alcoholism ranks behind cancer and heart disease as the number three disease killer. Excessive use can kill or cripple the drinker and in the process wrench apart families. It causes countless street fights, marital quarrels, and homicides.

But when alcohol is mixed with drugs, especially tranquilizers, the toll is far worse. With 100 million drinkers of alcohol in the United States and 120 million or more tranquilizer prescriptions written each year, the combination constitutes society's worst addiction problem. When Dr. Gitlow began practicing about twenty-five years ago, only about one-third of his alcoholic patients were users of prescription sedatives. Now the percentage is up to 50 percent, and it is growing, particularly among women. Treatment centers throughout the nation say that 50 to 70 percent of their patients are hooked on alcohol plus one or more prescription drugs. Karst Besteman, acting director of the National Institute on Drug Abuse, says poly addiction is the major topic of concern expressed by state and local officials working in the drug abuse field.

One of these dually addicted persons is Ann, who "survived horrors not even Dante could have dreamed up" during twenty years of drinking, drugs, hospitalizations, suicide attempts, and finally commitment for life to a state mental institution in New York. A warm and kind woman, Ann, at the age of forty-eight, was slowly putting her life back together, living and coping without chemicals for the first time in two decades. During her drinking and drug-taking years, she had been diagnosed as anxious, depressed, repressed, manic, neurotic, and psychotic. With each new diagnosis came a new pill, and with each new pill came a new set of symptoms. With each new set of symptoms, Ann found a new doctor, until she "finally found a doctor who really knew what the problem was. I was none of the above. I was just a plain, run-of-the-mill Irish drunk. Whew, I was glad to hear that. And hearing that, I gradually started to recover—from all the doctors and all the pills and all the alcohol. Today I know that I am an alcoholic or, as Dr. Gitlow says, a sedativist. The solution for me is simple: life without chemicals, without liquor, and everything will be all right. But I paid a price for this knowledge, and I think the doctors are partly to blame for that." Now a member of both Alcoholics Anonymous and Pills Anonymous, she told how it began:

"I guess I was an alcoholic the day I received my first tranquilizer prescription, somewhere back in the fifties. I still have a hard time sorting out the years. When I go back through my very clouded memory, I think, 'That was the year I was on Miltown, and that was the year they tried me on Elavil.' Hell of a way to remember your life, isn't it? Anyway, that first prescription was for Miltown. I was very anxious and nervous—I guess anyone who started the day with a glass of white wine would be nervous—and went to my gynecologist and told him I had a terrible case of nerves. He nodded knowingly, wrote out the prescription, and I was on my way. I did not tell him I had a drinking problem, and he did not bother to ask.

"I liked the Miltown, and I liked it even better when I had a drink or two or three or even more. Before I knew it, the delivery men from the pharmacy and the liquor store were making more trips to my house than any place in town. This is a long story, but it is all the same. More booze, more pills. You know how I finally ended up? In the nut ward, zonked out of my mind on Thorazine because they said I was violent. Who wouldn't be violent with all the chemicals I put into my body on doctors' orders over a twenty-year period? I lost a lot along the way: my self-respect, my looks, almost my mind, not to mention the house in Greenwich—there are a lot of women like me in suburbia— the Ivy League husband, and the kids. I haven't seen the children for three years because somewhere along the line my husband had me declared mentally incompetent. He got custody. I fought it, and the judge decided it would be bad for the kids—I have two, a girl, ten, and a boy, fourteen—to be exposed to me. I am not a 'stable influence,' the judge said.

"And that's the real tragedy of this. Today, with both Pills Anonymous and Alcoholics Anonymous in my life, I have a lot to offer those kids. But few people understand what I've been through. They all think I am crazy. Well, if I am crazy, then what about the doctors and the drug companies? I think they should shoulder some of the blame, too."

Today Ann has hope, "and that's something you don't find in a pill or in a doctor's office. It's something you find in your soul and in other people. I have hope and faith that my suffering has not been for nothing. If nothing else, my story can help other people see what is happening to them and get off the merry-go-round before it is too late."

Once Ann understood she was an alcoholic or a sedativist and should not take mood-altering drugs of any kind, whether in pill or in liquid form, she was able to find help to break the vicious cycle of pills and booze and start on the road to recovery and a new life free of chemical addiction. She accepts the responsibility for her own sickness but thinks the medical profession and the drug industry must, as she says, "shoulder some of the blame."

Dr. Pursch, the physician who treated Senator Herman Talmadge and Billy Carter for alcoholism in addition to Mrs. Ford, agrees. Out of ignorance or indifference, many doctors find it easier to prescribe psychoactive drugs to a patient with emotional problems without bothering even to inquire about a patient's drinking habits. Often doctors think they can treat alcoholism with sedatives. This is the kind of treatment that leads to dual addiction, because although doctors may think drugs are the solution, they fail to recognize that often they can become part of the problem, aggravating, distorting, and hiding it. Also, a high percentage of alcoholics—some of whom are aware of their drinking problem and try to hide it, and some of whom are not able to recognize it—visit their doctors for tranquilizer prescriptions because their complaints mirror the symptoms of anxiety or stress for which tranquilizers are promoted. These complaints—nervousness, anxiety, insomnia, and so on—sound to some doctors like a classic case of anxiety when they are, in fact, a reflection of the early stages of alcoholism. Doctors are too quick to reach for the prescription pad when they hear such complaints. Instead, they should conduct a more thorough physical examination and a more probing interview of the patient. Doctors complain, however, that most patients with drinking problems rarely tell the truth about their drinking habits.

Doctors like Pursch and Dr. David Knott, director of the Alcohol Rehabilitation Center for the city of Memphis and a member of the board of the National Council on Alcoholism, contend that any doctor can spot the signs of alcoholism if he takes the time to learn about the disease and does a sufficient patient examination and interview.

"There are ways a good doctor can tell if he has a patient who is merely anxious or who has been abusing alcohol," says Knott. "Any doctor can detect alcoholism—even in its early stages—by running the right kind of blood chemistry tests, by doing a good physical and finding out what the patient's real problem is. A conscientious doctor will do this because the last thing he wants to do is cross-addict anyone."

But many people do become cross-addicted at the hands of their doctors. According to Dick Bast of the National Clearinghouse for Alcohol Information, "only five percent of the doctors in this country conduct a thorough questioning and examining of their patients." Bast doubts that "very many even bother to explain to their patients that they should not mix alcohol and tranquilizers."

Dr. Pursch, who has been director of the navy's Alcohol Rehabilitation Center since 1968, is trying to do something about the medical profession's ignorance of alcoholism and pill addiction. He feels so strongly about the use of Valium and Librium that he banned their use on an outpatient basis at Long Beach Naval Hospital in 1973. He believes that "if you are sick enough to want or need Valium or Librium, you're sick enough to be in the hospital."

Pursch, a psychiatrist, believes that any doctor who gives anxious patients, especially alcoholic ones, Valium, Librium, or any other tranquilizer "really is not treating them. If I give you a pill, I am really not treating your problem. You will go away, but your problems will not. A concerned physician should let his patient talk through his crises, and if he cannot help enough, he should refer the patient to someone who can help him solve his problem—a psychiatrist or, in the case of an alcoholic, someone who is in Alcoholics Anonymous."

Unfortunately many doctors do not take this approach because they suffer from what Pursch calls the 4–2–1 syndrome. "In four years of medical school, we spend two hours studying America's number one health problem, alcoholism or sedative-hypnotic drug dependency." He is convinced that until doctors learn to treat alcoholism and sedativism properly and are so educated, the problem will get worse. He says fifteen out of twenty physicians in the United States are unable to deal with the problems of alcoholism, sedativism, or dual addiction because they:

1. lack useful training or education in alcoholism or drug addiction;
2. may have unresolved alcoholism or pill problems themselves or in their own families;
3. may be treating their own alcoholism through self-administration of psychoactive drugs;
4. are continually preoccupied with significant negative experiences with alcoholic patients in their own backgrounds;
5. often have rigid personalities with little or no ability to deal with patients on an emotional or feeling level; and
6. fear that if they were outspoken about alcoholism, they would lose some patients, lose some personal and social friends; colleagues would frown on forthrightness, or their career advancement might be impaired.

Dr. Pursch's answer to these problems is a course he runs at Long Beach for physicians. It is a training program that could serve as a model for a nationwide program for educating the fifteen out of every twenty doctors Pursch says are unable to deal with alcoholism or sedativism. The Long Beach program involves navy doctors and includes some measures that many find humiliating at first. They include humanizing the doctor by taking away all the symbols of his authority when he checks into the program. This means taking away his white coat, stethoscope, beeper, doctor name tags, and even the title of doctor itself. The doctor trainees are required to associate with the patients—all of whom are recovering alcoholics or dually addicted persons—on a first-name basis. Pursch thinks this initial demystifying plays an important role in the educational process that follows, and he takes some glee in it. "Can you imagine how naked a doctor feels when you take away his beeper?"

Stripping the doctor of his authoritative symbols and his electronic gadgetry and forcing a first-name familiarity between doctor and patient allow the doctor trainees to get to know patients as something more than patients, maybe for the first time in their lives. The doctors are forced, Pursch says, to deal with the patients as real people, not just another patient sitting across a desk who needs a prescription.

The trainees are required to abstain from the use of alcohol and drugs while taking the course. This has produced another side benefit. Pursch says 9 percent of the doctors who come for training end up staying for treatment. This is not a surprising statistic either, as it just about corresponds to the national average of alcoholics in the population.

The trainees are intimately involved in the recovery program for the patients. They attend group therapy sessions. They listen to the patients' stories of the agony they suffered while drinking and taking pills. They hear patients tell how they conned their doctors into giving them more pills. They hear patients tell how doctors were too quick to reach for the prescription pad and were too busy to listen. The trainees also attend AA meetings and see firsthand that it is a therapy that works far better than any nostrum they can pull out of their medicine bags.

The end result of this training, as simple as it sounds, is that doctors develop a new respect for alcoholism or sedativism as a disease, not as a sign of human weakness or moral decay. These navy doctors also gain a degree of optimism they never had before about diagnosing and treating alcoholism and pill addiction. They go away with new respect for the growing number of paraprofessionals, many of whom are recovering alcoholics or dually addicted persons, who treat other addicted persons far more successfully than doctors can.

As Pursch noted, one reason some physicians do not like to confront alcoholism in their patients is that *they* are alcoholics or drug addicts. In fact, physicians as a class have the highest rates of alcoholism and drug addiction in the United States. Dr. Morris Chafetz, director of the National Institute of Alcoholism, estimates that 18 percent of the nation's doctors are alcoholics. This compares to a national rate of alcoholism of about 10 percent. The AMA more conservatively estimates the number of alcoholic doctors at 10 percent.

Dr. John A. Renner, director of the Boston Drug Treatment Program, described the typical drug-abusing doctor in a 1978 article in the *Boston Herald-American*: "He may very well be white, middle-class professional, in his mid-30's, established, with a practice and a family. He usually is under a lot of stress with a heavy workload, financial demands and pressures from his family. And he starts looking for relief—in drugs.

"He may begin with Demerol and eventually get to the stage of injecting narcotics intravenously. He continues until he can no longer function without it." Drug-addicted doctors are hard to spot because their "social life appears normal. They get started on drugs because of pressure or psychological problems. And, most difficult of all, they have easy access to drugs."

Alcoholic doctors compound their problem by self-prescribing the same mood-changing drugs they too often prescribe for their alcoholic patients, thus setting up a cross-addiction.

"Many alcoholics substitute several drugs for alcohol, some of which do not necessarily show a pharmacological cross-tolerance with alcohol," wrote Dr. Le Clair Bissell, director of the Smithers Alcoholism Treatment Center in New York City, and Dr. Al J. Mooney, director of the detoxification unit of the Jefferson Alcoholism and Drug Abuse Center in Louisville, Kentucky, in an article in the medical journal *Resident & Staff Physician.* "Most of the time, sedative-hypnotic drugs sold as soporifics or as 'minor' tranquilizers are used this way. The alcoholic physician will also frequently take mood-changing drugs, such as amphetamines, Darvon or Talwin." Because the alcoholic doctor is able to make these substitutions rather freely, he "may present a rather convincing and technically accurate argument that he is not drinking excessively or perhaps even at all."

Dr. Robert Jones, a Philadelphia psychiatrist, says other doctors "have a tendency to protect their medical colleagues from labels which might be considered damaging—such as schizophrenia, alcoholism, or drug addiction. Instead, treating physicians label them with 'depression.' Thus, the incidence of depression among these doctors may be erroneously high and may cover other disorders."

Alcoholic and dually addicted doctors often have difficulty seeking help and getting into recovery programs because they have been conditioned to treat ailments with pills and have difficulty accepting nonmedical solutions. Drs. Bissell and Mooney urge drug-dependent doctors to seek help from "those experienced and effective in dealing with this problem rather than from colleagues who may know little or nothing about it."

The most "direct step toward treatment might be joining AA," they advise. Probably the most effective group working to educate doctors about the perils of alcoholism and dual addiction and the best therapy for treatment is the International Doctors in AA, an organization of some 1,000 recovering alcoholic and dually addicted physicians and dentists.

In Memphis, Dr. Knott is trying to change the chemically oriented treatment attitudes of the medical profession by carrying his message to the doctors of tomorrow, the medical students and interns. He believes that the new crops of doctors are more aware of the problems and that things will change. However, he feels that drug companies must assume more responsibility for the nation's dual addiction problem. "The way this drug [Valium] has been advertised has made doctors aware of its uses and very unaware of its problems. Roche created the idea—and doctors bought it—that you can have better living through chemistry. They have created what Aldous Huxley envisioned in

Brave New World. They have given us soma, and it is called Valium."

In the early 1960s, when Librium came on the market, Hoffmann-La Roche promoted the tranquilizer as an effective cure for alcoholism. Earlier Carter-Wallace, which grew from a small unknown drug company to a thriving concern because of Miltown, had pushed its tranquilizer as a chemical treatment for alcoholics, and Roche was following this lead in its competition with the better-known sedative. Dr. Richard Heilman, a psychiatrist and director of the Alcohol and Drug Treatment unit at the Minneapolis Veterans Administration Hospital, says he tried to warn Hoffmann-La Roche early in the 1960s that Librium would not cure alcoholism but rather would make it worse by fostering dual addiction. Heilman's concern arose from the fact that a number of his patients being treated for alcoholism were also addicted to Librium. At the same time he was noticing this growing dual addiction problem, he was receiving "frequent, expensively done brochures suggesting that Librium was an effective cure for alcoholics. . . . I was amazed and greatly disheartened by this approach," Heilman recalls, "because this did just not fit into my experience with the drug. I talked frequently with the Roche detail man and told him that their promotion of Librium for use in long-term alcohol therapy was defeating my work here with alcoholics. People were having their addiction transferred from one drug to another or reinforced. I also told them that they would end up harming themselves if they continued to promote Librium for the long-term treatment of alcoholics by eventually discrediting the drug completely, even for use in withdrawal."

Heilman pauses in his recollection, sighs, and says, "Do you know what Roche did? They sent a Roche-employed physician out here from Nutley [New Jersey] to argue with me about my point of view, and in essence he told me that I was unethical and definitely lacking in compassion. 'You just have to give them [alcoholics] something,' the Roche doctor told me."

Roche denies it actively promoted the drug for treatment of alcoholism at any time. However, a Roche spokesman did concede that in the early 1960s the company circulated medical papers written by independent authorities showing that Librium was an effective cure for alcoholism. The spokesman said circulation of such literature should be construed not as promotion but rather as part of the company's ongoing effort to keep physicians informed of new developments. But, as Heilman points out, it was Roche's detail man who contacted him about it initially, and later the company sent a doctor to Minneapolis to defend the use of the drug for alcoholism and "to argue with me about my point of view." The drug companies say they are doing their best to combat the problem of dual addiction. Dr. Bruce Medd, medical director of Roche Laboratories, acknowledges there is a problem. "It would be naive to think that every patient placed on Valium therapy would refrain from taking an alcoholic beverage," he said in an interview in his Nutley, New Jersey, office. He says Roche is fulfilling its obligations by placing special ads in medical journals highlighting the problems of dual addiction and urging physicians to be vigilant in their prescribing practices. The company also warns doctors to caution patients that by mixing Valium and alcohol they may experience side effects such as dizziness, decreased alertness, and muscle incoordination.

At a medical writers' seminar sponsored by Roche in January 1979, several experts did, in fact, warn against the use of Valium and Librium in combination with alcohol, but one of the drug's staunchest defenders, Dr. Leo Hollister of the Stanford School of Medicine, expressed some disappointment that the tranquilizer is not an effective substitute for alcohol. Said Hollister: "If I had a choice between dipsomania and Valium mania, I'd choose the latter." Alcohol, he said, is "more toxic." Hollister offers no apology for his enthusiasm for Valium and jokingly admits he must remind himself that he "cannot for a moment believe that God works for Hoffmann-La Roche."

Although the practice has been discredited for many years, the idea of treating alcoholism with tranquilizers and other cross-addictive drugs still persists in segments of the medical profession. No less an authority than the Food and Drug Administration, which should know better, said in the October 1978 issue of the FDA Consumer, an official monthly magazine with a wide circulation in medical and consumer health circles, that minor tranquilizers such as Valium "are of value in treating such conditions as alcoholism and epilepsy. . . ." Despite the fact that tranquilizers are medically indicated *only* in the acute withdrawal phase of alcoholism, many doctors continue to prescribe them as a cure in the long-term treatment of alcoholism, and such statements of ignorance by the FDA only contribute to this dangerous practice. Wayne Pines, the FDA's commissioner for public affairs, acknowledged the mistake after checking his *Physicians' Desk Reference*, the most commonly used authority on prescription drugs, but allowed that the reporter who brought it to his attention was "too sensitive to the nuances" of alcoholism.

Another equally dangerous myth—that alcoholism is caused by an underlying mental disorder and, therefore, treatable with psychoactive drugs—persists within the medical profession. In 1979 the American Psychiatric Association in its *American Journal of Psychiatry* sought to link alcoholism with depression, a condition some articles said was treatable with antidepressant drugs. Sadly, this amounts to foisting upon the alcoholic another potentially addictive drug.

For years, medical researchers have been frustrated by their inability to identify specific mental, emotional, or physical causes of alcoholism. Invariably what they find is that there are as many variables as similarities. An Indiana University survey of thirty-seven different studies found that any type of personality— "happy, sad, introvert, extrovert"—could be alcoholic.

In 1978 Hoffmann-La Roche did indeed begin running a series of display advertisements in medical journals cautioning doctors against prescribing Valium for alcoholic patients, but people like Dr. Knott in Memphis say the company is not doing enough: "All Roche is doing by saying that is sidestepping their responsibility. They are partially responsible for the creation of this problem [of dual addiction], and they should be doing more." Dr. Heilman of the Minneapolis VA Hospital worries that the cumulative effect of drug promotion has "institutionalized the dispensing of pills as the only way to treat sickness. This is not good therapy for anyone who is suffering from a simple problem such as anxiety, and for the alcoholic it is very dangerous. More alcoholics were harmed during Roche's promotional pushing of Librium than all the treatment centers helped."

The medical institutionalization of pills has helped foster social acceptance. Paul, a television producer, became addicted in a way that has become increasingly common. He was casually offered a Valium by a friend in a moment of stress and decided to go get his own prescription. Such a casual offering and use of a potent prescription drug in a society that so freely accepts the casual use of alcohol is a poignant reminder of how ingrained the easy chemical solution has become in our way of life.

Paul started his drinking career at the age of seventeen and took his first sedative drug at the age of twenty-one. During the sixteen years he was addicted to alcohol and pills, his life disintegrated slowly until one fateful day he chose suicide as his only way out. The suicide attempt failed, and Paul finally made it to a drug-free life; but in the interim there were lots of times he "thought dying would be far better than living."

Paul feels he was an alcoholic from the day he took his first drink because he had a blackout that day, one of the early and sure warning signs of alcoholism. As he tells it:

"I did not really know what blackouts were until I came to AA. If I thought anything about them, I thought they were normal. It's hard for anyone who is not an alcoholic to understand them. About the best way to describe them is the 'waking up with a strange person, in a strange bed, in a strange place' syndrome. That is, after a few drinks, I just went away mentally and could and usually did end up almost anywhere with almost anyone."

Paul's blackouts were not bad at first, usually of short duration and infrequent. But that changed when he found pills while in the army. "My first pill was legitimate. I had been wounded in the leg and evacuated from Vietnam. I had a lot of pain from the wound and had a hard time getting to sleep at night. They gave me some phenobarbital to help me sleep. I loved phenobarbital, especially when they let me go to the Enlisted Men's Club at the hospital and I could have a few beers on top of the phenobarb. I really felt like I was floating."

Paul eventually was sent back to Vietnam, where he found a friendly medic to keep him supplied with barbiturates. "I really got hooked on booze and pills in Nam. No one really wanted to be there, and there was no way to get out until your tour ended, so I found that mixing booze and pills was the best way to get away from it all. I also started my morning pill and my morning drink then, a practice I did not think was very unusual, because it seemed everyone else was doing it. So, if it was normal for everyone else, why not me?"

When he returned to the United States and entered college, Paul made a rigorous effort to control his drinking and pill taking. "I saved my drinking for the weekend, but I always took my morning barbiturate." When Paul was twenty-five, he was introduced to Valium by a coworker in a television news department where he had gone to work as a trainee. The long hours, his morning hangovers, the stress and strain of a new job—all combined to make the middle of the day very rough for him. "I took one Valium—given to me by a lady I worked with who saw how uptight I was—and after it took hold, I decided right then and there I was going to spend the rest of my life on Valium."

The next week he went to an internist he had seen only once before and described to the doctor the pressure he was under at work and the anxiety he often felt. "The doctor listened to me for about five minutes, reached over to his prescription pad, wrote out a prescription for Valium, and said, 'Take these; they will help you cope.'" This was in 1969, and Paul spent the next seven years ingesting increasing amounts of Valium and alcohol. As his Valium intake increased, so did his liquor intake. He soon found that the longer he continued to drink and take pills, the more of both he needed just to stay even. One pill and one beer were enough to get him started in the morning in 1969, but by 1971 it took three Valiums and as many beers just to get out of the house. He also began experiencing "the sweats and a bit of the shakes in the middle of the morning and also around four in the afternoon. So I started taking Valium during the day, just to keep the sweats down, and I found that I was popping pills about every hour or so."

Paul's work started to deteriorate noticeably in 1970. "People would ask me something, and then an hour later I would have forgotten what they asked me. I started misplacing files, memos, instructions. I was literally losing my ability to think, yet I never connected it with the pills. I knew I was a heavy hitter on the booze, but I figured that was not my problem either. I just put all these signs down to the stress and strain of my job, not to mention the stress and strain of living in New York." Paul also began to experience even worse blackouts, and his behavior became more unpredictable. Once he came out of a blackout to find himself screaming at a film crew on the streets of New York. His blackouts no longer lasted hours; they lasted days. He would wake up not only in strange places but in strange cities with no idea how he got there.

"By this point I realized that I probably was an alcoholic—no one could drink like I did and not be an alcoholic. I was going through a case of beer a day at least, plus a scotch here, a martini there. But I still did not think pills were part of the problem. In fact, I thought the pills were keeping me from becoming even a worse alcoholic. After all, a doctor gave me Valium to calm me down, and now that I was an alcoholic, I really was nervous."

Paul hit bottom in 1976 after a car accident. "I was driving back from the Hamptons after a long and very drunk weekend. I was drinking beer while driving and had taken two Valiums before starting out. All of a sudden I blacked out and woke up off the road with the car upside down." Although he was not injured, he was charged with drunk driving. The incident filled him with despair. He knew alcohol was ruining his life, but he did not know how to stop drinking. "I took a look at my life and realized how loused up it was. I did not like myself; I had few friends, was an alcoholic, and was very close to losing my job. I decided I might as well kill myself. So I took a hundred milligrams of Valium and drank a fifth of bourbon. The next thing I knew, I was in a hospital having my stomach pumped out. That really depressed me. I could not even succeed at killing myself." That day he called Alcoholics Anonymous and went to his first AA meeting. There he found not only that he suffered from the disease of alcoholism and had to give up drinking but that he also was addicted to Valium. The pills he was taking to ease the pains of living were as much a part of his problem as the alcohol.

Paul found getting off Valium far more difficult and painful than getting off alcohol. "The withdrawal from liquor was not bad at all—three days of aches and pains, shakes and sweating. But about a week later I started to go through Valium withdrawal, and it was ten times worse than the alcohol withdrawal. I think the withdrawal from Valium went on for months; at least it seemed it took that long for me to stop having the shakes and paranoia. I tell you, I never want to go near a drink or a Valium as long as I live."

Paul's difficult withdrawal from Valium was similar to what others who have abused the minor tranquilizers have gone through. It is a common occurrence in rehabilitation centers throughout the nation, and many in the field say they would rather take someone off heroin than Valium. Dr. Pursch says Valium withdrawal "is very dangerous. In fact, it is far worse than any kind of withdrawal from any substance that I have ever seen." He warns people against taking themselves off alcohol or Valium by themselves outside a hospital setting. He says, "A lot of people come into Long Beach for treatment of their alcoholism, but they don't tell us about their pill problems. But we know the signs, and somewhere around the first week these dually addicted people start bothering the nurses with complaints about aching joints, the shakes, or insomnia. Some of them throw fits. Then we know the individual has a pill problem as well as an alcohol problem."

The drug companies and the defenders of the minor tranquilizers of the benzodiazepine class claim that such popular drugs as Valium, Librium, Serax, and Tranxene are not normally addictive, and therefore, withdrawal is rare when the drugs are removed, and that when withdrawal occurs, it is the result of another abused drug, usually alcohol, in the system, not the tranquilizer. Professionals working in the rehabilitation field strongly dispute this, suggesting that the drug companies and many medical scientists are blind to the overwhelming episodic evidence that is available.

There is, however, no question that the most dangerous and life-threatening reactions are caused by the drugs in combination with alcohol. Using tranquilizers like Valium or any of the sedative-hypnotic drugs with alcohol adds to the potency and dangers of each drug. This is called a synergistic effect, in which one drug plus one drink does not add up to two but rather to four or five or six. The combination of any of the tranquilizers with alcohol starts a chemical time bomb ticking that can explode with disastrous effects. In one of the most dramatic illustrations of the potential dangers, Karen Ann Quinlan combined alcohol and tranquilizers the night she went into a coma in 1974. The New

Jersey woman's parents won a celebrated right-to-die decision and had their daughter's life-support mechanisms removed, and years later Karen Ann Quinlan still lay in a vegetable state in a nursing home.

Exactly why alcohol and sedative drugs have this synergistic or potentiating effect is a question that still baffles medical researchers. Probably the person who has come closest to the answer is Dr. Charles S. Lieber, professor of medicine at the Mount Sinai School of Medicine in New York and director of the Liver Disease and Nutrition Research Center at the Bronx Veterans Administration Hospital.

According to Dr. Lieber, the potentiation process begins in the liver, the chemical-processing plant of the body. The liver breaks down or metabolizes all the substances a person ingests, and potentiation occurs because the same microenzymal system that processes alcohol also processes the tranquilizing drugs. Dr. Lieber warns that mixing the two is hazardous because alcohol and tranquilizers compete with each other for a place in the processing operation, with alcohol always getting priority. Therefore, the tranquilizing drug remains in the blood longer, waiting for the alcohol to be processed in the liver, and its effect on the body and mind is exaggerated. This slower metabolizing of drugs results in their potency's being doubled, tripled, or quadrupled when they enter the central nervous system.

The classic case of such potentiation occurs when alcohol is taken with barbiturates. This creates such a potentially toxic cocktail that Dr. Heilman says, "The quickest way I know to kill yourself is to mix alcohol with barbiturates." This is because it takes only a very small amount of alcohol to potentiate even a small dose of barbiturates.

The barbiturates—amobarbital, secobarbital, butabarbital, and phenobarbital to name a few—are killers in their own right. According to figures compiled for the government's Drug Alert Warning Network, acronym DAWN, barbiturates accounted for more drug-related deaths in 1975 than any other psychoactive drug, whether legal or illegal. Use of the barbiturates is declining because they have been implicated in so many deaths. According to the National Institute on Drug Abuse (NIDA), only 18 million barbiturate prescriptions were written in 1976, a 47 percent reduction since 1971. The military, which operates worldwide hospital facilities, has drastically cut its use of barbiturates not only because of their dangerous potential when used alone but because of their lethal potential when used with alcohol. "The military is a drinking society," a Defense Department spokesman said, "and we were just seeing too many people in our hospitals as a result of barbiturate and alcohol overdose." The military started a crash program to reduce barbiturate use and by 1976 had eliminated amobarbital from its pharmacy system. Similarly, other barbiturate prescriptions in the military system have been cut 80 percent. A major reason for the decline is that barbiturate prescriptions were placed under tighter federal controls.

Like Dr. Lieber, Dr. Stanley Gitlow, a pioneer in the treatment of alcoholism, believes the potentiation effects of combining alcohol and psychoactive drugs, particularly the tranquilizers and sleeping pills, are extremely dangerous. "All the sedatives and the soporifics—alcohol being one of them—are irregular depressants of the central nervous system; and when alcohol (or another sedative) depresses the brain, it diminishes psychomotor activity. Diminished psychomotor activity level means relief from anxiety," Dr. Gitlow explained in an article in the AA publication *The Grapevine.*

The lower psychomotor level and the relief from anxiety it brings pass in about two hours. Dr. Gitlow says this short-lived sedative effect is itself not bad, but it brings with it another problem—agitation. To counteract this agitation, many people take more drugs, including alcohol and pills, and thus set themselves up for the kind of merry-go-round on which Paul, whose story we told earlier, found himself.

As Dr. Gitlow explains it: "The second effect of the sedatives is to *increase* psychomotor activity levels. This increase takes place immediately, right after the drink, but is not immediately felt because it is a change of less intensity than the sedative effect. This latter lasts two or three hours while the opposite or agitating effect lasts for about 12 hours after the first drink. Therefore, as the short-term sedative effect wears off, the other effect of alcohol (or other sedatives) becomes apparent. No one in this world can get a sedative effect from any known drug without it being followed by an agitating effect which wears off more slowly. The piper must always be paid."

Dr. Gitlow says this sedating-agitating process continues as long as an individual continues to take drugs or alcohol, and the agitation is magnified with each pill or drink. At high consumption levels over a long period of time, the effect can be disastrous. As Gitlow describes it: "A person whose psychomotor activity level is extremely elevated may suffer from one of several effects. He may start to shake and shiver, he may pace back and forth, palpitate and show great agitation and tremulousness. He may get hallucinosis, which basically means that his brain is so irritated it sees, hears and feels things that aren't there.

"If the individual gets one step sicker, he will go into a condition known as delirium tremens (D.T.'s) in which not only sensory input but the motor output has become tremendous and he is literally unable to stop moving. He might pace around, and hallucinate actively. A sine qua non to this delirium is not only tremulousness but absolute terror. The individual behaves as though someone were attempting to kill him. His psychomotor activity may reach the point of causing spontaneous convulsions."

This chain of events is speeded up and exaggerated when individuals combine drugs with alcohol. There is some evidence that people are entering drug treatment programs such as AA at an earlier age than in the past. One popular theory is that the combination of tranquilizers or other psychoactive drugs and alcohol is bringing them in for help sooner.

Dr. Gitlow notes that most people do not want to repeat the sedation-agitation experiment after their first brush with it, and these people avoid abusing drugs. They are the social drinkers. But the alcoholic or addictive person for unexplained reasons repeats it again and again until he is driven to treatment or to death. Although there are no clear reasons why one person is addictive and another is not, Dr. Gitlow believes the answer lies partly in the alcoholic's compulsive nature and partly in what he identifies as an abnormally high psychomotor activity level that drives an alcoholic to drink or use pills excessively. The alcoholic or sedativist, as he sometimes calls him, repeats the experiment "again and again, even though he suffers loss of job, loss of health and family. The definition of the disease includes not just addiction, but compulsivity. Now why, when he suffers so much, does he do it again and again? The reason to drink may be psychological, I used to think that, but now I am not so sure. These individuals may just have a different level of psychomotor activity."

The agitating effect of sedative drugs may explain why there are so many adverse reaction reports on file with the Food and Drug Administration. Many of the reports on Valium, filed by doctors with Roche, which is required to pass them on to the FDA, tell of something called a paradoxical rage reaction. The reaction is paradoxical because drugs like Valium are supposed to bring calm and peace, not rage.

A lot of the paradoxical rage reaction reports show the reaction often occurs when Valium is combined with alcohol, potentiating the agitation and hence the possibility for rage. With so many such reports on file, many researchers, including Dr. Knott of Memphis, are starting to think rage is a true reaction to Valium, especially in combination with alcohol, not a paradoxical one. The price many people pay in anger and hostility when they combine such rage-producing substances as Valium and alcohol can be high indeed. One of the more chilling examples of this adverse reaction in the FDA files is of a woman who had several drinks and then engaged in an argument with her husband. When he left the house, she took several Valium tablets to calm down. She went to sleep but woke up when her husband returned, took out a pistol, and shot him dead. The FDA file tersely refers to the incident as "an obvious paradoxical rage reaction."

Another example is Susan, an attractive, lithe, and soft-spoken woman, who at the age of twenty was prescribed Valium by her therapist to help her get over her shyness. By the age of twenty-seven, she was a kicking, screaming barroom brawler. Susan started out innocently enough, taking Valium "sparingly at first" and drinking little. With the aid of these "magic pills," as she called them, her shyness seemed to drop away; she became more assertive and less bothered by strain and anxiety. At first, she followed the Valium instructions on the label but gradually found she needed to exceed the dosage "to handle little events during the day." About the same time she began to frequent neighborhood bars, discovering that she could better wind down from a hard day on the job by drinking a few beers on top of the Valium. The feeling was "almost euphoric."

After two years on Valium and with her alcohol consumption steadily increasing, Susan found herself unable to get up in the mornings without Valium, which she was taking in increasingly large doses of twenty or thirty milligrams at a time. "That was the first thing I did when I woke up—reached for the Valium bottle, took one, and just lay back and waited for it to start to work. When it started to work, then I knew maybe I could." She also began taking "whole handfuls" during the day to counter job stress. Within five years she had lost her job—a responsible editorial position in a publishing house—but quickly landed another one. At this point Susan began to worry about her increasingly large consumption of alcohol, so she sought help from another therapist, one she hoped would listen to her fears and anxieties. The therapist listened but did not ask Susan about her drinking habits, and she did not volunteer any information about how much she drank. Nor did he ask her whether she had been on medication. What he did do was give her another prescription for Valium, for which Susan was grateful. "I had a hard time getting the first one refilled after all those years, and I was beginning to get worried about running out of Valium." She tells how she "hid that stuff—from whom, I don't know, seeing I lived alone. But I put the pills into a vitamin bottle, and then I hid the vitamin bottle in a shoebox, and then I hid the shoebox in a closet. I remember one day I was so foggy I could not even find the shoebox, and I sat there on the floor and cried because I could not find my pills."

Susan continued to go downhill, becoming promiscuous, more out of a desire not to be alone than anything else, and experiencing long blackouts. Her drinking escalated. She was eating little, living on Valium, beer, and just enough food to get by. As her drinking and pill taking went up, the kind of bar she chose went down.

"I found a rough neighborhood old-timers' bar filled with what I called at the time 'real people.' Actually, those people and I had a lot in common. All we wanted to do was drink, because there were a lot of alcoholics in that place. But due to my pill habit, I was probably the worst of them all. I started to develop a fierce temper. I'd pick a fight—and I mean a fistfight—with almost anyone in the place who looked at me wrong. The last six months I drank in that bar, I think I had a fight almost every night. I'd curse people out, I'd yell at them at the top of my lungs, and then I'd get physical, kick 'em, hit, whatever." She also got very frightened. "It got so I would not go out on weekends. I'd have the booze delivered and have the man leave it in the hall because I was afraid, very afraid, of the world." In the last six months of her drinking and pill taking, Susan overdosed three times—"not on purpose, just accidentally because I could not keep track of how much Valium I had in my body or how much booze." She stopped going to work because "I thought people were after me and after my Valium."

Seven years after taking her first Valium pill, she was on 150 milligrams a day plus about a case of beer. "Finally, I ended up in the hospital one more time. They made me stay overnight, and in the morning a doctor told me about AA. Said he was in it, told me he had the same problems I had, told me about the fears he had—and I thought they were unique to me—and told me that he had found a way to live without alcohol or pills."

Susan went to her first AA meeting that night in 1975. She has had one drink since, a beer, because she took Valium, and the Valium "set up some sort of craving for beer. When I first went to AA, they suggested that I put down both the big bottle and the small bottle. I could admit that alcohol had fouled up my life, but I did not want to give up Valium. I carried my Valium bottle with me everywhere, but didn't take any. Then, one day after I was in AA for about a year, I had a very stressful situation and decided I had better take a pill. Before I even realized it, I was in a bar ordering a beer. That was, hopefully, my last drink and my last pill. I've put both bottles down and realize today that if I want to live and handle all the stresses in life, I have to stay away from booze and pills and go to AA meetings. AA helps me handle life—and I still have a tough job—much better than any pill ever invented."

Dan Andersen, founder of Hazelden, a pioneering alcohol and drug rehabilitation facility in Center City, Minnesota, has seen a lot of dually addicted patients like Susan. While the medical profession has to accept a lot of the responsibility for fostering the

pill mentality that so pervades our society, patients also are cul-
pable, he believes. "These are people who want to modify their
environment, and they cannot do it themselves. They cannot seem
to change the way they feel about things, how the world affects
them, so they go to their physician seeking help, and the help
they get is a pill. They accept this pill because it enables them
to will what cannot be willed—happiness, calm, and peace. Drugs,
to a lot of people in our addictive culture, represent repeated
opportunities for this attempt at altering what really cannot be
altered."

Andersen says they don't see "many 'pure' alcoholics anymore"
at Hazelden. "We find that anywhere from forty to seventy percent of the patients are not only alcoholics but also people who
have abused pills. We have had women come in denying they
have ever taken medication, and when we go through their luggage, we find a shoebox full of tranquilizers."

The reverse was true for Betty Ford. The former First Lady
says in her autobiography that when first confronted by her
family about her problems, she was willing to admit to having
become addicted to painkillers and tranquilizers but not to alcohol. "The reason I rejected the idea I was an alcoholic was
because my addiction wasn't dramatic," she explains. "So my
speech had become deliberate. So I fell in the bathroom and
cracked three ribs. But I never drank for a hangover, and in fact
I used to criticize people who did." But the combination of
alcohol and pills she was taking to relax, sleep, or soften pain
pushed her to the edge. "When I add up the number of pills I
was taking, and put a drink or two on top, I see how I got to the
breaking point."

Mrs. Ford, who was assisted in getting into a rehabilitation
program through the forceful intervention of her family and Dr.
Pursch, at first resented the medical profession for "fourteen
years of [her] being advised to take pills, rather than wait for
pain to hit" but now feels doctors are being educated about the
dangers of psychoactive medication "right along with the rest
of us."

Pursch, her doctor, says patients should hesitate when a pill is
offered by a physician and should ask about alternative means of
treatment for emotional or psychological problems. He looks

"upon giving a patient something to swallow when he has an emotional problem as destructive. If you come to me with an emotional problem, you want help. I really can't help you by giving you a pill. The act of giving you a pill reduces your humanness. If I give you a pill, I reinforce all the negative forces in you. By giving you a tranquilizer prescription for an emotional problem, I am saying that you are inadequate, that your humanness does not count, and that you need a pill to live. By giving you a pill, I diminish you."

People with emotional problems or with alcohol and/or drug problems should do as Pursch and many other experts in the field suggest. The first step is to realize that more drugs or more alcohol will not solve the problem but only make it worse. The second important step toward recovery is to seek help from self-help groups such as AA or through nonchemical therapy such as counseling, meditation, or prayer—anything, Pursch urges, other than a pill. The medication that works the best is the help two people can give each other—help born of common suffering, common problems, and common solutions. This is the help born of love that Betty Ford describes in summing up her recovery: "You get better when you least expect to, when you're not even trying, when you're down by the coffee machine kibitzing with two black seamen who are playing cards. In my everyday life, I would never have met these men, but they and I helped heal each other."

Following the public announcement of Betty Ford's hospitalization, thousands of persons, mostly women, called treatment centers, hot lines, AA, and the various national councils on alcoholism to talk over their own concerns about pills and alcohol. Women's magazines featured articles on dual addiction, and newspapers carried stories about the dangers of mixing alcohol and drugs. This new public awareness is healthy not only for those who are addicted and potentially addictive but also for those who are casual or social drinkers and may have to take medication of any kind for a short or long period of time. One does not need to be alcoholic to run a grave risk by mixing alcohol and drugs.

Valium topped the federal government's Drug Alert Warning Network list for emergency room mentions with 54,400 such incidents in the twelve-month period ending April 1, 1977. Librium accounted for another 9,300 emergency room visits, and Dalmane, a chemically related sleeping potion, was listed as responsible for 11,500 visits. Listed separately, alcohol in combination with other drugs was responsible for 47,700 emergency room incidents. The majority of the emergency room incidents involving Valium, Librium, Dalmane, and other psychoactive drugs were the result of using these drugs in combination with alcohol or other drugs. Even aspirin, which ranks number three behind Valium and alcohol in emergency room incidents, can be dangerous, even fatal, to certain allergic individuals or when abused or taken in combination with other drugs.

The National Institute on Drug Abuse estimates that 900 people died of adverse reactions to Valium in the twelve-month period. Another estimated 200 deaths were attributed to Librium, 200 to Equanil and Miltown, 100 to Dalmane, 500 to Luminal (phenobarbital), 200 to Mellaril, and 100 to Thorazine. Again, many of these deaths—94 percent in the case of Valium—were caused not by one single drug but by the combination of drugs, usually one or more of the prescription drugs in combination with alcohol, and not all of the victims were addicts, alcoholics, or abusers of drugs. Some simply made the fatal mistake of taking a drink with a prescription drug.

The best way to avoid the potential hazards is to avoid mixing alcohol with any prescription drug. Dr. Frank Seixas, former medical director of the National Council on Alcoholism, says diabetics, for example, should not drink if they are taking certain antidiabetic drugs. Mixing these drugs with alcohol can raise blood lactate to a danger level.

People taking antidepressant drugs classified as MAO (monamine oxidase) inhibitors, such as Nardil, should not think, "A little bit of wine won't hurt me," and then have some with dinner, because some wines, particularly Chianti, when combined with MAO inhibitors can be fatal. Chianti contains a substance called tyramine, which, when combined with these antidepressants, can cause a hypertensive crisis known to be lethal.

Even aspirin can be fatal when combined with alcohol. According to Dick Bast of the National Clearinghouse for Alcohol Information, deaths have occurred from a mixture of alcohol and aspirin because it brings together two extremely acidic substances that irritate the stomach lining. This irritation has been known to become so severe as to cause stomach hemorrhage. Also, Bast warns, mixing alcohol with aspirin can produce a low-blood-pressure crisis, leading to dizziness or fainting spells. A lot of home accidents can be traced to this combination, he says.

Similar risks are run by people who combine alcohol with such seemingly innocent home medicine mainstays as Anacin, Bufferin, Bromo-Seltzer, Cope, Empirin, ASA Compound, APC Compound, or Excedrin. Mixing even wine with cold or cough preparations, such as Cheracol D, Vick's Formula 44, or Nyquil, can cause central nervous system depression. The same reaction could occur when alcohol is used with other over-the-counter (OTC) preparations, including Allerest, Contac, Coricidin, Super Anahist, Triaminicin, and Sinutabs, to name some of the common cold medicines. The same is true for the OTC sleeping preparations: Sominex, Dormin, Nytol, or Sleep-Eze.

To alert citizens to the dangers of mixing alcohol with prescription drugs, the National Clearinghouse for Alcohol Information has proposed a sample prescription form that provides room at the top for the doctor's prescription and a detachable section at the bottom that lists several commonly prescribed types of drugs with a box to be checked next to each. At the top of the detachable section, which is to be kept by the patient, is this statement: "Caution: The medication I have prescribed for you has been reported to interact with alcoholic beverages. Some of these interactions are particularly dangerous, and I have checked below the class of drug which covers the one I am prescribing." (See sample on page 53.) Bast of the Clearinghouse says the proposed universal prescription pad has run into stiff opposition from doctors and drug companies, and the chances of its being adopted by a significant number of doctors are slim.* Such a prescription pad, Bast believes, could prevent someone from innocently mixing a fatal combination of drugs and alcohol and could at the least serve as an early-warning system to keep some people from heading down the path of dual addiction.

Prevention is the best medicine, and the best way you can avoid dual addiction or simply an adverse reaction is to be on

---

* Many doctors feel that such a prescription pad would discourage patients from taking necessary medications.

Sample prescription form proposed by
National Clearinghouse for Alcohol Information

Phone:
(123) 765-1321 **Office**
(123) 123-1567 **Home**

Dr. J. SMITH
1234 Main Street
Dayton, Ohio 09876

Office Hours:
Week Days
9:00 A.M.—3:00 P.M.
Saturday 11:00—2:00

℞

**A CHECK-MARK HAS BEEN PLACED IN THE BOX PRECEDING THE CLASS OF DRUG
WHICH BEST DESCRIBES THE ONE WHICH I HAVE PRESCRIBED**

CAUTION: The medication I have prescribed for you has been reported to interact with alcoholic beverages. Some of these interactions are particularly dangerous, and I have checked below the class of drug which covers the one I am prescribing.

If you have any questions concerning your medication, do not hesitate to ask me. The pharmacist who fills this prescription can also give you valuable information on alcohol and other drugs, and you may wish to send for the free alcohol and drug information provided by: The National Clearinghouse for Alcohol Information, P.O. Box 2345, Department RX, Rockville, Maryland 20852.

☐ **ANALGESICS, NARCOTIC**
(Demerol, Darvon, Dilaudid, etc.)
When used alone, both alcohol and narcotic drugs cause a reduction in the function of the central nervous system. When used together, this effect is even greater, and may lead to loss of effective breathing function (respiratory arrest). Death may occur.

☐ **ANALGESICS, NONNARCOTIC**
(Aspirin, APC, Pabalate, etc.)
Even when used alone, some nonprescription pain relievers can cause bleeding in the stomach and intestines. Alcohol also irritates the stomach and can aggravate the bleeding, especially in ulcer patients.

☐ **ANTIALCOHOL PREPARATIONS**
(Antabuse, Calcium Carbamide)
Use of alcohol with medications prescribed to help alcoholic patients keep from drinking results in nausea, vomiting, headache, high blood pressure and possible erratic heartbeat, and can result in death.

☐ **ANTICOAGULANTS**
(Panwarfin, Dicumarol, Sintrom, etc.)
Alcohol can increase the ability of these drugs to stop blood clotting, which in turn can lead to life-threatening or fatal hemorrhages.

☐ **ANTICONVULSANTS**
(Dilantin, Diphenyl, EKKO, etc.)
Drinking may lessen the ability of this drug to stop convulsions in a person.

☐ **ANTIDEPRESSANTS**
(Tofranil, Pertofrane, Triavil, etc.)
Alcohol may cause an additional reduction in central nervous system functioning and lessen a person's ability to operate normally. Certain antidepressants in combination with red wines like Chianti may cause a high blood pressure crisis.

☐ **ANTIDIABETIC AGENTS/HYPOGLYCEMICS**
(Insulin, Diabenese, Orinase, etc.)
Because of the possible severe reactions to combining alcohol and insulin or the oral antidiabetic agents, and because alcohol interacts unpredictably with them, patients taking any of these medications should avoid alcohol.

guard and to be skeptical of the drugs your doctor prescribes, finding out what they are, what they will do (the good and the bad), how long they need to be taken, and, most of all, what alternatives are available. The National Institute on Drug Abuse suggests that you be sure you can always answer the following questions:

1. Do I know what drug I am taking, why I am taking it, and what it is supposed to do for me?
2. Do I know when I am supposed to stop taking the drug?
3. Have I asked my doctor if it is all right to have alcohol while using the medication?
4. Do I know what side effects or problems to watch for? (Although NIDA didn't include this, it is wise to get a copy of the adverse reactions and warnings the government requires the drug companies to offer. If your doctor won't give it to you, your pharmacist will.)
5. If I question the drug I've been prescribed, have I talked with my doctor about it or considered getting a second medical opinion?

As the Betty Ford story dramatically demonstrated for the public, dependency on alcohol and psychoactive drugs, including painkillers and tranquilizers, is not an uncommon thing, and even those who might be receiving what they consider the very best medical attention can be victimized. But Mrs. Ford's story and the others in this chapter also clearly demonstrate that people with drug-dependency problems can get help to restore their health and start on the road to fuller and more rewarding lives free of drugs. For the alcoholic, AA works best, and every telephone book lists a number for the nearest AA group. All one has to do is call, and help will be on the way. AA also seems to work best for those who are dually addicted or even those hooked only on pills. Pills Anonymous, which follows the AA program but is not an AA organization, is a growing organization specifically for prescription junkies. For the family or friends of the alcoholic or dually addicted, AA has affiliate groups called Al-Anon to help them cope with problems they experience in their relationships with alcoholics. There are many other self-help groups with proved records of effectiveness, including one for women called Women for Sobriety. For those who need more intensified assistance, there are a number of excellent public and private rehabilitation centers throughout the nation.

The best treatment is, however, prevention. To avoid trouble, Karst Besteman of the National Institute on Drug Abuse has a simple rule worth following: "If you aren't in trouble, less is better. Once you are in trouble, best is none."

If you have a problem with drugs, the first step toward recovery is to recognize it. The second step is to ask for help. Once these two steps are taken, the healing process can begin.

In the chapter that follows, we will show how women are victimized by the health care system in a way that makes them particularly vulnerable to prescription drug addiction.

What Could Happen If You Drink While Taking Any of These Drugs

The chart below lists classes of drugs which have been reported to interact with alcohol. Some of the dangers that may result from combining alcohol with the other listed drugs are described. If you asked for information on a specific drug, a check-mark has been placed in the box preceding the class of drug which best describes the one for which you requested information. It must be emphasized that this chart, or any other like it, only represents the smallest part of the whole alcohol/drug interaction picture. It is not meant to replace the advice of your family doctor or your pharmacist.

☐ **Antihistamines**
(*most cold remedies, Actified Coricidin, etc.*)

Taking alcohol with this class of drugs increases their calming effect and a person can feel quite drowsy, making driving and other activities which require alertness more hazardous.

☐ **Antihypertensive Agents**
(*Serpasil, Aldomet, Esidrix, etc.*)

Alcohol may increase the blood-pressure-lowering capability of some of these drugs, causing dizziness when a person gets up. Some agents will also cause a reduction in the function of the central nervous system.

☐ **Antiinfective Agents/Antibiotics**
(*Flagyl, Chloromycetin, Seromycin, etc.*)

In combination with alcohol, some may cause nausea, vomiting, and headache, and possibly convulsions, especially those taken for urinary tract infections.

☐ **Central Nervous System Stimulants**
(*most diet pills, Dexedrine, Caffeine, Ritalin, etc.*)

Because the stimulant effect of this

class of drugs may reverse the depressant effect of the alcohol on the central nervous system, these drugs can give a false sense of security. They do *not* help intoxicated persons gain control of their movements.

☐ **Diuretics**
(Diuril, Lasix, Hydromox, etc.)

Combining alcohol with diuretics may cause reduction in blood pressure, possibly resulting in dizziness when a person stands up.

☐ **Psychotropics**
(Tindal, Mellaril, Thorazine, etc.)

Alcohol and the "major tranquilizers" cause additional depression to central nervous system function, which can result in severe impairment of voluntary movements such as walking or using the hands. The combination can also cause a loss of effective breathing function and can be fatal.

☐ **Sedative Hypnotics**
(Doriden, Quaalude, Nembutal, etc.)

Alcohol in combination further reduces the function of the central nervous system, sometimes to the point of coma or the loss of effective breathing (respiratory arrest). This combination can be fatal.

☐ **Sleep Medicines**

It is likely that nonprescription sleeping medicines, to the degree that they are effective, will lead to the same kind of central nervous system depression when combined with alcohol as the minor tranquilizers (see below).

☐ **Tranquilizers—Minor**
(Miltown, Valium, Librium, etc.)

Tranquilizers in combination with alcohol will cause reduced function of the central nervous system, especially during the first few weeks of drug use. This results in decreased alertness and judgment and can lead to household and automotive accidents.

☐ **Vitamins**

Continuous drinking can keep vitamins from entering the bloodstream. However, this situation changes when a person stops drinking.

☐ **Other**

Either we have not been able to identify the drug you mentioned, or data are not sufficient to provide an answer. Check with your doctor or pharmacist to be sure.

Women as Victims | **3**

Sharon West * lay on the couch unconscious, one arm loose at her side, the other dangling to the floor. The television was on, the volume set high for the loneliness-breaking voices of a late show. Now the grating din of a kiddie cartoon told of morning.

Sharon's husband came down the stairs, walked indifferently to the couch, and quickly checked his wife's vital signs. She was alive, and Dr. John West * left for work.

Five years later—a year after divorce and several weeks after her last pill and months after her last drink—Sharon describes this first of three attempts to commit suicide with Valium. To her best recollection, she had a few drinks and then swallowed forty five-milligram yellow tablets. In the third attempt, Sharon almost succeeded, taking more pills and more alcohol. She ended up in an emergency room of a nearby hospital, much to the embarrassment of her husband.

Today, as she tells about it, she seems detached. Sharon says she knew even then it wouldn't work—that she could never take enough to kill herself and really didn't want to. All she wanted was to end the terrible cycle of booze and pills, loneliness and sadness, fear and anxiety, and self-loathing and distrust. Most of all, she wanted someone to take her seriously, to pay some attention to her as a person, perhaps just to listen and understand.

* The names Sharon West, Dr. John West, and Jean Daley (page 73), which appear in this chapter, are fictitious, and certain circumstances have been changed to protect the identities of those involved.

Her husband knew the morning he found her passed out on the sofa that she would be okay. A doctor, he knew the pills his wife took were safe. The Librium and Valium she had been taking for several years were, after all, prescribed by him or by his (and her) friends: the gynecologist, the internist, the dentist, and later the psychiatrist. Sharon also was in the unique position of prescribing her own. When she ran out of Valium, she would call the local pharmacist, with whom her husband did most of his business, and place an order. If her renewable prescription had run out, the druggist would call her husband's nurse or receptionist and have a prescription sent over to satisfy the legal requirements.

Since the early 1960s, tranquilizers had been a major part of Sharon's life. "I started taking them when Librium first came out," she recalls. "John took it, too. He was a surgeon, so I figured it had to be okay. We were just starting out, and he was working hard to build a practice. He didn't drink much, so he used Librium to relax. I wasn't much of a drinker then, either, and so I got into the habit of using Librium whenever I seemed nervous or uptight."

She used Librium and later Valium almost daily. She used tranquilizers to sleep at night and to stay calm but awake during the day. She used them to relieve minor aches and pains. She used them when she anticipated a crisis, during a crisis, and after a crisis. "Even today, it doesn't make me uncomfortable to talk about it. It was so acceptable, even expected. I never thought much about it. For many years I never abused the dosage, and at first I used it mostly to sleep. I was careful in the beginning not to mix tranquilizers with alcohol. I knew that much. Later, I didn't care and deliberately mixed them."

As her husband's practice grew, the Wests settled into a comfortable suburban neighborhood in Michigan. Dr. West busied himself at the office and the hospital, and Sharon busied herself at home, taking to housekeeping and child rearing at first with relish but later with resentment. She grew "uneasy and uncomfortable." She had a degree in communications from a major university and yearned to find a job. "But I felt guilty about leaving the children, and my husband thought it was a silly idea because he was making a good living. He really wasn't interested in talking about it and couldn't understand why I would be restless with such a fine home and such healthy children."

Sharon began to rely more on pills to settle herself down. Everyone she knew used them. "Of our entire circle of friends— all doctors and their wives—only one didn't take Valium. He was an internist and wouldn't give any to his wife either, so she would get a prescription from my husband and hide the pills." Taking pills was acceptable in Sharon's circle of women friends, but drinking was not, except at night. "I began to look forward to the cocktail hour before dinner, and in a few years I was taking a drink at lunch or fixing my dinner cocktail earlier." The daytime drinking habit grew worse, and Sharon found it abhorrent, so she would cut back on alcohol and increase her use of Valium. By this time the marriage was in trouble, but the Wests weren't talking about it. Sharon began to pour out her troubles to other doctors, and "each time they told me to keep taking the Valium."

Surrounded by doctors and given the "best medical care" in her community, Sharon West, a well-educated white suburban mother of two, became first a prescription junkie and later an alcoholic. It wasn't until she became very sick and very scared that she sought help from nonmedical sources. She looked up Alcoholics Anonymous in a phone book, called the number, and went to a meeting that night. With the help of friends, she gave up alcohol within a few days, but it took two months to taper off Valium. She describes the withdrawal from Valium as "the worst experience of my life. For no reason at all, I would burst into tears. I couldn't sleep. I couldn't work. I would be doing the simplest task and would break into the shakes. I was really scared, absolutely paranoid. I really am just beginning to get over it."

It wasn't until she sought help through nonmedical sources that she learned she had become addicted to tranquilizers as well as to alcohol. As she looked back, she could not recall ever being told by her husband or any other doctor of the potential for addiction. She did remember a long time ago an internist's saying at a party that he didn't like to prescribe them for his patients, but "everybody else, including my husband, thought they were really good drugs." She also recalled the time she was sitting in a park in the middle of the day, about to take a Valium and feeling uneasy about it. "I went down the street to this doctor friend and asked him if I really should be taking these things. He reassured me. I think he was upset because I barged into his office, though he didn't say so." Sharon said she approached her husband a couple of times about taking tranquilizers when she was beginning to feel in the back of her mind she was in trouble with them. "He'd say things like: 'You're just upset, take it easy, settle down.' Or he would lose patience and say, 'Why the hell can't you be satisfied and settle down?'"

Sharon is not unlike millions of women who are victimized by a health care system that pushes pills as solutions to everyday problems and singles out women as the chief candidates for psychoactive drugs for emotional support.

She was not unlike Betty Ford. The wife of the former president checked into Long Beach Naval Hospital's Drug and Alcohol Rehabilitation Center on April 10, 1978, for what she described as a condition brought about by "overmedicating" herself with drugs prescribed for arthritis and a pinched nerve. Later she described it as an addiction to alcohol, tranquilizers, and painkillers. How could the wife of a former congressman, vice-president, and president become addicted to this life-threatening combination? Surely, she of all people had the best medical care available. She had always been open and honest about her personal health, and she had talked freely about the painkillers and Valium she was using well before she entered the hospital.

Four years before entering the rehabilitation center and while the Fords were still in the White House, she told the Fairchild News Service that she took Valium three times a day and had received letters from citizens wondering if this made her a "drug addict." "I'm candid," Mrs. Ford said. "I wouldn't deny it. I do take tranquilizers. People just don't understand. They are for my neck. I find I get nervous when I realize how much I have to do each day and that I won't get here or there when I'm running late. So rather than wait until I get the pain when my neck goes into a spasm, I take Valium."

This statement is in sharp contrast with the account written four years later for her autobiography, *The Times of My Life*, of her addiction to alcohol and prescription drugs, her rehabilitation, and the education she received in living a chemically free life. "At first," she said, "I was bitter toward the medical profession. Fourteen years of being advised to take pills, rather than wait for the pain to hit. I had never been without my drugs. I took pills for pain. I took pills to sleep. I took mild tranquilizers. Today things are changing. Doctors are being educated right along with the rest of us, but some of them used to be all too eager to write prescriptions. It was easier to give a woman tranquilizers and get rid of her than sit and listen to her."

Like millions of others, Betty Ford became hooked on prescription drugs. So did Loretta Lynn, the first lady of country music. In an interview published in *US* magazine on March 21, 1978, she told how she had become addicted to tranquilizers taken to calm her nerves: "Too many responsibilities, too many conflicts and too many guilts made me take too many pills. It felt like everybody was pulling on me—my kids, my husband, my fans, my career. And there were these really bad migraine headaches. I began taking 'nerve pills.' City folk call them tranquilizers, but either way they're drugs. Everytime I felt nervous, I'd take a pill. And at bedtime, I had me still other pills to get to sleep. I guess you can say I was addicted 'cause that's the truth."

Sharon West, Betty Ford, and Loretta Lynn were addicted not to illegal—and, for them, socially unacceptable—street drugs, but to drugs prescribed for them by their doctors. What was given to make them better made them worse. Like millions of other women, they were victims in a health care system that increasingly depends on chemical solutions for human problems. They were victims of a medical mentality that reflects a strong male bias toward medicating women for displaying normal human emotions and frailties that are perceived as a sickness requiring chemical treatment. They were victims of the medical profession's ignorance of the effects of psychoactive drugs, and they were victims simply because as women they availed themselves of a health care system they trusted and did not challenge. Finally, they were victimized by the slickest, most expensive and successful advertising and sales campaign ever conducted on behalf of a prescription class of drugs—the so-called minor tranquilizers.

In the tranquilizing of America, women are the chief targets and the major victims, constituting the largest percentage of the newest drug abuse phenomenon—the prescription junkie. The National Institute on Drug Abuse (NIDA) estimates that 1 to 2 million American women are hooked on psychoactive prescription drugs alone, and many drug abuse experts believe the NIDA estimate is conservative. If the number of women addicted to both alcohol and pills is considered, the toll of dually or poly addicted women probably is at least twice as high—2 to 4 million. (For purposes of comparison, NIDA estimates the number of heroin addicts of both sexes to be half a million.) According to government statistics, 1 out of every 5 women—or 16 million women eighteen or older—will take tranquilizers for short or long periods of time in any given year. Of that number of tranquilizer users, the FDA estimates that 2 in 5, or 6.5 million, are regular users of alcohol, and 1 in 5, or more than 3.2 million, is a heavy user. The number of women alcoholics in the United States now is estimated at a staggering 5 million, and on the basis of the numbers of women entering rehabilitation programs with dual addiction, at least half are hooked on both alcohol and pills, chiefly Valium. The magnitude of the prescription abuse problem illustrated by these usage figures is highlighted by the government's reports on the number of women admitted to hospital emergency rooms for accidental and purposeful overdosing on prescription tranquilizers in combination with alcohol or other drugs.

Of the 78,400 reported emergency room incidents in a twelve-month period ending April 1977 involving minor tranquilizers, usually Valium, in combination with alcohol or other drugs, 60 percent of the cases, or about 47,000, were women. Of the 1,500 estimated deaths from minor tranquilizers in combination with another drug and the 100 deaths from minor tranquilizers alone, 60 percent were women. Of all drug-related deaths, including overdoses from illicit street drugs, 57 percent are men, and 43 percent women, further confirming the sexual pattern of men making up a disproportionate share of illicit drug abusers and women a greater share of prescription drug abusers. In an FDA survey of four hospital emergency rooms in representative geographic areas, two-thirds of the drug-related visits involved prescription drugs, and 70 percent of these patients were women, most of whom were between the ages of seventeen and thirty-five. In a study conducted by the state of Rhode Island, 57 percent of the hospital overdose cases in 1975 were women, and 86 percent of the "people in trouble" with drugs calling for help were women. In all these surveys, minor tranquilizers, mostly Valium, either alone or in combination with other drugs, usually alcohol, are implicated.

These statistics, as alarming as they are, represent what many believe to be only a small portion of a much larger and largely hidden problem. According to a 1978 report by a NIDA-sponsored Alliance of Regional Coalitions on Drugs, Alcohol and Women's Health, the statistics show "only the tip of the iceberg." The alliance's report, based on information gathered from forty-nine states and the District of Columbia over an eight-month period, concludes that "substantial numbers [of women] are using drugs and/or alcohol, have not yet had visible trouble, and that large numbers are in trouble but remain unidentified." The report shows that "drug and alcohol abuse appears to cut across all economic, social, racial and cultural boundaries, but many—perhaps the majority—of women substance abusers are 'hidden.' They do not become 'statistics' until confronted by a crisis that forces them to seek help. The stigma attached to the abuse of drugs or alcohol by women makes it difficult for them to admit their problem, seek help, be rehabilitated and then accepted by society." Later in this chapter, we will examine the roadblocks that hinder women in recognizing their addiction problems and in getting help through the health care system.

It is no accident that prescription psychoactive drugs are a common and serious problem for women, and it is not coincidental that more women than men become prescription junkies or cross-addicted to tranquilizers and alcohol. Women are the major users of prescription—and over-the-counter—psychoactive drugs. Women are prescribed tranquilizers at a consistent two-to-one ratio to men. In addition, they take 71 percent of all antidepressants and 80 percent of all legally obtained amphetamines. NIDA estimates that an astounding 32 million women—or 42 percent of the adult female population—have taken minor tranquilizers at some time; 16 million—or 21 percent—have used other prescription sedatives; and 12 million—or 16 percent—have used stimulants. By contrast, only 16 million adult males—or 21 percent of all men—have used minor tranquilizers; 12 million—or 16 percent—have used other sedatives; and 5 million—or 8 percent—have used prescription stimulants.

The number of women exposed to psychoactive prescription drugs is growing rapidly as the medical profession increasingly relies on chemical solutions. In 1977, NIDA says, 8.5 million women used prescription tranquilizers for the first time. An additional 3 million women were prescribed other sedatives for the first time, and 1 million became first-time users of stimulants.

The most apparent reason women receive and take more tranquilizers and other psychoactive drugs is that women see doctors more often than men. According to the National Center for Health Statistics, nearly 60 percent of all visits to physicians are made by women. In 1976 the average number of physician visits per person was 5.6 for women and only 4.3 for men. Men are more likely—at least in the early to middle years—to visit doctors for specific and easily identifiable physical ailments. Women, on the other hand, are accustomed to seeing their gynecologists or obstetricians at least once a year whether they have a specific complaint or not. They also are more likely to see an internist or family doctor for routine checkups. Routine tests such as Pap smears also bring women into more frequent contact with the medical profession. Women traditionally have placed more trust in the medical profession, and many women active in the feminist health movement think this trust has been misplaced. In an introduction to a resource guide on health care for women, Belita Cowen writes: "When men go to the doctor, it is usually because they are ill. Women, however, seek medical care when they are healthy—for birth control, abortion, prenatal care, childbirth, Pap smears and breast exams, not to mention the countless times that women with small children see the pediatrician. Women, more so than men, rely on doctors, make more office visits, consume more pills, are admitted to hospitals more frequently, have more surgery, and are committed to mental hospitals more often than men. This dependence on the medical profession has created a situation where healthy women are given medications and even surgery that may be medically unjustified."

It generally is true of doctors and patients that there is an expectation of treatment, and in the last twenty-five years the preferred method of treatment has been drugs. Indeed, it is not uncommon today to be asked after one sees a doctor, "What did he give you?" Built into that question is the assumption that if the doctor didn't give you anything, you really must not be sick and perhaps are a hypochondriac. It also is characteristic of the medical profession's emphasis on treatment instead of prevention that there is an expectation on the part of the doctor that something be given to the patient to satisfy his need to provide treatment. Leaving the doctor's office with a prescription satisfies the patient's expectation of receiving something that confirms an ailment, and at the same time the doctor's needs are satisfied by his providing the prescription.

Another major factor in prescription writing is economic. Doctors keep patients moving in and out of the office quickly, terminating patient visits by taking out the prescription pad. The more patients a doctor can see during regular office hours, the more money the doctor makes. Statistics furnished by the National Center for Health Statistics show that the average patient visit is surprisingly brief. Some 16.4 percent of patients see a doctor for five minutes or less, 31.8 percent see the doctor for six to ten minutes, 20 percent for sixteen to thirty minutes, and only 5.4 percent for more than half an hour. With many doctors spending only about ten minutes with each patient, it is not surprising they take the easiest and most economical approach to therapy—the prescribing of medications. With anxiety, stress, and nervousness having replaced the common cold as the major patient complaint, prescribing of the tranquilizing drugs like Valium becomes almost an automatic reflex, just as the prescribing of antibiotics for cold symptoms is routine for cold viruses despite the fact that they are of no value in treating viruses. As one physician put it so well, "It takes thirty seconds to write a prescription for Valium but thirty minutes to explain why a patient shouldn't have it." The brief patient-doctor visit also does not permit enough time for much more than a cursory physical examination, let alone time for a dialogue between patient and doctor to determine the root causes of the anxiety, to explore alternate nonchemical therapy, to determine accurately life-style habits such as alcohol consumption, or, for that matter, to explain the side effects, drug interactions, and usage warnings should drugs be prescribed. Significantly, about half of all prescriptions for tranquilizers are written on a patient's visit to a doctor, giving the ring of truth to the frequently made charge that doctors are too quick to put patients on psychoactive drugs on the basis of quick diagnoses and without trying nonchemical approaches—even including doing noth- at all—before resorting to chemicals.

It also is frightening that most prescriptions for psychoactive drugs are written by doctors with little or no training in pharmacology, family physicians, general practitioners, internists, obstetricians-gynecologists, and osteopaths. Psychiatrists and neurologists prescribe only 17 percent of all psychoactive drugs, including the "major" tranquilizers, such as Thorazine, used routinely in the treatment of severe psychotic conditions and controlled under stricter regulations.

Barry Blackwell, chairman of the Department of Psychiatry and a professor of pharmacology at Wright State University in Dayton, Ohio, notes in a study that 97 percent of all family practitioners and internists prescribe Valium, but that two-thirds of its use "is accounted for by only one-quarter of M.D.'s." Citing five independent studies published in the United States, Great Britain, and Canada, Blackwell drew profiles of doctors who prescribe tranquilizers freely and of those who do not. Says Blackwell: "Physicians who use psychotropic drugs stringently have been characterized as better educated, holding progressive views, and as treating the patient as a whole person. Fewer prescriptions are given when the doctor finds the patient easy to talk to and considers the consultation to be satisfactory. This contrasts with the heavy prescriber who is characterized as being *pessimistic about outcome and more angry toward the patient.*"

These negative attitudes of heavy prescribers of tranquilizing drugs make women especially vulnerable to receiving and using unnecessary and perhaps dangerous mood-altering drugs because women are the most frequent users of physician services. Because they see more doctors more frequently, it follows that they will take and use more drugs. But another important component is the fact that women report symptoms of an emotional nature more often than men, who are more apt to report physical symptoms. Women are caught in a bind of reporting their feelings to a medical profession that is overwhelmingly male and views emotional expression as a weakness.

Noting that women make more visits to physicians, are more likely than men to report emotional symptoms, and receive more prescriptions of all kinds, Dr. Linda Fidell, a psychologist at California State University at Northridge, points out that the three variables are indeed related but do not tell the whole story. In a widely quoted article, "Put Her Down on Drugs: Prescribed Drug Use in Women," she writes: "Since physicians tend to terminate interviews by giving prescriptions, it isn't surprising to find the sex with the greater number of visits getting the greater number of prescriptions. The problem is that the numbers are disproportionate. Women get more drugs than they make visits. Therefore, a relationship that appears straightforward has, in fact, a heavy overlay of sex-role stereotyping." In the stereotyped female-patient, male-physician confrontation, which unfortunately is more real than hypothetical, the woman describes her feelings of frustration, inadequacy, guilt, fear, anger, and resentment in, say, her relationships with her husband and children. Hearing this expression of emotional feelings from a male view that accepts physical symptoms as real but emotional symptoms as unreal, the doctor reacts negatively toward his female patient. He is uncomfortable, unwilling to understand, unable to communicate in a like language, frustrated by his inability to provide a cure, discouraged in his desire for a favorable outcome, impatient to end the interview, and angry that his time is being wasted. To bring a quick end to the consultation and at the same time to fulfill his expectation of providing treatment and the woman's expectation of receiving it, the doctor writes a prescription for Valium, assures his patient the pills will help, and sends her on her way with the parting information that the prescription is refillable and can be renewed with a telephone call to the office.

In one of the pioneer studies on the sexist bias demonstrated by the medical profession, Ruth Cooperstock, a sociologist at the Toronto Addiction Foundation, asked general practitioners to describe the typical "complaining patient" without reference in the questionnaire to sex. A substantial 72 percent "referred spontaneously to female patients," only 4 percent mentioned men, and 24 percent made no mention of either sex. According to the sexual role models of Western society, men are strong and stoic and women are weak and emotional. Even when women complain to their doctors of physical ailments, they often are not taken seriously and are dismissed as being "hysterical." Men who complain of physical ailments are taken seriously on the ground that they wouldn't be complaining if they were not really sick. The negative attitudes toward women are even more sharply focused when women present emotional symptoms whether in conjunction with physical symptoms or not. Cooperstock found that when men and women presented the same symptoms of unhappiness, crying, depression, nervousness, worry, restlessness, and tenseness, doctors prescribed tranquilizers more frequently for the female than for the male patients. On the other hand, men received slightly more physical therapies and laboratory tests. Follow-up therapy produced similar results: "Prescriptions for tranquilizers increased in proportion to total female visits, but this was not so for male visits."

Why do women get all this attention? Are women more emotionally and mentally unstable than men, or are they just perceived that way? Are women under greater cultural, social, and economic pressure than men, or are women just more likely to admit they feel stress and other feelings? Says Cooperstock: "Briefly stated, the first component of the model holds that contemporary Western women are permitted greater freedom than men in expressing feelings. Because of this, women are more likely to perceive or recognize their feelings and, more specifically, to recognize emotional problems in themselves. Since the woman is permitted greater expression of emotion (whether it be pleasure, pain or dependency) and hence recognizes emotions more readily, she feels freer to bring her perceived emotional problems to the attention of the physician." The doctor expects women to come to him with "emotional problems" and thus expects "a higher proportion of female than male patients will need mood-modifiers."

Dr. Donald Bennett, a pharmacologist on the staff of the American Medical Association in Chicago, thinks women are indeed under greater stress than men in our current environment because they have more direct responsibility at home and with the children. Women are constantly involved with the children and the home, and if anything goes wrong, they are sitting on it. Therefore, they have a greater need for tranquilizing drugs. They have more stress than men do. I'm not saying they should receive more, but they probably need more help, and they seek more help," he said in an interview. Bennett, who was careful to note he is not a spokesman for the AMA or in a policy-making position, also said women as a group may receive more medication than they need: "I honestly believe that a number of them receive antianxiety drugs when they shouldn't receive them. I think because of the pressure of having to see a number of people in a short period of time, there are instances when a doctor should consider alternate therapy but can't. There isn't enough counseling as there should be in an office practice."

Dr. Charlotte H. Kerr, president of the 6,000-member American Medical Women's Association, believes women, particularly those who work, are under greater pressure because they "still have the responsibility of the home. No matter how cooperative the husband, some of them can't cope with all this." Dr. Kerr, a gynecologist in private practice in Florida, finds many of her patients try to do too much themselves, are reluctant to ask their husbands and children to help out around the house and feel guilty when they do. "I go over their life-styles, finding out what they do. I try to get them to take some time for themselves, take an exercise program, for example. In other words, I sit down and help them work out some of their family problems and fix up a work schedule with everyone having some responsibilities so they will have more time for themselves and won't feel they are on a roller coaster." Dr. Kerr feels female doctors are better equipped to counsel women because as a rule they schedule fewer patients to spend more time with each patient and because they have the "potential of being more perceptive of problems. As women physicians they are in a position of coping with the same problems, having to cram their time effectively for family, home, and practice. Women physicians usually are successful at it because otherwise they wouldn't be practicing. Male physicians can read about it, but it is impossible for them to fully comprehend how women feel."

The difficulty is finding a woman doctor in private practice. Without question, American medicine is one of society's most male-dominated professions. Only about 9 percent of the nation's 373,000 practicing physicians were women as of 1978. Not much progress has been made since 1905, when women represented 4.1 percent of the total or, for that matter, since 1955, when they totaled 6 percent. Even the traditional female medical specialties are dominated by men in the modern medical system. Of the more than 21,000 active specialists in obstetrics and gynecology, only 1,887 were women in 1978. By far the most open area for women doctors is in the field of pediatrics, where the AMA lists 5,306 women practicing, about one-quarter of the total. While women have been systematically excluded from the "doctor" categories of the health care system in the United States, they traditionally have constituted an overwhelming percentage of the work force subservient to male doctors, administrators, and teachers. Women constitute 70 percent of all nurses, aides, laboratory technicians, clerks, maids, and cooks. "From the nurses' aide, whose menial tasks are spelled out with industrial precision, to the 'professional' nurse, who translates the doctors' orders into the aide's tasks, nurses share the status of a uniformed maid service to the dominant male professionals," wrote Barbara Ehrenreich and Deirdre English in a history of women healers published by the Feminist Press.

Until the federal government forced change through anti-discrimination regulations in the allocation of funding for medical schools, few women could gain admission, and those who could often were badgered and ignored. In 1973 "Dr. Margaret A. Campbell" published a damning critique of the attitudes of male medical school administrators, professors, and students toward both female students and female patients. On the basis of seventy-six responses from women medical students at forty-one medical schools, "Campbell" traced a persistent pattern of male discrimination and domination. Respondents reported that lecturers often referred to women patients as "hysterical," "hypochondriacs," "douche bags," and "crocks." "Dr. Margaret A. Campbell" was a pseudonym for Dr. Mary Howell, who published her survey while serving as associate dean of students at the Harvard Medical School, one of the nation's most prestigious institutions. At the time she was the highest-ranking woman in any medical school. Out of fear of being fired, Howell, a pediatrician, did not reveal her authorship until after she resigned. In the 1973 study, Howell showed how medical education conditioned doctors in "the assumption that the ills of women are less important than those of men; repeatedly the students comment that the medical and psychological illnesses of women are slighted in the medical curriculum. If signs and symptoms of disease are regularly *assumed* to be of a psychological origin then, in the 'scientific' atmosphere of present-day medical education, they are of no further concern to the physician."

Not only are almost all doctors, administrators, and professors men, but nearly all the standard medical textbook writers are men, further assuring a male view in the perception of ailments of women. In *The Hidden Malpractice: How American Medicine Mistreats Women*, author Gena Corea documents many instances of misinformation and unscientific conclusions in medical textbooks written by men about female conditions. To cite one example, Dr. Thomas H. Green, Jr., in a 1965 textbook, *Gynecology: Essentials of Clinical Practice*, claims one of the causes of menstrual cramps is "immaturity and dependency, or rejection and misunderstanding of the female role." In fact, says Corea, "there is almost no research to back up many of the assertions physicians make about the causes of cramps and other menstrual disorders. They pull this sort of thing right out of their hats."

In a more recent example of the tendency of male doctors to dismiss as exaggerated the health problems of women, the January 4, 1979, issue of the *Journal of the American Medical Association* featured an article on the cancer-causing properties of estrogens, entitled "What You Should Know about Estrogens or the Perils of Pauline." The author, Dr. Richard L. Landau of the University of Chicago Medical School, starts out by wondering what happened to America's sense of humor and bemoaning that "the world should throw away so many good things merely because they are unwholesome." The tragic irony is that on the same day most doctors received their *JAMA* with Landau's article they also received a current edition of the *New England Journal of Medicine* which included a study showing that women using estrogen during menopause were six times more likely to develop uterine cancer. Such a risk is hardly "the perils of Pauline."

To women like Gena Corea and many others in the growing women's health movement, the issue boils down to one of male control of women. Says Irene Javors, a therapist who helped establish a unique clinic in New York to help women free themselves from dependency on male doctors and psychiatrists: "The way the system is now set up in the patient-doctor relationship, the patient necessarily is giving up power to this all-knowing expert. This is a passive role, and it corresponds with the passive role women are taught. It is men telling women what to do. We get women who have been on drugs and in psychotherapy for from five to twenty years. Instead of the psychotherapy encouraging them to be independent and make choices, they are taught to be more dependent. Physicians prescribe so many drugs because they see feelings and emotions as a sign of being sick. The orientation is to drug a feeling so you don't feel it. From our orientation, we do not see feeling as a disease but as a very human experience and something to explore. The point is you're feeling, you're not sick. It's okay to feel."

Doctors, whether in general medicine or in psychiatry, like to drug women patients with tranquilizers to make them easier to work with, says Javors. "Drugs make the person more manageable. You're in control more. If you can diagnose a feeling as an entity to be treated, then you don't have to deal with the patient as a human being."

Gena Corea believes women "sometimes appear to confirm the sexist views of male physicians" by their behavior and thus reinforce a parent-childlike relationship. "So while some women object to the condescending way doctors relate to them—the pats on the head, the slow baby talk, the gentle refusal to explain the diagnosis or treatment—other women like it," she wrote. Whether they like it or not, she added, "It can harm them" by exposing them to "unnecessary surgery, unproven drugs, and population-control experiments."

Women more than men place almost a blind trust in their doctors, and doctors like it that way, according to Dr. Diana Scully, a sociologist at Virginia Commonwealth University. "Doctors like patients who obey, who do as they are told," she said in an interview. In a two-year study of thirty interns in obstetric and gynecology wards in the Chicago area, Scully concluded that doctors just starting out look forward to an "ideal" practice of white, middle-class, well-educated women. "They are the most trusting, the most easily controlled, the most malleable, and the most likely to obey orders," she said. What the doctors don't want, she found, is a woman patient who "knows health care from A to Z" and would challenge, question, and not obey.

Jean Daley * was an ideal patient—female, white, middle-class, and college-educated. She trusted doctors, and she had her first tranquilizer when she was five. According to her baby book, the family doctor prescribed it because she had trouble sleeping. "I had a mentally retarded brother who got sent away when I was five, and I suppose I wasn't handling that very well," she said in an interview, looking back at a long history of drug dependency.

"I started on Librium when I was twenty. I was in a depression when I started taking it. It was prescribed by a psychiatrist in a hospital where I was for clinical depression. I was very withdrawn, and I was suicidal. Maybe he thought it would bring me out of it. I never really got off it.

"I continued taking Librium from 1962 until 1967. Then for some reason, I don't know why, my obstetrician put me on phenobarbital. Maybe it was because I had been drinking heavily and was trying to get clean of everything, including the Librium. I had no history of convulsions or anything like that but I was falling apart. That's how I got into phenobarbital.

"I started taking Valium around 1973. I had been clean and dry for a year but had a very bad spastic colon, and a stomach specialist prescribed Valium. I was either on Valium or trying to withdraw from it for about four years. It was horrible. I was basically dry, but I did go on a toot or two after taking a lot of Valium. The psychological addiction for me was incredible. It made me feel extremely grandiose. It gave me an unusual feeling of well-being way out of proportion. I wasn't at all in touch with my limitations. It made me very insensitive compared to what I normally am. Before I would take it in the morning, I would experience a lot of rage. I got to the point where I was convinced that I couldn't function without it."

At the time Jean had an open-ended prescription from her family doctor. "I could get it anytime I wanted it. By the time I really got dependent on it, I went to another doctor with another set of symptoms. By this time I knew what to say to get a prescription of Valium. So I had two separate prescriptions at two separate drugstores. It was really insane because I never had any trouble getting what I needed—and I never took more than the prescribed dose—under the original prescription. I think I was really afraid of my one source running out, and I wanted to open another one."

After about two years of continuous use of Valium, Jean went back to her doctor and asked if it might be a good idea to go back into psychotherapy. "'No, don't be silly. You don't need a shrink. Just keep taking the Valium,'" Jean recalls his telling her. "This was the stomach guy."

Jean stayed on Valium for another two years while at the same time going to Alcoholics Anonymous for alcoholism. In AA she became concerned about continuing to take Valium, which, like alcohol, acts as a depressant on the central nervous system, and made a special trip back to her doctor to "educate" him about her addiction to alcohol and pills.

"I had to sit down with him for about forty-five minutes. I had to literally scream at this guy, my doctor for nine years, that I'm alcoholic and I can't take Valium. That I knew Valium was lethal for me. I had the feeling he wanted me to shut up, get out of his office, and not bug him. Finally, I asked him what he would do if I were his wife. That's when his attitude changed toward me. I was the one that had to tell him that I was addicted to Valium and that he was not to give it to me, or anything else with a mood changer in it."

Jean had been off Valium for a year and alcohol for nearly three years at the time of the interview. "When I came off Valium the last time, I had to walk and run five to ten miles a day. The agitation was unreal. I had to spend a lot of time taking baths to calm down. It was awful. The really, really bad part was the first three weeks. I don't know how I kept from going back to them, except that I was so scared." Even now, a year after her last pill, Jean still goes through "periods of agitation very similar to what I went through when I first came off. I don't know if it is my anxiety or if it has something to do with them."

Jean still suffers from a spastic colon. "Today the spastic colon is livable. I know it is not going to hurt me organically. When I get into this with my stomach, I know something is going on emotionally, and I should pay attention to it. Being psychosomatic was a hard thing for me to accept because I wanted all these things wrong with me to be legitimate. What this doctor finally helped me do after we had our knock-down, drag-out was to accept that the spastic colon is functional, that I was not going to die from it, and that I was psychosomatic and had to live with it."

Jean Daley no longer can be considered an "ideal" patient who passively follows doctors' orders. "Every time I go to a doctor they take one look at me, spot a psychosomatic person, pull out a pad, and write a prescription for Valium. They always want to give me Valium, whether I go to the OB, the gynecologist, or the stomach doctor. Any complaint they don't consider real, that's their solution. I had an example of it the other night. I went to my OB with a bad vaginal infection. He examined me and said, 'I don't know what this is from. Have you been under any stress lately?' I knew damn well that if I hadn't stopped him right there, he would have given me Valium.

"The whole attitude of doctors is, why live with it if you can get relief? I don't think it ever occurs to them to tough anything out. I really don't.

"The sad thing was that I got hooked because it was so very okay, for my super, super doctor told me to take these pills. They made my stomach like glass, and I said, 'Hmm, they sure work.' But at the end I was like a chemical robot. Something in me knew that this wasn't me. The only thing I could do was take the risk of the pain to find out who I really was."

At the age of thirty-three, Jean Daley, the wife of an advertising executive and mother of two, took charge of her own life and her own body. Hardly a fiery feminist, she took responsibility for maintaining her health and, confronting her own addictive nature, has forced her personal physicians to consider her whole being in diagnosing and treating her when she's sick. Jean sees the same "stomach doctor," but it's no longer a quick look-see and off to the pharmacy. "Until I had the blowup with him, he never took me from the examining room to his office. Now he'll take me into his office and talk to me for fifteen minutes. But I was the one who had to educate him, or he would still be treating me the same way."

What took place between Jean and her doctor is as important to the health care system as the development of a new miracle drug, a new computer, or a new surgical technique. The human element was restored to the one-to-one relationship between a patient and a doctor. The problem with the medical profession today is that not enough doctors are either willing or able to take the time to talk and listen to their patients and not enough patients are willing to accept responsibility for their own care by openly and honestly telling doctors everything they know about their ailments and life-styles and what other drugs, alcohol and/or medication, including over-the-counter drugs, they use and perhaps abuse.

Because women are the major consumers of health care services, be it in the doctor's office, the hospital, the clinic, or the pharmacy, they are the most obvious victims of the flaws in the system. Women are beginning to insist on better treatment, and the growth of the feminist health care movement is one of the most encouraging developments of the last decade. But for many women and sympathetic men, change is coming too slowly in the overwhelmingly male-dominated medical profession and in the pharmaceutical industry, which capitalizes on and profits by playing to the sexual bias of doctors.

In 1968 Dr. Robert Seidenberg, a psychiatrist and psychoanalyst in private practice in Syracuse, New York, and a professor in clinical psychiatry, attended a regional organizational meeting for a chapter of the National Organization on Women (NOW). Out of this meeting came a lonely and frustrating crusade against the pharmaceutical industry, the professional medical and psychiatric associations, and medical journal publishers. "About ten of us sat around sorting out sexism in our work," Seidenberg recalls. "I went home and started going through the scores of professional journals I get." What he found and continues to find is a deliberate sales campaign to drug women. He discovered a conscious effort by Hoffmann-La Roche and other makers of psychoactive drugs to condition doctors in the practice of prescribing drugs for every conceivable life situation—from going off to college to losing a loved one—and to "relieve the anxiety accompanying practically every medical illness and surgical procedure." The targets for this sales campaign were—and are—women.

No one ever accused drug companies and Madison Avenue of not knowing their market or the potential for creating one. At a time of social unrest and when women, the major consumers of health care services, were challenging their traditional societal roles, the market was clear. The advertisements leave no doubt. The surveys by Seidenberg and others, including the authors, show that while women are almost always depicted as the patients in the advertisements for psychoactive drugs, the doctors are always white men, and they all look a little like Marcus Welby —kindly, concerned, distinguished, intelligent, competent, and confident. Until the late 1970s the female patients typically were depicted as distraught, anxious, harried, unhappy, unkempt, tired, overwhelmed, frustrated, scared, and even frigid. Furled brows, nail chewing, sagging shoulders, baggy and circled eyes, and unkempt clothing left no doubt that here is a person who isn't coping with life and is in dire need of a tranquilizer.

The advertisements even utilized the language of the women's liberation movement. A two-page spread by American Home Products' Wyeth Laboratories for Serax, a chemical equivalent of Valium, depicts a nail-chewing housewife imprisoned behind bars of mops, brooms, brushes, irons, and other symbols of household drudgery. The text tells the doctor: "You can't set her free, but you can help her feel less anxious." The underlying message is that when a bored housewife comes into your office, you should drug her so she'll stop being bitchy about having to clean house. Valium was recommended for the overeducated woman who got married, had children, and grew bored, finding her master's degree in fine arts going to waste in volunteer work. Librium was advised for the woman who was beginning to feel like the kitchen appliances. Sandoz Pharmaceuticals pushed tranquilizers for "the woman who can't get along with her new daughter-in-law" or "the newcomer in town who can't make friends." Librium was suggested for the college girl whose "newly stimulated intellectual curiosity may make her more sensitive to and apprehensive about unstable national and world conditions." Ritalin was recommended as a pick-me-up for "environmental depression," such as when an air conditioner is "turned down, or off."

Another common theme running through advertising for psychoactive drugs is the suggestion that they are an effective way to get someone (usually a woman) off someone else's (usually a man's) back. Tranquilizers are suggested for the nagging wife, so the husband can get some sleep; for the "impossible" woman, so her husband or boyfriend can relax; and for the elderly mother, so that life will be simpler for her daughter. Through some slick Madison Avenue techniques, doctors are told that if they drug their female patients who disrupt their office schedules by unnecessary visits and phone calls, their offices will run more smoothly and they can make more money.

Although some of the more blatant abuses have been curbed under a directive from the Food and Drug Administration, women remain the number one sales target in tranquilizer ads. "Times change. Today's patient has changed." With that declaration in 1974, Abbott Laboratories announced a "different tranquilizer" in bold print. In the small print, Abbott admits its new tranquilizer, Tranxene, is "clinically equivalent to diazepam [Valium]." What's different about Tranxene is the Tranxene woman. To be sure, it is still a male hand handing a prescription to a woman patient. But instead of an anxious, unkempt housewife, we have a pretty blond neatly and simply groomed and dressed. The blue eyes are clear, and there is no sign of fatigue or despair. For more than fifteen years, advertisers of psychoactive drugs presented pictures of women who at least looked as if they needed help; suddenly they present pictures of women who look as if they don't need help. By 1978 the Tranxene woman is sitting at a typewriter "calm but awake" on tranquilizers. Medical science hasn't changed, but marketing strategy has. In its battle for a share of the $2.3 billion tranquilizer market, 80 percent of which is held by Hoffmann-La Roche with Valium, Librium, and Dalmane, Abbott was out to persuade doctors to prescribe Tranxene for the young working woman.

With depression catching on as a growing medical problem for women, Pfizer Laboratories heavily promoted Sinequan, a powerful antidepressant, in 1978–79 with two-page full-color ads showing a female hand cleaning a dusty window with a rag. When the dirt clears from the window, we see the sun coming up over a mountain range and glistening through fresh pine trees onto the cool waters of a mountain lake. The ad says that "clearing of depression" with up to 150 milligrams of Sinequan a day is as easy as washing windows with a terrycloth rag. (We take a detailed look at the advertising and sales practices of drug companies in Chapter 8.)

Not only are women victimized by drug promotion, misdiagnosis, and drug therapy, but they are victimized in recovery should they seek help for drug addiction. "While women make up more than half of the population of the United States, they do not account for half of those being treated for alcohol and drug problems—even though some estimates suggest that women's substance abuse problems may be as great as those of men," according to the report of the Alliance of Regional Coalitions on Drugs, Alcohol, and Women's Health. One obvious reason is that most drug rehabilitation programs originally were established to treat alcoholism, considered a man's disease, not women alcoholics, whose numbers are growing, or prescription junkies, or those dually or poly addicted to prescription drugs and alcohol. For example, of the 600 federally funded halfway houses in the United States as of 1977, only 30 were for women; the rest were only for men. Although drug treatment programs primarily are a state affair, the federal government has tremendous clout in policies and programs because the states are heavily dependent on Washington for funding, and federal agencies are beginning to require the states to make more rehabilitation services available to women. Still, in 1978, of the 54,000 treatment slots funded by the National Institute on Drug Abuse, only 26 percent were for women. Most of the monies flowing from Washington are directed at heroin programs, however, and very little is designated for persons, most of whom are women, addicted to tranquilizers and other psychoactive drugs prescribed by their doctors.

One woman working with a federal agency described her frustration in trying to "get the system moving from a very male-oriented extra-illegal drug abuse program to starting to think along broader lines of programs for abusers of legal drugs." The woman, who was in a policy-making position and asked not to be named, said she went to work for the agency "all fired up" after personally working with poly addicted women for ten years as a social worker. "My experience in government tells me that government is reactionary and not proactive, meaning that if enough pressure is put on a single issue, the government will eventually move. If there is no pressure, it ain't going to happen. It's been an extremely frustrating experience to get the system to change in midstream and circle in another way." One major reason why the system is resisting change is that neither the medical community, which prescribes psychoactive drugs, nor the federal government, which sanctions their use, wants to admit there is a prescription drug problem.

Also standing in the way of women who want or need help for addiction to licit drugs and/or alcohol and other drugs are forceful societal attitudes that prevent women from seeking treatment. "While society tends to accept the fact of alcoholism and drug abuse in men, women's drug problems are neither accepted nor tolerated," concludes the report compiled by the women's Alliance of Regional Coalitions. "A woman is labeled, instead, as unfit, deviant, weak and 'fallen' often by herself as well as by society." This pressure often prevents early detection by creating a strong atmosphere of denial. State drug abuse authorities reporting to the alliance said women typically seek help at later stages of dependency than men.

The problem of prescription drug abuse among women is further complicated by forces that keep it hidden. As we have seen, women are likely to turn for help to their doctors, who prescribed the drugs for them in the first place and who are least sensitive to the problem. "More often than not the women coming to us have been on drug therapy for many years," says Irene Javors of the Feminist Center for Human Growth and Development in New York. "They don't usually come to believe the treatment they are in is really destructive. They are very frightened and distrusting because they think we're going to be doing the same thing."

Despite the handicaps, there is reason for hope.[The most important thing any person, regardless of sex, can do is take primary responsibility for his or her own health care.]By taking charge of our lives and forcing our doctors to deal with us as people to be helped when we need help, not as objects to be drugged whether we need it or not, we can force the medical profession to become more human and caring and less oriented to the scientific and chemical solution. By becoming knowledgeable about what drugs can and cannot do, we can weigh the risks against the benefits of drug therapy and insist that our doctors allow us to be partners in this evaluation.

We examine some of the resources available to help us take charge of our mental and physical health in Appendixes 2 and 3. In the chapter that follows, we examine some of the problems, many of which are just surfacing, associated with drugging women during pregnancy, labor, and delivery. The consequences of heavily medicating women is not an issue of concern only for women but rather one of overriding significance for all of us, women and men, child and adult.

Poisoning Our Future | 4

In the United States many people view pregnancy and childbirth not as a natural process, but as a medical condition or illness, requiring monitoring every step of the way by a physician. Despite the growth of the natural childbirth movement in this country, a great number of physicians believe that pregnancy and birth require more—not fewer—drugs than other conditions.

The drugs prescribed for pregnant women in this country, either in the early stages of pregnancy or in the delivery room, often are the same tranquilizing substances that permeate other stages of life. Some of the drugs prescribed for women in labor are extremely potent, such as the phenothiazines, normally used to treat the insane but sometimes used in the delivery room as sedatives and early in pregnancy to treat morning sickness. Others are less powerful, such as the over-the-counter drugs used by many pregnant women to ease some of the pains that accompany the growth of the fetus.

While tranquilizers, such as Miltown, Librium, or Valium, have been routinely prescribed for many years during pregnancy and have been considered relatively benign substances by both mother and physician, a growing body of scientific evidence now implies a causal relationship between these drugs and birth defects. Even the ubiquitous aspirin, supposedly a safe painkiller, has been linked to a number of children born with cleft palate after their mothers took this most common of all drugs.

Medicated childbirth is the routine practice in this country, and it is growing. While the public may believe the natural childbirth movement, with all the attendant publicity, is sweeping the country, the opposite is true. In written testimony submitted to the Senate Subcommittee on Health and Scientific Research in April 1978, Dr. Yvonne Brackbill, professor of psychology at the University of Florida in Gainesville and a pioneer in the field of behavioral teratology, estimated that "95 percent of births in United States hospitals nowadays are medicated. This means 3,500,000 medicated births out of 3,700,000 births a year."

Dr. Paul Doerning, a researcher, puts the number of drugs in terms of doses. He estimates that in 1973 obstetricians in private practice prescribed a staggering total of 3.7 million doses of narcotic analgesics, 1.1 million doses of nonnarcotic analgesics, and 1.1 million doses of tranquilizers to women in the hospital waiting to give birth, before they even entered the delivery room.

For many years doctors routinely prescribed Miltown to help their pregnant patients cope with prenatal stress. When Librium was introduced, it too was prescribed for pregnant women. Valium came on the market, and doctors found it to be a panacea for stress and strain experienced by pregnant patients. These drugs were prescribed not for any compelling medical necessity, but rather to treat anxiety.

The results of such large-scale tranquilizer use by pregnant women were clear. A series of medical studies in the 1970s suggests all these "best-sellers" as the possible cause of a variety of birth defects. Nowhere in the whole age of chemical tranquillity is the risk/reward ratio between the use of drugs and the consequences more apparent than in this area.

Reports of birth abnormalities associated with Miltown, Librium, and Valium have been routinely forwarded by doctors to both the drug manufacturers and the FDA, but it was not until 1976 that the FDA finally took heed of this growing evidence and put a warning label on all the minor tranquilizers, cautioning against their use by pregnant women. Hoffmann-La Roche steadfastly maintains that one of its products, Valium, has not been implicated in birth defects, despite the FDA's warning notice.

There are cases of these drugs being routinely administered

from "standing orders" which many obstetricians leave with hospitals where they practice. When a woman is admitted for delivery, the drugs are started without consultation between mother and doctor.

Dr. Brackbill, in a chapter she wrote for *The Handbook of Infant Development*, presented a typical standing order for medication to be administered to *all* private patients of one Florida obstetrician (that is, without taking into account the woman's age, physical condition, or other variables):

Routine Ante Partum Orders

Nembutal 200 mg by mouth, as necessary
(for mothers delivering first child)

Demerol 75–100 mg
Largon 20 mg
} Intramuscular, first dose

Scopolamine 0.4 mg
Demerol 50 mg
Largon 20 mg
Scopolamine 0.3 mg
} Intramuscular, every
two hours as necessary

Deladumone Ob, 1 ampule intramuscular at
6 cm dilation, as necessary

1000 cc Ringer's lactate, intravenous
All patients to have regional anesthesia

Dr. Brackbill contends that the use of such standing orders is widespread. She cannot make a national estimate, but in a survey she conducted with the directors of pharmacy of ten hospitals located in Florida, she found that the percentage of obstetricians in those hospitals issuing such orders for routine medication of their patients ranged from 50 percent to 100 percent, with the median being 85 percent.

Public protest against the widespread use of these drugs has been weak. Doris Haire, president of the American Foundation of Maternal and Child Health, attributes this to the social conditioning of mothers, a desire by the medical profession to have tractable patients, and laxity on the part of the Food and Drug Administration.

Mrs. Haire, who has been in the forefront of a small but increasingly vocal and effective movement to control the use of obstetrical medications, says part of the problem lies with women themselves. They have been led to believe that the pain of childbirth is continuous and unbearable and that the technology of this country has developed to the point where women no longer have to bear the pain. But Mrs. Haire, who delivered her first child naturally in 1951—a time when hardly any women opted for natural childbirth—says the misleading information surrounding the pain of a natural experience deprives women of the "central, core experience of any woman's life. When I gave birth to my first daughter—fully awake, alive, seeing, and hearing—it was like I had given birth to the sun—I was all aglow with the spirit of it."

But Mrs. Haire opted for natural childbirth for a more pragmatic reason than just the experience—she wanted to do everything possible to ensure she had as "intelligent a child as possible." She knew instinctively what later research proved true: drugs can and do interfere with the child's development.

"When I was pregnant, I was determined that my children be given the best head start possible. So I insisted that I have no drugs, and in that time it was hard to find a doctor to go along with this. But I persisted and finally found one who would let me deliver naturally—and with my husband in the delivery room.

"This was the beginning of an experience that would finally lead me to petitioning the FDA, to badgering doctors, to giving lectures about the dangers of drugged childbirth and the beauty of natural childbirth.

"But what really convinced me that I was on the right track was an experience I had while auditing a course in obstetrics at a major university medical school in 1973. I had become very active in the whole field of childbirth at that time—I was president of the International Childbirth Education Association and had just completed a tour of thirty-seven countries around the world, observing their obstetrical techniques. I went, more to confirm my suspicions about U.S. obstetrical practices than anything else.

"The suspicions were confirmed one night in the delivery room, after I had observed what happened to seven healthy women.

Each of the women was brought into the delivery room and automatically given a spinal anesthetic. Then, because the mothers' pushing reflexes had been deadened, the doctors had to deliver the babies with forceps.

"I was so upset by this I called the resident aside and asked him what he was doing. I pointed out to him that if the women had not been given anesthesia, they would have been able to 'push,' and the babies all could have been delivered normally, without the use of those terrible forceps.

"He just looked at me very strangely and said, 'Mrs. Haire, if all women gave birth naturally, we would have no one to practice our techniques on.' That's what he said. Absolutely deadpan.

"The reaction I get to this story when I tell it shows the attitudes of obstetricians toward childbirth compared to the attitudes of women. When I tell the story to a group of obstetricians, they chuckle nervously. But when I tell the story to women, they are shocked."

Mrs. Haire knew why the residents at the medical school wanted to practice their techniques: because these techniques would give them the ideal patient when they went into practice —tractable, malleable, and quiet.

"Have you ever walked into a delivery room?" Mrs. Haire asks. "It's eerily quiet because that's how the doctors want it. They want all those women knocked out. If they don't feel pain, they don't cry out, make noise, or otherwise upset the routine."

This convinced Mrs. Haire that something had to be done about the state of obstetrical practices in this country.

"So I made my first trip down to the FDA, and I met with Dr. Richard Crout, director of the Bureau of Drugs, and asked him what he was going to do about the use of these drugs. I pointed out to Dr. Crout that no one had ever determined whether or not these drugs used in labor and delivery had an adverse effect on the fetus which would affect the subsequent development of the child. I requested that the FDA advise expectant mothers, by means of a 'Patient Information Package,' that the delayed long-term effects of the drug on the subsequent neurologic development of the offspring are unknown.

"Yet the FDA continued to let the manufacturers sell the

drugs. The FDA told me they had no power over that, no control. Well, it took me awhile, but I have finally proved them wrong."

Doris Haire went to work as a concerned layman, with the intuition that many professionals seemed to lack. She traveled all over the world observing obstetric practices. She attended FDA hearings on drugs. She wrote letters; she badgered senators and congressmen. Along the way she met people who had the same concern she had—giving infants the best start in life possible.

Mrs. Haire's work is far from over. Yet she has had several successes that have gone a long way in protecting infants from exposure to potentially threatening drugs. In July 1977 she delivered a technical paper to the Food and Drug Administration that resulted in that agency's finally barring the use of oxytocin, a uterine stimulant, as a means of inducing labor. In April 1978 Mrs. Haire and many of the individuals she met in her research into the problems of obstetric medications told a special committee of the United States Senate the results of their decade-long efforts.

At that hearing, Richard Butcher, associate professor of pediatrics research at the Institute for Developmental Research, Children's Hospital Research Foundation, in Cincinnati, Ohio, said, "The fetus is vulnerable to brain damage throughout the entire period of gestation." In testimony to the Senate in April 1978 Butcher warned about the problems associated with drug use in pregnancy and delivery:

"We have no system whatsoever for identifying drugs and chemicals that, when administered during pregnancy or delivery, may permanently impair psychological functioning in the offspring. There are neither human investigations to study behavioral outcomes of pregnancy nor requirements for animal studies, as there are in Britain and Japan, where behavioral teratology of new drugs must be studied before they are marketed. Thus, there is the threat that events during pregnancy and delivery are reducing the intellectual capacity of a sizable number of children. Because these impairments are not accompanied by physical signs, they are going completely undetected. . . ."

Butcher told the Senate that because the effects that drugs

used during pregnancy and delivery have on the mind are subtle and cannot be seen—unlike the birth deformities caused by thalidomide—the problem may have been overlooked. He pointed out that it took a long time to link thalidomide with the birth defects, even with such visible defects, and suggested that the Senate "consider, in the light of the history of thalidomide, how small would be the probability of detecting the cause and effect relationship between an agent administered during pregnancy and [brain] impairment. Such an impairment would not be an uncommon event, would represent a rather subtle effect, and would be diagnosed almost certainly after the first year of life."

Dr. Yvonne Brackbill believed she had found further evidence linking obstetric medication with the kind of impairment Butcher told the Senate about. The evidence was contained in an analysis of data collected by an obscure agency of the Department of Health, Education and Welfare called the National Institute of Neurological and Communicative Disorders and Stroke. This agency had gathered a massive amount of data on 53,000 mothers and their children in a study called the Collaborative Perinatal Project. Using researchers in hospitals throughout the United States, the CPP gathered every conceivable kind of medical data on the children and their mothers: drugs taken, the results of routine physical exams, and intelligence tests of the children at various stages of life.

Early in 1974 Dr. Brackbill and her colleague, Dr. Sally Broman, asked NINCDS for permission to use this data bank, and they conducted a study to determine the effects of obstetric medication on the development of the 53,000 children included in the data.

In 1979, after the authors filed a Freedom of Information Act request, NINCDS released the Brackbill-Broman study, which said that analgesics and anesthetics given to women during labor and delivery may have long-lasting effects on a child's behavior and development. In the scientific phraseology of the Brackbill and Broman report, "There were strong associations between the pharmacological agents that had been administered during labor and delivery and the infant's development during the first year.

"In some cases these associations decreased with age (e.g. oxytocin) or even disappeared with age (e.g. promethazine), but in others, principally inhalant anesthetics, the associations persisted throughout the first year. . . . The strongest relationships could be seen between the development of gross motor abilities, e.g., the ability to sit, stand and locomote."

Brackbill and Broman believed these effects to be particularly significant because they had chosen only the 3,500 healthiest women from the study to ensure that any developmental problem would be due to the drugs alone, not complications involved in pregnancy or birth.

The Brackbill-Broman report received widespread publicity, caused concern among a number of laymen, and also received sharp criticism from obstetricians, anesthesiologists, and perinatologists.

Medical writer Gina Bari Kolata summarized many of these objections in an article in *Science* magazine in April 1979: "But how solid are Brackbill and Broman's conclusions? One indication they may be questionable is that their statistical consultant, John Bartko of NIMH [National Institute of Mental Health], disassociates himself from their work because they would not follow his advice."

Brackbill also took her case directly to the public, a move that may have pleased natural childbirth advocates but greatly displeased her professional colleagues. As Kolata points out, Brackbill's public stance may have exaggerated the test results beyond the scientific findings.

Milton Alper, an anesthesiologist at the Harvard Medical School, contends that Brackbill has exaggerated her findings when talking to the public. He cites Brackbill's speculation in Senate testimony and elsewhere that obstetrical medications may cause an average loss of four IQ points per child.

Statistician Ralph d'Agostino of Boston University reviewed the Brackbill-Broman report, and he too disagreed with its findings. According to Kolata, "d'Agostino made it clear that he thought Brackbill's and Broman's conclusions unwarranted on the basis of what he had seen of their work."

Emmanuel Friedman, professor of obstetrics and gynecology at Harvard Medical School, was even harsher than d'Agostino in his criticism of the study. Friedman, who has a follow-up contract from NINCDS to analyze the same data Brackbill and Broman looked at, said of their work, "In tone, it is shrill and strident, leaving no doubt of the authors' preconceptions."

According to Dr. Philip Goldstein of the Sinai Hospital department of obstetrics in Baltimore, "I would have no problem with the Brackbill-Broman report if they said obstetricians used these medications injudiciously. But they went much further than that, causing a great deal of alarm and panic."

Behavioral teratology is a new discipline, and little work has been done in the field. While the Brackbill-Broman report might have provided many answers to the real concern many doctors and scientists have about the use of drugs in obstetrics, its tone and its flawed data may have been self-defeating. As medical writer Kolata summarized the controversy in *Science*: "While gaining points with natural childbirth groups, she [Brackbill] and Broman polarized the scientific community against them. Now, even if they are right about the effects of obstetrical medications, they will find that other scientists no longer have anything like open minds on the matter." This is tragic, because, as Dr. Goldstein points out, "we definitely need to do more work in this area—it's an area that needs good, sound studies."

Brackbill and Broman inserted in their report a recommendation made by the American Academy of Pediatrics' Committee on Drugs that could serve as a guideline for any pregnant woman faced with a decision about whether or not to have anesthesia during delivery. The statement reads:

"The committee recommends that until further studies are available, it would be advisable to avoid the use of drugs or drug dosages that are known to produce significant changes in neurobehavior of the infant. This statement does not mean that the patient in labor should be denied reasonable relief of pain by analgesic or anesthetic agents, but rather that the minimum dose of these agents should be administered when indicated.

"Moreover, the committee recommends that the physician discuss with the patient, whenever possible before the onset of labor, the potential benefits and side effects of maternal analgesia and anesthesia on both the mother and the infant."

Brackbill and Broman ended their study by commenting on the Academy's statement: "Implicit in this statement is the recognition of several facts. The first is that, unlike other situations in which physicians prescribe drugs for patients, *pregnancy and childbirth are not illnesses or disease states that can be improved by drug therapy* [emphasis added]. Administering drugs prenatally and perinatally may sometimes be essential but is most often optional and is done to relieve pain, not to remedy a disease. In addition, the mother is the only one who can gauge the pain and her tolerance for it. These considerations re-focus attention on the mother as consumer and active participant in the decision-making process."

On September 1, 1978, New York became the first state to enact a law requiring physicians and nurse-midwives to inform expectant mothers, in advance of birth, of the drugs they expect to employ during pregnancy and of the obstetric medications they expect to use at birth. The law also requires the doctors and midwives to inform expectant mothers "of the possible effects of such drugs on the child and mother." New York physicians complained that the law was impractical and infringed on the doctor-patient relationship.

One of the people for whom the obstetric medication warning comes too late is Benjamin Cohen. A young man, twenty-eight years old in 1979, he is one of the victims of the practice of medicated delivery in this country. He finds it difficult to hold a job, is unable to concentrate, and spends much of each year remembering the horror of the preceding one. Benjamin is not brain-damaged enough to be institutionalized, yet he was classified as an MBD child in the 1960s. His mother, Estelle Cohen, blames Benjamin's living problems on a medication she received in the delivery room. Her story illustrates not only the problems mothers face because of administration of drugs in the delivery room but also the insensitivity of the medical profession, the government, and the school systems to the voice of one angry, concerned average citizen.

While Brackbill was conducting her research on obstetric medications, Estelle Cohen was trying to make the country aware of the hazards of the drugs. She wanted to save other mothers from having to live with a new idea that was sweeping the ranks of obstetricians, "babies by appointment." Benjamin had been such a baby, and she knew the practice could lead other children to a life in an angry twilight. Estelle recounts her problems and her saga:

"Benjamin was born in 1951 and was beautiful. When I was ready to deliver, I had to go to a doctor recommended by my regular obstetrician, who was on vacation. He was at Columbia-Presbyterian in New York, and years later I was to find out he was more of a researcher than an obstetrician.

"This doctor called me up and asked me to come in for an examination. After the exam, he told me that he wanted me to come into the hospital on a certain day, and he would induce labor. I really did not know what he was talking about, questioned him a bit, but finally gave in. You have to remember that was the 1950s, like millions of women, my knowledge of childbirth was nil, and I put all my trust in the doctor.

"I had a highly abnormal birth. I had one very strong, long-lasting, deep, painful contraction. I did not realize for the next fifteen years that this contraction was caused by the drug the doctor used on me."

The contraction that Estelle Cohen describes was the result of the drug Pitocin (oxytocin) which for years was routinely used to induce labor. Pitocin is manufactured by Parke, Davis. The warning carried for the drug in the *Physicians' Desk Reference* states that Pitocin "causes overstimulation of the uterus by improper administration and can be hazardous to both mother and fetus." In fact, so hazardous is this drug—often used more as a matter of convenience for doctor and mother than for any compelling medical reason—that in October 1978 the FDA banned the use of Pitocin to induce labor, but at the end of a four-year effort by Doris Haire, in a bureaucratic sleight of hand the FDA did not ban its use as an adjunct to labor. This has resulted, according to Norma Swenson of the Boston Women's Health Book Collective and coeditor of *Our Bodies, Ourselves*, in "doctors first piercing the amniotic sac and then using Pitocin anyway. The reason—doctors like to use this drug. It makes their job easier."

Estelle Cohen did not know about the possible hazards that a fetus could experience if exposed to Pitocin, but she did know, as Benjamin went through the various stages of childhood, that something was drastically wrong with her son.

"Benjamin entered school at the age of five, and from day one it was an absolute disaster. There was an assistant principal there who told me that in twenty years of experience in education he had seen only two children as bad as my son.

"And I knew there was something wrong with Benjamin. I thought he was emotionally disturbed and wondered if I had done something wrong in bringing him up. He just could not get along in school—I used to go meet him at the school, and when he came out, instead of walking down the steps like all the other children, he came running down, flailing his arms and knocking all the kids out of the way.

"He seemed to have no conscience. He constantly behaved in a very bizarre way. He had an inability to play with other children. His coordination was damaged. He could not hit a ball with a bat.

"Benjamin had a hard time comprehending the simplest of concepts. He could not grasp the fact that when he came to a street corner, he should stop, look both ways, and then cross. Instead, he just dashed across the street—and when you live in a city like New York, this is very hazardous.

"In school, he had trouble learning. It took him a long time to learn to read and write. Finally, when he was nine, I took him to Columbia and had him examined by a group of doctors. They said he had minimum brain damage sustained at birth."

When Estelle received this diagnosis about Benjamin, she enrolled him in a special school. "How is it that in the 1960s we all of a sudden had so many children like Benjamin? Was it a coincidence? I don't think so. I think they all had the same problem.

"Anyway, at that time parents' groups were also being formed, and I joined a group called the New York State Association for Brain Damaged Children. I was grateful for the help people in this group gave me and volunteered my services as an unpaid secretary. This put me into contact with a lot of people whose children had the same problem Benjamin had, and we all wondered how and why such a thing happened to so many children at the same time. I found out later it was probably due to drugs used at childbirth."

During her work with the parents' group, Estelle Cohen

searched for the "why" of her son's problems, and in 1966 she finally found the answer not only for Benjamin but for all those other children as well.

"In 1966 I picked up a copy of *Family Circle* magazine—I don't know where, the beauty parlor, the dentist's office. It really changed my life, though. As I was leafing through that magazine, the July 1966 issue, I came across an article entitled 'Babies by Appointment,' and it was authored by the obstetrician who persuaded me to have induced labor, Dr. Anthony D'Esopo, M.D.

"I could not believe that article. It told in glowing details about the advantages of scheduling your delivery. It talked about the certainty involved, the fact that labor when induced would be slower and less painful. But it also mentioned toward the end of the article some of the problems associated with the drug used to induce labor. The drug was the one I was given, and the article pointed out that if the kind of prolonged contraction I had occurred, it could deprive the fetus of the oxygen its brain needed, and that could cause problems.

"This article turned my life around. I had finally found out what was wrong with Benjamin. You see, for many years I had blamed myself for what had happened to him. I wondered if I had been a good mother; I wondered if his diet had been wrong; I felt maybe I had damaged him emotionally. But after reading that article, I realized it probably was not my fault, but rather the fault of the drug. I also realized that all these other children whose problems their parents could not understand maybe had the same kind of damage in delivery that Benjamin had."

In 1966 Estelle wrote the National Institutes of Health, hoping that they could initiate a research project into the whole problem of drug-related birth defects. She received a reply from Dr. Philip N. Corfman, M.D., director of the Reproduction Program, National Institute of Child Health and Development, dated November 15, 1966, that reads in part:

". . . when oxytocins were first introduced at the turn of the century it quickly became apparent that the very large doses in use then were clearly harmful to both mother and child, and shortly thereafter a conservative approach to the use of these drugs developed. Since then, they have been carefully re-introduced into medical practice. Newer, more potent and safer synthetic drugs have been developed and they are now in wide use. . . .

"You refer to a problem which has not been resolved, namely the establishment of a relationship between the use of labor stimulating drugs in a well controlled medical situation and fetal damage. . . .

"It is because of this important issue that NIH established a number of years ago a collaborative research project with a number of leading obstetrical services throughout the country . . . some goals of this project are to answer some of the questions you raised. Although no definitive answers are yet available, research of this type takes a great deal of time, in part because the children born must be followed for a number of years. There is nothing available so far which implicates the judicious use of oxytocins in childbirth."

Drugs used to induce labor—shortcuts, a means to avoid pain, any kind of pain—like many other drugs described in this book, really are not used for medical reasons. According to Dr. Ronald Rindfuss of the Department of Sociology of the University of North Carolina, elective, or induced, labor is for "personal preference, not medical reasons." Dr. Rindfuss told the Senate Subcommittee on Health and Scientific Research that while medical textbooks almost unanimously discourage the use of elective induction, it is becoming a common practice in the United States, because it is more convenient for the physician.

"One obstetrician told me," Dr. Rindfuss related to the Senate committee, "that he induced 40 percent of his patients. When asked why, he said that he preferred to have weekends with his family—something we can all understand. Another obstetrician told me he preferred scheduled deliveries because they did not interfere with his office schedule. . . .

"It is also easy to understand why obstetricians would want predictability in their lives. What I cannot understand is why a person desiring a predictable daily and weekly schedule would become an obstetrician.

"This is a question that needs to be faced by medical students. What the public has to ask and answer is first whether any medical procedure that might introduce an increased risk to patients, no matter how small the risk is, can be tolerated on the grounds that it is convenient for the physician, and second, if yes, then what level of risk is acceptable."

While the drugs themselves are a real problem, many concerned women say they are only part of the problem. Birth defects resulting from medication used in delivery are as much a result of the attitudes surrounding childbirth in this country as anything else. The women contend that an attitude of looking upon gestation and birth as an illness creates a climate in which drugs not only are routinely used by many doctors but also are routinely expected by many mothers. This is the view espoused by Norma Swenson of the Boston Women's Health Book Collective: "One reason behind the increase in medicated deliveries is simple. Women are increasingly acculturated to believe that the pain of childbirth cannot and should not be endured. They have been taught not only is it a good idea to have a medicated delivery, but it is their right in this society to have it that way. They have been convinced they are lucky medical science in this country has advanced to the point where they do not have to endure the pain that women in less civilized countries must endure."

Swenson explains this desire to escape the pain of childbirth in the same kind of language used to explain many other aspects of the tranquilizing of America: "The problem is that women are told that they should not have to endure this very natural pain. They are taught that there are chemical ways to enable them to cope with it. They are taught that science has found ways to totally eliminate this pain, that while it may be natural, it does not have to be endured, particularly by the American woman."

Swenson contends that most women cooperate with the system, that they willingly allow themselves to be drugged in the delivery room. Many not only ask for "painless" childbirth but expect it. "These women allow themselves to be manipulated and controlled. This kind of practice and these kinds of drugs would not exist unless the women went along with it all."

As Swenson sees it, the first step is to educate women that birth is a joyful, wonderful experience that should occur with all their faculties at peak, natural condition, not drugged into submission. Women, she contends, should also be educated that as natural a childbirth as possible is essential to having a healthy, normal baby. Such education is, of course, too late for many women and many babies, and Swenson believes we have not yet realized the extent to which medicated childbirth will ultimately affect our society.

"I really believe that the moment of birth is one of the key experiences of life, one that is incorporated into a person and affects his behavior for many years to come. Following this line of reasoning, it is my theory, and while it's only a theory, I believe it is a pretty good one, that the real reason for the drug generation is that many of the people who turned to hallucinogens had been delivered under the effects of scopolamine. I think that all those kids who took to the hallucinogens in the 1960s were just trying to create the key experience of their life—being drugged at birth."

Estelle Cohen also believes that the effect of obstetrical medication lingers for years. She theorizes that one of the reasons behind the steady decline on College Board exam scores is a result of obstetrical medication and its effect on the learning process. "College Board scores first started to decline in 1963—that's the year the first children of the postwar baby boom started to take the tests. And the postwar baby boom is the time period when doctors really started using a lot of these drugs." Estelle Cohen points out that the average scores on the College Boards have continued to decline year after year, reflecting, she contends, the increasing use of obstetrical medication and the effect it has on a person's development, intelligence, and behavior.

Estelle Cohen and Doris Haire first met at a meeting on birth defects in Queens, New York, in 1973. Since then they have formed a partnership designed to change the way obstetric drugs are used in this country. Estelle provides the personal experience and the emotion; Doris provides the methodical examination of the laws, the issues, and the scientific literature that have allowed the two of them to achieve some degree of success with the FDA and the medical profession.

In 1973 Mrs. Haire became convinced that the best way to rectify many of the problems associated with the use of medications in pregnancy and childbirth was to change the labeling laws. She had a law firm research the issue and then filed a brief with the FDA, which until that time had maintained it did not have the power to require manufacturers to provide patient-packaging labeling on their drugs—that is, clear, concise, and easily understandable explanations of the drugs in terms the average person could understand. (There is labeling on prescription drugs today—but it is written in medicalese and more often than not the patient never sees it. The doctor can look at it in the *Physicians' Desk Reference*, and the pharmacist can read it on the box; but few patients see the labeling.)

The FDA finally has agreed that it does have the power to require consumer labeling and does require it on three classes of drugs—birth control pills, estrogens, and progesterones. But Mrs. Haire continues to spend a good part of each month testifying at FDA hearings and corresponding with FDA officials. "I tell those people down at the FDA that they have two choices. They can act on my suggestions to protect mothers and babies, or they can drag their feet and look irresponsible. Either way, sooner or later we are going to get what we need for the consumer—and it's up to these officials how they look. And you know, in this country it's very hard to be against motherhood."

Despite that viewpoint, FDA officialdom still seems a long way from instituting measures Doris Haire and other concerned women and doctors believe are necessary to protect the health of future generations. A statement made by FDA Commissioner Donald Kennedy at the Senate subcommittee hearings in April 1978 particularly alarmed Mrs. Haire. At that hearing Commissioner Kennedy said, "Demerol, like other narcotic analgesics, causes mild respiratory depression in some cases [of delivery]. But when the drug is used judiciously, the depressing effects are readily reversible by modern resuscitating techniques."

Mrs. Haire wrote a letter to the commissioner, expressing her concern about that statement particularly in light of the research done to date that implicates Demerol as impeding a child's development. She received a reply from Kennedy dated August 14, 1978, which read in part:

"My statement about Demerol should be interpreted in terms of judicious administration. The labeling for this drug does mention that it . . . may have an effect on the newborn. . . . As mentioned in my [Senate] statement, properly utilized in labor, Demerol is usually not a serious problem. I believe there is extensive clinical experience to support this statement since Demerol has been used in obstetrics for almost 40 years. Demerol is today perhaps the most widely used analgesic for labor."

This statement is unsupported because little or no work had been done on the effect of Demerol on the infant brain all through those forty years. Doris Haire also observed that it is hard to determine whether or not any drug is a problem because "there is widespread underreporting of adverse drug effects."

Two other bits of Commissioner Kennedy's testimony sounded questionable to Doris Haire. He applied the phrase *useful drugs* to obstetrical medication and also claimed that "considerable experience . . . shows that obstetric analgesia and anesthesia when judiciously employed are usually beneficial rather than detrimental to the mother; adverse effects to the infant are not usually a serious problem." The FDA commissioner's view was quite a contrast with a statement from the American Academy of Pediatrics, which recently warned its members that no drug when taken by or administered to a childbearing woman has been proved safe for the unborn child. Mrs. Haire queried Dr. Kennedy about this statement, and he replied:

"Your letter could lead one to the conclusion that you are advocating that all analgesia and anesthesia, as well as many other drugs useful in obstetric practice, should be abandoned until such time as complete information regarding any possible long-term adverse effects has been gathered. . . ."

Mrs. Haire has stated at FDA hearings that she does not want all obstetrical drugs banned. What she wants is something the FDA has failed to produce: a full-scale investigation of the safety of all drugs being administered during pregnancy and labor. The FDA contends that it would be unethical to conduct such research on pregnant women. Doris Haire replies, "In other words, the FDA condones the administration of drugs which have never been proven safe for the unborn child, but it deems evaluation of those drugs, once given, unethical!"

The FDA allows drugs used in labor and delivery to exist in a legal vacuum, according to Doris Haire. "The FDA does not require drug companies to establish the safety of a drug in regard to its delayed or long-term effect on the neurological, mental, or physical development of the offspring in order to gain approval as 'safe' for use in obstetrics." This, in her view, gives implicit, if unstated, FDA approval to the drugs, leaving the consumer literally at the mercy of the drug companies and physicians. She has urged the FDA to adopt strict labeling standards that would clearly warn the patient that drugs given to her during labor and delivery may affect her child not only in the short term but also in the long term. Until such a warning is made, she feels that unborn generations of American children may suffer the consequences.

Dr. Brackbill agrees. She points out that although most drugs used so casually by so many obstetricians may have been approved by the FDA for use in nonpregnant adults, they have not been approved for use in pregnant women or in children.

All the mother really knows is what she has been educated to believe: that pregnancy and birth in this country, as Norma Swenson puts it, are an "illness that has to be medically managed and controlled. Drugs, the mother is told, are the best way to manage the situation."

Dr. Brackbill says that this viewpoint must be changed if we are to try to protect future generations from harmful exposure to obstetric medications that many millions of Americans have already been exposed to. "For many illnesses today, drug therapy is the only effective therapy. Under these circumstances, there's very little real decision making involved. But pregnancy is not an illness. Childbirth is not an illness. Administering drugs perinatally and prenatally is often more optional than essential, and there is plenty of room for decision making." She makes two recommendations that she believes will solve many of the problems presented by obstetrical medication:

First, she says that "the mother is a consumer; she must be treated as an intelligent human being capable of understanding information on drugs when it is written in plain English. She is capable of evaluating drug risks and benefits and capable of choosing alternatives. Her doctor should allow her some alternatives."

And second, the best way for the consumer to be aware of her alternatives, Dr. Brackbill claims, is to get the right kind of information, and this, she believes, is a role the Department of Health, Education and Welfare should play: "HEW has two offices to deal with consumer information and education—the

Office of Health Information and Health Promotion and the soon-to-be-established Office of Health Technology."

This availability of information to both the expectant mother and her doctor will allow the woman to make the right kind of decision on whether or not she should receive any obstetric medication, Dr. Brackbill says.

Doris Haire suggests that mothers about to go into labor ask the following questions when they arrive in the hospital, questions that may save mother and child from the kind of grief Estelle Cohen experiences every day of her life:

"When you go to the hospital and everyone is a stranger, ask this question first: 'Who are you?' The next questions should be: 'What are you planning to do?' and 'Will it possibly hurt me or my baby?' If the answer is no, then ask, 'Could I see something from the manufacturer that guarantees this drug or device is safe?'"

Such a line of questioning, Doris Haire contends, will enable the mother-to-be to discover what drugs she is being given. Once the mother finds that out, she will also find out that no drugs have been approved as truly safe in labor or delivery, and it is then up to her to weigh the risks to which she may expose her baby against the momentary relief from pain the drugs may give her.

Pregnant women should be asking questions about drugs long before they get to the delivery room, for in the United States drugs are routinely prescribed throughout pregnancy. Dr. Reba Hill reports that 29 percent of all pregnant women in 1977 received a prescription for one or more psychotropic drugs, despite recent FDA warnings that minor tranquilizers have been linked with a variety of congenital malformations. This warning, first put on the minor tranquilizers in 1976, was too little too late, according to critics of the FDA and the drug companies. They say that it still allows doctors to prescribe the minor tranquilizers for their pregnant patients. This warning states that these drugs "should almost always be avoided" in pregnancy, but it does not prohibit their use.

Denise Woods, of the NOW Women's Health Network, warns that unless pregnant women are warned never to take these tranquilizers during pregnancy, they run the risk of ending up with a deformed child. "The problem is, though," Woods says, "that doctors don't tell women that anxiety or stress is not much of a problem to cope with compared to that of having a malformed child. I believe that if the kind of risk pregnant women run by taking tranquilizers was stated openly by all the doctors in the country, we would not be seeing many tranquilizer-related birth defects."

One woman who is very well aware of the risks associated with such drugs is Laura Cohen of Chatham, New Jersey. Her son was born with a birth defect. Laura Cohen claims that her son's malformation is the direct result of her taking an antidepressant drug, Tofranil (Ciba-Geigy), during the first six weeks of her pregnancy. Her story illustrates the pain and suffering many mothers go through because their doctors wanted to alleviate stress, strain, depression, or anxiety by chemical means. Laura Cohen's story also shows that it takes a very determined woman to go against the advice of a doctor when he makes a routine decision to prescribe a medication. As she tells it, her problems began in 1972.

"At that time I was seeing a psychiatrist because I was very depressed, almost suicidal. He offered me two choices: electric shock or Tofranil. So, naturally, I took the Tofranil. He was, looking back on it now, a doctor in the classical modern role—take any person who steps into the door, especially if that person is a woman, and put them on medication.

"Well, shortly after the doctor put me on Tofranil, I thought I had become pregnant. I had missed my period, and while it was too early to find out conclusively whether or not I was pregnant, I was very concerned about the drug. I knew that the first six weeks of the fetus's development are crucial—that's the time when a process called organogenesis takes place, when all the baby's limbs and organs are formed—and I wanted to know if there was any chance of Tofranil affecting the fetus.

"So I contacted my obstetrician and asked him if I should be taking the drug, and he told me it would be a good idea to get off. I went back to my psychiatrist—who told me he was very concerned about my mental state—and he told me that Tofranil would not harm my baby in any way at all if, indeed, I was pregnant. So I decided to stay on the drug for a while.

"Two weeks later I went back to my obstetrician and he confirmed that I was pregnant. I asked him again if I should stop taking Tofranil and told him what the psychiatrist said. At this point the obstetrician backed up the psychiatrist and said it was all right for me to stay on the drug."

But Laura Cohen still had nagging doubts about the health and safety of her baby. She weighed all the merits of staying on the drug and then decided that she could live with any depression she might have, especially if it meant the difference between a healthy child and a possibly deformed one. She decided to stop taking the drug. But it was too late. As she tells it:

"The damage had already been done. My son, Douglas, was born with a urinary tract defect. He also had a hole in the side of his penis. I was really shook up over this. I was convinced that the damage had been done by the drug and compounded by my doctors who dismissed my fears so quickly.

"Well, Douglas bore the scars of their laxity. He was unable to urinate naturally and had to have three operations. Today he is finally all right, but that's not the point. He should have been born all right in the first place. He would have been if it had not been for the desire of doctors to keep me on medications, even when I asked them questions."

Laura Cohen was not content just to let the damage be done, though. She was convinced that the damage to her son had to be linked with the Tofranil she took in those first six crucial weeks of pregnancy. She wanted to help other women avoid the heartbreak she felt when her son was born. So she decided to take action. "I decided that I had to warn someone about this. If it happened to me, how many other women was it happening to? So I wrote the Food and Drug Administration, outlined Douglas's birth defect, the drug I was taking, and also the fact that it was the only medication I was on, which is very important, because it is hard to prove a cause/effect relationship if you are taking more than one drug.

"I did not expect much to happen. But the least I expected was a reply. I received none.

"I also wrote the drug company at their headquarters in Summit [New Jersey]. They replied, and a gentleman from their professional staff talked to me. I also believe he talked to my doctors and looked at my records. Do you know what his conclusion was?

There was no linkage between my taking Tofranil and my son's birth defect.

"I just can't believe that. I just can't believe that they could dismiss something that seems so clear-cut to me. But they did.

"I'm not a crusader. I let the matter drop there. But I am still angry about the whole thing.

"I also learned a valuable lesson—drugs are not the answer to my problems; in fact, they caused me and my son one. I have learned now how to live drug-free, to handle my problems with other kinds of therapy, and I am very happy."

The drug company's action in flatly denying there was any causal relationship between Laura Cohen's child's problem and its drug is common, according to critics of the drug industry. "These companies don't want to admit there are any congenital abnormalities," says Dr. Mary Howell, a Boston pediatrician and former member of the FDA's Neuropharmacological Advisory Committee. "They shy away from any discussion of teratogenicity because they are very afraid it will hurt their most important market—women. They really do not even want to look into the problem because the one thing that might stop a woman from taking a drug is the possibility she may have a malformed baby."

The drug companies do not do research on the possible birth defects their drugs could cause, Howell points out, and this makes the general population "guinea pigs" for the drugs, she says. So, while a drug company may have met the FDA's standards for "safety and efficacy" by testing the drug on adults, there really is no test of the drug in infants or on the human fetus.

This leaves the test of safety and efficacy up to researchers, who must do their studies from a retrospective viewpoint. That is, they must examine its effect on the population after the drug is already on the market. These studies are complicated because it is hard to isolate exactly what substance can be linked with a birth defect, and in an industrial society sometimes the very air a mother breathes, the water she drinks, and the food she eats can be the cause of birth defects.

These studies are also expensive. In order to have any validity at all, they must track a large sample population, and the cost of this, understandably, is usually financed not by drug companies but by the government. Government money for such research is not given out freely. Only a few researchers are financed, so it sometimes takes years to assemble enough data on any given drug to prompt the FDA to take action.

One of the pioneering studies on the effects of tranquilizers on the fetus was conducted by Dr. Bea J. Van Den Berg and Dr. Lucille Milkovich of the Child Health and Developmental Studies Department, School of Public Health, University of California at Berkeley. This study, first published in the *New England Journal of Medicine* in December 1974, linked the use of the two most-prescribed tranquilizers, Librium and Miltown, with a high incidence of birth defects.

As Milkovich and Van Den Berg pointed out in that 1974 study, "Although both compounds are still widely prescribed, little is known about their effect on human fetal development, and their safety in pregnancy or in women of childbearing potential has not been established." According to their study, that safety had to be questioned. Milkovich and Van Den Berg had a statistically large sample to study—20,501 pregnancies with a broad socioeconomic base representing all races present in the San Francisco Bay area: white, Oriental, black, and Mexican.

Milkovich and Van Den Berg conducted a retrospective study. That is, they tracked down the mothers and the children years after they had enrolled in the study (enrollment was from 1959 to 1966) and examined the children born to these 20,000-odd women to discover what birth defects, if any, the sample population had. Their findings were startling: "Most striking were the high rates of severe congenital anomalies after prescription of meprobamate (Miltown) or chlordiazepoxide (Librium) during early pregnancy (the first 42 days of gestation). With respect to meprobamate, the findings suggest that the early period of pregnancy is crucial. . . . The important findings relating to chlordiazepoxide were similarly confined to early pregnancy."

The congenital anomalies Milkovich and Van Den Berg found linked with Miltown usage included congenital heart disease, Down's syndrome, partial deafness, and deformed elbows and joints. The birth defects they found linked to Librium usage included mental deficiency, spastic children, deafness, retardation, and duodenal atresia.

The two women concluded their paper by stating: "Although our findings support the suggestion that meprobamate may be teratogenic in man and point some suspicion at chlordiazepoxide, they are not conclusive. Our data merely imply associations that need further confirmation. On the other hand, they suggest that meprobamate and chlordiazepoxide may not be safe during early pregnancy. We conclude that these minor tranquilizers were often prescribed when it was not yet obvious that the woman was pregnant. We conclude that the prescription of these drugs to women of childbearing age should be restricted to cases with strong indications, and it would be prudent to assure that the woman is taking precautions against pregnancy."

Looking back on this study, Dr. Milkovich recalls that she did not believe it was the definitive and final one. She felt that more studies would have to be done before a definite cause and effect relationship could be established between the drugs. She was also willing to be proved wrong. She saw help in this area from an unexpected source: Hoffmann-La Roche.

The day the Milkovich and Van Den Berg study appeared in the *New England Journal of Medicine*, the *Wall Street Journal* had an article on the study. Dr. Van Den Berg read the article and was intrigued by a statement attributed to a Hoffmann-La Roche spokesman that seemed to refute her work. Intrigued, Dr. Van Den Berg wrote to that drug company on January 17, 1975, requesting more information. In a letter addressed to the Roche Laboratories' Professional Service Department, Dr. Van Den Berg said:

"In an article in the *Wall Street Journal* (Dec. 12, 1974) relating to a publication of Lucille Milkovich's and mine in the *New England Journal of Medicine* . . . , a reference was made to a study that we were unable to find in reviewing the literature. The reference was, 'A spokesman for Hoffmann-La Roche cited another study, of 671 women who had taken Librium early in pregnancy, which found that the birth-defect rate was lower than could be expected in the normal population. . . .' We are very much interested in the design and the results of that study and would much appreciate receiving a copy of it or a reference for it."

Dr. Milkovich recalls that her colleague's letter was prompted by a desire to serve the cause of science, not by a desire to "get" Hoffmann-La Roche. But the two authors were very curious to find out how they could have missed such a study in their literature search while preparing their article for publication.

They soon had their answer. On February 10, 1975, Dr. Van Den Berg received a letter from Dr. C. Bliss Monroe, assistant director of professional services at Roche Labs, that said, "Our study is an internal document not prepared for general distribution."

This brushoff still rankles Milkovich and raises her suspicions about Roche's methods. "The statement in the *Wall Street Journal* by the Roche spokesman raised questions about our research. We wanted to see their study to see how they reached their results. And they would not send it to us. I think they have a human responsibility to let the public know what is in their research, especially if it shows the drugs are all right to use.

"I never have seen that study. I have never seen it published, and I really wonder what is in it. If their research is so good, why don't they publish it?"

Milkovich still wonders if Roche was not trying to impugn the results of her careful, well-documented, scientific work, for in 1975 another article on the effects of tranquilizers in early pregnancy appeared in the *New England Journal of Medicine*. This article, written by members of the staff of the Boston Collaborative Drug Surveillance Program, refuted the work done by Milkovich and Van Den Berg.

The Boston study, however, used a different method of sampling and depended on the women in the study recalling the drugs they used in pregnancy, rather than on the detailed medical records used in the Milkovich-Van Den Berg study. What troubled Milkovich then, and what still troubles her, is not so much the results or the methodology, but who did the study and where they received their funding.

"This kind of research, on thousands of subjects, costs a lot of money," Milkovich says, "and about the only people who can afford that kind of research are the drug companies. They put a lot of money into research, and a lot of the studies that show drugs do no harm have been supported by drug company funds."

Roche spokesman Al Zobel was asked if his company did

support the Boston Collaborative Research Project with funding. At first, Zobel declined to tell the authors whether or not Roche supported the Boston Collaborative, saying, "We do not stoop to this kind of questioning and what it implies. It's not ethical." However, Zobel did check his files and told the authors, "We do contribute funds to the Boston Collaborative Surveillance Program, but you should not construe this to mean we try to influence the results."

Whether or not Roche's money influences the results of medical research would be hard to say and even harder to prove. One fact does stand out: of the four medical studies the FDA cited when it issued its warning limiting the use of minor tranquilizers, three of the studies strongly linked the drugs with congenital malformations, and only one, the Boston Collaborative study, attempted to find other causes.

The Milkovich and Van Den Berg study was just the beginning of research into the connection between the tranquilizers and birth defects. Dr. Hill points out, "Isolated reports have appeared in the literature suggesting that psychotropic agents classified as mood elevators are teratogenic agents."

Isolated or not, Denise Woods believes it is a "dangerous area to fool around with. All women should be warned of taking these drugs in pregnancy. At the moment the only way we know of these drugs causing any danger is by studies done after the damage has already occurred." The casual prescription of drugs to pregnant women is, to her, just an extension of how doctors tend to treat any woman. "All the doctors think when they get a woman in their office is how to get rid of her. And the best answer they have is to give her a pill. They don't even think about the consequences."

The consequences are, in some cases, extreme. A recent study, published in the October 1978 *Journal of the National Cancer Institute*, implicated the use of barbiturates, such as phenobarbital, with brain tumors in children. Cancer is the second leading cause of death in children under the age of fourteen in the United States, and according to the study, brain tumors account for 20 percent of all cancers in children. According to the authors of this study, Ellen Gold and Leon Gordis, "Mothers of children with brain tumors more frequently reported having used barbiturates during their pregnancy than did mothers of children without brain tumors."

The brain cancer study also found that children who had been prescribed barbiturates in their youth also were susceptible to brain tumors, which led the authors of the study to say, "These results suggest that barbiturates may play an etiologic role, and it is estimated that as many as eight percent of brain tumors in children may be attributable to the use of barbiturates by either the child or the mother perinatally."

Another study, conducted in Finland by Dr. Irma Saxen in 1975, linked benzodiazepine tranquilizers with birth defects, particularly cleft palates. Using data from the Finnish Central Registry of Congenital Malformations, Dr. Saxen tracked down cases of cleft palate and then examined the mothers' drug histories. After analyzing the data, Dr. Saxen concluded: "During the first trimester, analgesic, chemotherapeutic, and antineurotic drugs had all been significantly more frequently used by the mothers of children with clefts than by the control mothers. The consumption of drugs in general was more frequent among mothers of children with cleft lip."

Another study linking the use of tranquilizers in pregnancy with birth defects was conducted by two doctors at the Center for Disease Control in Atlanta in 1975. The authors, Dr. Mark Safra and Dr. Godfrey Oakley, summarized their findings as follows: "Valium use was examined among the mothers of infants with birth defects who were interviewed by the Metropolitan Atlanta Congenital Malformations Program. Exposure during the first trimester of pregnancy is four times more common among mothers of infants with cleft lip or cleft palate as among mothers of infants with other defects."

These three studies finally prompted the FDA to take action. On July 22, 1976, the agency issued a warning cautioning women to avoid the use of minor tranquilizers in pregnancy because they had been implicated as a possible cause of birth defects. The commissioner of the FDA at the time, Dr. Arthur Schmidt, said, "These studies do not demonstrate conclusively that these drugs, taken early during pregnancy, can cause cleft lip or other birth defects. But use of these tranquilizers during pregnancy is rarely a matter of urgency and their use during this time should almost always be avoided."

The drug companies, which had no choice but to go along with the FDA's order, did not think the problem was all that bad. Dr. Bruce Medd, medical director of Roche Laboratories, steadfastly maintained in an interview that there has been no direct cause/effect relationship established between Librium or Valium and birth defects. He said, "We should not jump to false conclusions from these studies."

Asked to elaborate on his feelings about the FDA ruling, Dr. Medd replied that as far as he was concerned, the number of birth defects reported by women taking Valium probably was not significantly much higher than the number of babies born with birth defects to mothers who did not take the drug.

Asked to comment on this viewpoint, Lucille Milkovich said, "I think that is a highly irresponsible comment to make. But, if I was the medical director of Roche, I would make that kind of statement. It sounds to me like Dr. Medd is a very good PR man."

Other mood-changing drugs, such as the antidepressants, may also cause birth defects. Lithium, a natural salt that has gained much credence in the 1970s as a "natural" way to treat depression, has also been implicated as a possible cause of birth defects, according to Dr. Hill. "There is suggestive evidence that an increased incidence of heart disease occurs in infants born to mothers treated with Lithium during the first trimester of pregnancy."

Dr. Hill warns that infants born to mothers taking psychoactive substances face another problem: withdrawal. She says that children born to mothers taking Valium, Librium, Serax, Elavil, Equanil, Doriden, Benadryl, Talwin, Darvon, or other "mood" drugs may spend the first days of life undergoing the rigors of withdrawal because they became hooked on drugs their mothers were taking.

Problems for the newborn are also caused by analgesics taken by their mothers. Aspirin is the most common analgesic, and Dr. Hill reports that 65 percent of all pregnant women take aspirin, sometimes totally unaware of the consequences for the child.

Extreme use of the analgesics, she says, can lead to hemorrhaging or to problems with the infant's respiration. These kinds of drugs are often purchased over the counter by women who do not even realize they are drugs, Dr. Hill says.

One woman whose baby was born with an extremely high aspirin level was asked by Dr. Hill why she had taken so many aspirin, despite warnings to avoid drugs during pregnancy. The woman replied, "If I had known that aspirin was a drug, I would not have taken it."

How can a pregnant woman avoid exposing her child to the hazards of drugs? Simple, says Norma Swenson. Use common sense, ask a lot of questions, learn to say no when a drug is offered, and in childbirth, be willing to put up with some pain in order to ensure the safety of your child.

Laura Cohen endorses this common-sense approach, but she also feels that it is up to the government, the drug companies, and interested consumers to ensure that the problems she had with her son do not happen to other women. A child's life, she believes, is the most valuable thing in the world, and steps should be taken to ensure that all children born in this country start life drug-free.

Chemically Controlling Children | 5

Looking back on it, Carol DiMuro welcomes the chance to tell of her son's accomplishments. Recently he was taken out of a special education classroom and accelerated into fifth grade in a regular public school class. He's ten now and "doing beautifully." It wasn't always this way. For five years the DiMuros went through hell with their boy. As she tells it:

"My son started being a problem at the age of three. We lived with him for two years without drugs. He started fires, stole, you name it. We had a younger child, and he took vengeance on him. When he reached five, we couldn't take it anymore. We were willing to give him up. We went to a psychiatrist, and he gave him a brain-wave test. As a result of that, they diagnosed minimal brain dysfunction and epilepsy, although he had never had a seizure. The doctors treated him with massive doses of three or four medications at a time, including institutional-sized dosages of Thorazine. The medication dulled his body somewhat but not his mind. He remained on this for a year without much change in behavior.

"At this point we had been to seven or eight different doctors, and none could do anything but give me another drug. They tried every drug imaginable. Thorazine, Nembutal, Dilantin, Cylert, Ritalin, Librium, Dexedrine. We tried behavior modification. It was very difficult, and he didn't respond. I found I just couldn't cope with him anymore. By the time my son was seven, the only alternative the doctors presented was to institutionalize him. This is all they offered. I can't tell you how frustrating and lonely it was. It's like a thorn in your side, and you're willing to try almost anything. And many of the doctors laid the blame on my husband and me: you're not giving him enough love; you're not paying enough attention; you're too rigid, too structured, or too easy and permissive. It's an awful lot of guilt to carry around. You're afraid to talk about it. You want to hide in a closet."

About the time Carol DiMuro was making her desperate rounds of doctors in Smithtown, a New York City suburb on Long Island, another Smithtown woman, Vickie Giraldi, was withdrawing her five-year-old son from Ritalin. When he was just eleven months old, a child psychiatrist said the toddler was hyperactive and told Mrs. Giraldi, "There is no other mode of treatment but drugs." Eventually Vickie Giraldi relented and placed her son on Ritalin. While it seemed to calm him down, the boy suffered severe side effects. "One was suicidal tendencies," she recalls grimly. "He also had a loss of appetite and insomnia, and he mutilated his hands and fingers. The drug made him so nervous that he kept picking on his nails and cuticles. His skin was torn to his knuckles." When her son was five, Mrs. Giraldi had had enough, and so had her boy. "He used to ask me for the pills in the morning, he got into such a habit. He'd say, 'I feel so awful when I take them, I wish I never have to take them. I will do anything to not have to take these pills anymore.'

"When I stopped giving them, my son went through periods of depression, anxiety, sleeplessness. Then he would sleep all day. He wouldn't get up and get dressed. He would stay in his pajamas all day and not even wash himself. He was extremely unhappy and had pains in his stomach. Some doctors say there are no withdrawal symptoms from Ritalin. That's bull. If what my son went through is not withdrawal, I don't know what it is. It reminds me of heroin withdrawal on a milder level."

During the same period another Smithtown couple were worried about their son Brian, "a very active little boy, always into things, on the go from morning to night." Brian's mother, Carol Cummings, "would go to the pediatrician and ask him, 'What's the matter with this child?'" and the doctor would tell her he was just a "normally active boy and would outgrow" his exuberance. But when Brian got to first grade, the teacher "started to complain about him, wanting to know how he was going to learn to read and write when he was all over the classroom." Under pressure from the school, Carol Cummings had Brian examined again, and this time he was diagnosed as having minimal brain dysfunction with a learning disability. He was given a prescription for Ritalin.

What links these three children in a common bond is a vaguely defined and controversial medical disorder called minimal brain dysfunction, or MBD. The dispute centers not only on how it is diagnosed and treated but also on its origin and, in fact, whether it is a real disorder or a meaningless label to pin on children whose behavior is considered unacceptable by adults. The battle pits a small number of doctors and other health care professionals in alliance with an increasingly large and vocal number of parents against the most powerful institutions and industries in America—the federal government, organized medicine, the teaching profession, and the food, beverage, drug, and chemical giants of the nation. In the middle of the dispute are between 750,000 and 1 million children—almost all of them boys—labeled as suffering from MBD or one of its many behavioral symptoms: hyperactivity, hyperkinesis, learning disability, attentional deficiency, or simply distraction.

For more than ten years the common method of treatment for MBD children was to drug them with amphetamines and to a lesser degree with tranquilizers. In a reaction that remains unexplained by medical science, the amphetamines, which work as an upper on adults, act as a downer on children. Whether the reaction to amphetamines is paradoxical or not, the drugs seem to harness children so that they can concentrate more intently on routine and tedious tasks, sit still for longer periods of time, and be more attentive for longer periods. Benzedrine and Dexedrine were the early favorites for treatment of MBD and hyperactivity, but Ritalin, which is produced by Swiss-based Ciba-Geigy, soon captured the market and is the biggest seller today.

Although amphetamine prescriptions for MBD have waned in recent years, they still are prescribed for an extraordinarily high number of children. According to Ciba-Geigy, 750,000 children were seen for MBD by doctors in 1978. Of that number, Ciba estimates that 212,000 were put on medication, with about 57 percent of them, or 120,000, given Ritalin. In 1975, the company estimated, nearly 1 million children were diagnosed as having MBD, and more than half (515,000) were put on drugs, 265,000 of those being given Ritalin. In 1970, 150,000 children were on Ritalin, according to the company, and by 1972, after a major promotional effort by Ciba-Geigy and other stimulant drug manufacturers, the number leaped to 250,000.

There is no way to get an accurate fix on the number of children drugged with Ritalin or other stimulants or tranquilizers since the MBD phenomenon began to flourish in the late 1960s, but it is safe to estimate conservatively that 3 to 4 million children have been chemically harnessed for MBD or various MBD symptoms, ranging from hyperkinesis to fidgeting, in the past decade. Ciba-Geigy continues to identify a substantial number of children as candidates for an MBD diagnosis and Ritalin therapy. The company estimates that "one out of every twenty school children has MBD—three-quarters of them boys." This means an MBD target population of 1.6 million children—some 1.2 million of them boys—between the ages of five and thirteen. With the federal government estimating the number of children with learning disabilities at 10 percent of the grammar school population of 32 million, there is an even greater potential for indiscriminate drugging of youngsters. Real or perceived difficulties in learning often are the motivating force in diagnosing children with minimal brain dysfunction or with hyperactivity, although there is no conclusive link between hyperactivity and learning handicaps, other than the fact that the hyperactive child has trouble concentrating in school.

The causes of hyperactivity and MBD are uncertain, but there is growing scientific evidence pointing to licit and illicit drugs used by women during pregnancy and administered to them during labor and delivery. As we noted in the prior chapter on the poisoning of our future, a strong link has been determined between obstetric medications and impairment of a child's brain development, motor skills, and social behavior. Such a relationship has been suspected for many years, but a study by Dr.

Yvonne Brackbill and Dr. Sally Broman established for the first time a "clear-cut cause-and-effect relationship" between obstetric drugs and degradations in behavior and intelligence of children. There also is growing evidence linking alcohol use by pregnant women to hyperactivity in some children. New studies completed at Yale University in 1978 showed that of all children studied for MBD, hyperactivity, or learning disabilities, 10 to 15 percent of the problems were caused by the mother's drinking. Dr. Sally Shaywitz said the children of the drinking mothers were of normal intelligence, but all "had profound and pervasive school difficulties" and had been held back at least one grade. Although the association has not been proved scientifically, some authorities suspect that tranquilizer use by pregnant women can cause similar problems for infants. (The environment of the alcoholic family also could be a factor contributing to the acting-out of a child in the family.)

Further, there is a sizable body of information that links chemical food additives to hyperactivity in some children. This theory was first advanced in the United States by Dr. Ben F. Feingold, a pediatrician and allergist who at the age of seventy-four found a tie between food additives and behavioral disorders among patients at the Kaiser-Permanente health care clinic in San Francisco. In 1974 Feingold advanced his findings in a book, *Why Your Child Is Hyperactive*, which spawned a nationwide parent movement called the Feingold Association. Dr. Feingold's theory is relatively simple: hyperactivity in some—but not all—children is caused by artificial chemicals used in food and drink, and the hyperactivity in these children can be controlled by providing an additive-free diet. He claimed a success rate of about 50 percent with his diet, but local Feingold groups say that if the diet is followed rigorously and parents and children avail themselves of the self-help group therapy programs conducted by the Feingold parents, a success rate of 80 percent can be achieved. Drug companies claim a success ratio of 60 to 80 percent for stimulant drug therapy, if conducted as part of a program of special education, counseling for parents and children alike, and group or individual activity therapy.

The parents of the children in the three cases cited at the beginning of this chapter report good results in controlling the hyperactivity of their children with the Feingold diet. The parents turned to the chemical-free diet after their children had reacted adversely to drug use. Later in this chapter we will discuss how Vickie Giraldi and other parents in Smithtown, New York, banded together to spread the word about the Feingold approach to hyperactivity and how they have taken on the food, drug, and chemical industries in a David and Goliath struggle to rid food and drink of unnecessary additives and to force the government to require full disclosure in food labeling.

Minimal brain dysfunction is a catchall label that has been widely used—and as widely repudiated—to identify children, mostly boys, with behavioral problems of various and ill-defined origin. It is so vague and so abused as a diagnostic term that the FDA, after several years of debate and delay, finally ordered it eliminated as a diagnostic term as of February 21, 1979, although Ciba-Geigy continued to use it in a last-gasp promotional campaign throughout 1978 and at the turn of 1979. Over a line drawing of a young boy with his eyes closed and his head in his hands, Ciba described an MBD child as a "rebel without a cause" in an advertisement in the January 8, 1979, issue of *Medical News*. Here's how Ciba describes the MBD child:

"He seems to be at war with the world.

"In the classroom, he's the one who spills ink, breaks things, creates general havoc.

"On the playground, when he doesn't get his way he's apt to throw a temper tantrum.

"And at home, his parents try to understand but wish he could be more like his siblings. Less hyperactive. Better at doing things like tying shoelaces, buttoning a shirt, riding a bicycle.

"He's a rebel who doesn't understand why he rebels or what to rebel against."

Ciba recommended "stimulant drugs" to help the child "get his head together" and gain more benefit from other therapy, including special education and parental counseling. In this particular ad, Ritalin was not mentioned, thus permitting the company to omit the FDA-required listing of warnings and adverse reactions that must accompany drug advertisements in medical journals. The adverse reactions to Ritalin include nervousness, insomnia, skin rash, anorexia, nausea, dizziness, palpitations, headache, dyskinesia, blood pressure and pulse changes, angina, cardiac arrhythmia, abdominal pain, and toxic psychosis.

Actually, Ciba, which promoted the use of Ritalin directly to educators and parents as a means of controlling problem children until ordered to stop by the FDA, had toned down its advertisements for Ritalin by the late 1970s. Ritalin was still being pushed as "an effective member of the MBD management team," but in many advertisements the company had added this important and revealing caveat: "From Huckleberry Finn to the Katzenjammer Kids, the mischievous child has been an integral part of American folklore. But his normal, youthful overexuberance can be difficult to distinguish from MBD."

The term *minimal brain dysfunction* (or *damage*) has been a part of the medical literature since the 1920s, at first to identify specific organic damage to the brains of adults and later to refer to demonstrable brain damage in children leading to certain learning and behavioral problems. But in 1963 the U.S. Public Health Service and the National Society for Crippled Children and Adults sponsored in Washington a seminar on the "Child with Minimal Brain Dysfunction." The seminar's concluding report expanded the term to apply to every conceivable behavioral characteristic and effectively threw wide the doors for the indiscriminate drugging of hundreds of thousands of normal but perhaps mischievous children or, more specifically, mischievous boys.

Out of the seminar came a task force to identify and label what Dr. Richard L. Masland of the Public Health Service called "that group of children whose dysfunction does not produce gross motor or sensory deficit or generalized impairment of intellect, but who exhibit *limited alterations of behavior or intellectual functioning* [emphasis added]."

The task force was headed by Sam D. Clements, a psychologist at the University of Arkansas Medical Center, who later, along with his colleagues at Arkansas, became a paid consultant for Ciba-Geigy and wrote the company's physician's handbook on MBD. The Clements task force in its 1966 report acknowledged the "purist point of view" that MBD is "in most instances an unproven presumptive diagnosis," which can have little meaning in the absence of skills and techniques necessary to determine "physiologic, biochemical or structural alterations of the brain."

The Clements group then proceeded to reject the "purist" view and accept the more "pragmatic case" and approve the use of MBD to identify "children of near average, average, or above average general intelligence with certain learning or behavioral disabilities ranging from mild to severe, which are associated with deviations of function of the central nervous system. These deviations may manifest themselves by various combinations of impairment in perception, conceptualization, language, memory, and control of attention, impulse or motor function."

It would be difficult to write a more all-inclusive definition for this new disorder subsequently used to label millions of children, but the task force didn't stop there, offering ninety-nine symptoms to help doctors and teachers spot these otherwise normal children. The symptoms include hyperkinesis (too active) and hypokinesis (not active enough); hyperactivity and hypoactivity (activity opposites of a milder nature); "rage reactions and tantrums" and being "sweet and even tempered, cooperative and friendly"; "easy acceptance of others alternating with withdrawal and shyness"; being "overly gullible and easily led" and being "socially bold and aggressive"; and being "very sensitive to others" and having "excessive need to touch, cling and hold on to others"; and sleeping abnormally lightly or abnormally deeply. In addition, the task force listed a variety of common learning problems as MBD symptoms, including a short attention span and slowness in reading, spelling, and arithmetic skills.

After listing these ninety-nine symptoms, many of them characteristic of most children and many of them so contradictory as to be meaningless, the task force listed the ten most-cited MBD characteristics in order of frequency: hyperactivity; perceptual-motor impairments; emotional lability; general coordination deficits; disorders of attention; impulsivity; disorders of memory and thinking; specific learning disabilities in reading, arithmetic, writing, and spelling; disorders of speech and learning; and "equivocal" neurological signs and electroencephalographic irregularities.

It's unlikely that any child, no matter how normal or healthy, could escape classification under such a hodgepodge of "signs" pointing to an MBD child in need of treatment. The Clements report was, however, eagerly embraced by the government, the drug industry, educators, and many parents. Dr. Masland of the Public Health Service responded enthusiastically and charged the nation's doctors with the responsibility of seeking out and identifying MBD children "because they require special forms of management and education." The National Easter Seal Society for Crippled Children and Adults, which cosponsored the 1963 seminar on MBD, in 1971 circulated a booklet on learning disabilities that strongly endorsed the use of stimulants for treating hyperactivity, claiming drugs "can turn a non-achieving, hyperactive child into an *interested, alert, cooperative student within 20 minutes* [emphasis added]." The booklet containing this doubtful assertion of the chemical wonders of speedy and effective action to improve learning is still being circulated by HEW.

The Clements report in recent years has been repudiated by many authorities. Lester Grinspoon and Susan B. Singer in a 1974 review of medical literature on hyperkinesis and its treatment with drugs called it a "sophisticated statement of ignorance." Ten years after the Clements report and after thousands of clinical studies and reviews, medical science had shed little more light on the subject. Said Dr. Roger Freeman, a child psychiatrist at the University of British Columbia: "There is only one phrase for the state of the art and practice in the field of minimal brain dysfunction, hyperactivity, and learning disability in children: a mess. There is no more polite term which would be realistic. The area is characterized by rarely challenged myths, ill-defined boundaries, and a strangely seductive attractiveness. These categories and their management, because of massive support from frustrated parents, professionals, government, and the drug and remedial-education industries, constitute an epidemic of alarming proportions—but is the problem the disease or the treatment?" What is seductively attractive about MBD, hyperactivity, and learning disability is that they provide convenient labels to categorize children whose behavior or performance does not measure up to adult expectations. Once a label has been given, treatment can be applied, and, as we have seen, the easiest and most efficient, although in many cases the most destructive, method of treatment is chemical. With application of MBD to any child whose behavior or learning performance demonstrated a "mild to severe" deviation from what one subjectively would judge to be normal, the floodgates were opened to treat millions of children with stimulants to sedate them into being better learners and more obedient students at school and less active children at home.

Peter Schrag and Diane Divoky debunked many of the myths of the hyperactive child in their book *The Myth of the Hyperactive Child*, published in 1974. They attributed the quick and unquestioning acceptance of MBD to a middle-class need to explain failure, as well as to a need to control. "If one were to invent a means whereby the difficult children of socially respectable people—children who disrupt the routines of institutions and communities—were to be controlled without giving offense or generating political opposition, one could do no better than attribute to them an illness so new and so particular to one class of society that it carries no stigma, no innuendos of character and no denigration of ability, but which, at the same time, makes possible—indeed necessary—the controls and 'treatment' that the system deems necessary," they wrote.

The treatment of choice for minimally brain dysfunctioning children quickly became the amphetamine class of drugs. Without question, the stimulants seemed to work in calming children down, making them more docile and more attentive. The drug-treated children got better reports from their teachers and parents, and this positive feedback reinforced the recommended therapy and served as confirmation of the original diagnosis. Educational journals were filled with accounts of successful results—improved grades, less disruptive behavior, improved peer relationships—from using stimulants on hyperactive students. In 1971 Dr. Paul Wender, one of the early supporters of drug therapy for MBD, reported the ailment had become "probably the single most common disorder seen by child psychiatrists," and he happily reported the "correct treatment is often dramatically effective and is always cheap and readily accessible." By the early 1970s Ritalin had become so widely used that it was referred to as the "smart pill" in playground talk, and some cynics referred to the three R's as "reading, 'riting, and Ritalin." Ciba-Geigy, the manufacturer of Ritalin, spent heavily in the 1970–72 period to encourage the use of Ritalin, and the drug's sales peaked in 1971. Sales have been declining ever since, partly as a result of the indiscriminate prescribing practices that brought a public outcry and partly as a result of new evidence doubting the wisdom of drug therapy for hyperactivity. The reclassification of Ritalin under tighter government controls also reduced prescriptions.

By 1970 the public press had caught up with what was going on, and a television report from Omaha claimed some 20 percent of the city's elementary schoolchildren—most of them black —were on drugs for MBD. The claim proved to be exaggerated. But enough of a public outcry had been raised to prompt a congressional hearing by Representative Cornelius Gallagher of New Jersey. The committee's hearing served to demonstrate that medical science knew very little about this new childhood disorder and even less about the drugs used to treat it. The consensus of drug industry and government authorities was, however, that since the amphetamines seemed to improve the ability of children to concentrate on minimal tasks and to make them more manageable and, therefore, teachable, the disorder and the treatment were validated. In short, the treatment confirmed the ailment.

In response to the public concern raised by the Gallagher committee, Dr. Edward Zigler, then director of child development for HEW, hastily summoned a "blue-ribbon" panel to Washington for a two-day conference to draft a statement that would reassure the public. On January 11–12, 1971, the panel took such a general position on the safety and effectiveness of drug therapy for hyperactivity that all sides found confirmation of their positions.

Dr. Patricia Morisey, a Fordham University sociologist, was one of two nonmedical professionals on the fifteen-member panel, and in an interview seven years after their meeting she recalled that the view of the social scientists was relegated to "the bottom of the totem pole. On the whole, the bias of the medical profession dominated the discussions and was reflected in the report." Dr. Morisey felt then and now "that where there are proper services and supervision, children can be managed without drugs." The problem remains, she said, that "very often the tests are inexact and the children are wrongly diagnosed, and the pressure is on to keep them quiet and drugs are prescribed." In the poor and mostly black schools with which Dr. Morisey is familiar the type of total services, including special education, individualized attention, counseling for children and parents alike, and competent diagnosis, treatment, and follow-up if drugs are indeed necessary, simply does not exist. "I had to keep reminding them [the other members of the blue-ribbon panel], 'You just don't know the schools in central Harlem. They yell or send a note [home],'" she recalled, describing how teachers respond to troublesome students in inner-city schools.

Another concern of Dr. Morisey's was her fear that the use of psychoactive prescription drugs "seemed to be an introduction for inner-city children to the drug culture." The panel concluded that "clinical experience and several scientific studies have failed to reveal an association between the medical use of stimulants in the preadolescent child and later drug abuse." The panel did, however, weakly acknowledge—and quickly dismiss—the more subtle but more insidious fear of establishing early in life a predisposition to use drugs, whether legal or illegal, to induce a desired but not necessary mood or behavioral change. To the question "Does medication handicap the child emotionally?" the panel replied: "It is sometimes suggested that treated children may not be able to learn normal responses and master adjustments to the stresses of everyday life. These fears are understandable but are not confirmed by specialists who have experience with the conditions and situations in which medications are properly used." On the contrary, the panel concluded, after fewer than two days of deliberations, that stimulant drugs "help 'set the stage' for satisfactory psychological development." Considerable doubt has been cast on that assumption by recent studies, which we will look at later in this chapter, but we need first to take a closer look at definitions of "drug abuse" to put the issue in a broader context.

If the acceptable definition of a drug abuser is one typically identified by such street terms as *speed freak, dopehead, heroin addict,* and the like, then equally acceptable is the evidence of the drug manufacturers, their clinicians, and the federal government that there is no proof that a child who uses Ritalin is more likely to become a drug abuser in adolescence than a child who was not prescribed the medication. (It should be noted, however, that some studies do show that medicated children display the same patterns of behavioral problems in teenage years as do "normal" nonmedicated children, which means in the long haul little is gained by drug use.)

But drug abuse, whether by means of drugs purchased from a a street pusher or by prescription drugs, demands a broader definition. In one of the best discussions of the question, Henry L. Lennard, a medical sociologist at the University of California, and three colleagues make a convincing case for putting drug use into a broader social and cultural context. Their book, *Mystification and Drug Misuse,* makes a logical case that "the mere volume of increased drug use may also have dysfunctional side effects, leading to a subtle or secondary kind of drug abuse," causing a pollution of the human experience not unlike the ecological pollution and congestion caused by having too many cars on the road. Using another common illustration, they write: "In American society drugs have become as common as clothing, and a similar kind of dependency has come into existence. For many persons, to be stripped of their pharmacological wardrobe would be tantamount to facing the world naked. Yet to describe persons as being dependent upon or addicted to clothing because they suffer without it does not accurately characterize the situation. The sustaining forces in both instances—in both the use of drugs and the use of clothing—do not reside inside the individual person; they reside in the whole context of events that sustain his current pattern of behavior."

The widespread use of stimulants to harness chemically the activity levels of children and control their behavior is just one more link in the chemical chain that encircles us from cradle to grave. As pediatrician and author Robert Mendelsohn put it, "Sedation is as American as apple pie. You're sedated when you're born. You're given Demerol and scopolamine through your mother. When you start school, you're given Ritalin if you're hyperactive. If the teacher doesn't like the way you look at him or her, you're placed on Ritalin or Dexedrine. A little later you may be placed on tranquilizers, and finally at the end of life you may be placed on antidepressants. It's characteristic of our country to keep itself in a perpetual state of sedation. That's the kind of thing we have to fight against."

A sharp reduction in the prescription of stimulants and other psychoactive drugs for hyperactivity and MBD has come about in part because of a fear of bad publicity on the part of the drug manufacturers.

Felton Davis, Jr., Ciba-Geigy's vice-president for marketing promotion, indicated that the decline in sales was the result of a loss of interest on the part of the company in promoting the disorder and Ritalin for its treatment. Sales are down, he said, "because of, among other things, I suspect, a lack of promotion on our part and a lack of promotion about the indication. Few people are talking about minimal brain dysfunction, and we're not doing much talking about it. Nor are we doing much about the promotion of the drug. In its peak, we were doing a lot. We were promoting it vigorously to the physician." Davis also said that if the company were allowed, as it once was, to "educate" the public about the disorder "we would have more children on Ritalin than there are now." He said he is convinced there are children "not getting Ritalin who should" and equally convinced there are "some getting it who shouldn't."

The period of sharpest growth in Ritalin sales, from 1970 to 1972, corresponds with the period when MBD was a fashionable health problem among government officials and educators. It also is no coincidence that 1970–72 was a period of heavy promotion of MBD and drug therapy for its treatment by Ciba-Geigy and other manufacturers of stimulant drugs. The sales and promotion literature went not only into physician offices but into schools and homes. In their book, Peter Schrag and Diane Divoky document Ciba's efforts to carry the MBD message to teachers, parents, and community leaders. In one reference they cite a Ciba sales executive's exhortation to drug detail men to become "more effective pushers" for Ritalin at public meetings. The salesmen showed films describing the symptoms of MBD throughout the nation at PTA and teachers' meetings. The FDA subsequently cracked down on the company, forbidding it to promote either the disorder or drug therapy directly to the public.

To Davis the FDA order was illogical and does a disservice to parents and children "by denying them the opportunity to increase their knowledge about this condition."

Davis, who says his own daughter was helped by Ritalin, believes that if you accept MBD as a valid medical condition—and he does from personal experience and professional commitment—

then "educating" the public directly about it is no different from a drug company's educating the public, as is commonly done, about cancer or hypertension. Davis said: "If you accept the condition of minimal brain dysfunction and that it is not some real bad thing like drugging kids or labeling them improperly and it's not causing them problems for the rest of their lives, then there is no difference in our trying to spread information about the condition of minimal brain dysfunction than trying to spread the word about hypertension."

In an interview in his small private office in the Long Island community of Smithtown, Dr. Joseph D'Agrosa talked about the twelve-year trend to treat children with behavioral problems with Ritalin. Early in the 1970s, D'Agrosa and the two other pediatricians in private practice with him had 63 children on Ritalin, ten times more than they have on the drug today but not many for the time, considering the fact that they were seeing 60 children a day and on record there are cases of doctors having as many as 2,000 children on the drug at any given time. The pressure to drug the children came largely from the schools, explained D'Agrosa. It's a story best told in his words.

"Up until the past few years, generally a school system out here—I don't know about in general, but I get the same feeling from throughout the country—the first thing they wanted for a child who was not sitting still is to put him on medication. It's the easiest way out. You go on Ritalin or you go on Dex because it works. They give them psychological work-ups in the schools even before a physician is consulted. Unfortunately this has been the history out here. They'll find a doctor who will prescribe the drugs. The schools dare to tell us, 'Well, what are we going to do with this kid? We've worked him up psychologically, and he won't sit still, and we also sent him for a neurological work-up, an electroencephalogram—the routine that records electrical fluctuations of the brain and tells you very little—and now we'll put him on drugs. Now he'll sit still, and he'll be sedated, and then we can teach him.' That's the approach that was followed in the past few years. I think it's changing, though. I see a real awakening, a realization that we're not going to do it with drugs alone."

Dr. D'Agrosa said that during the early 1970s he had several children on Ritalin but would see them monthly for physical examinations to monitor the effects of the drug. "They came in with their mothers monthly and had their weight taken and their blood pressure checked. You don't do a very thorough follow-up, but you do a blood pressure and take their weight because you worry about stunted growth. As you know, it's there with the medication. I would say, on the average, I got better reports about these kids because the pressure was off them. It wasn't their fault they weren't learning. It wasn't the teacher's fault. It was this hyperactivity, which they sedated with medication. These drugs were supposed to make the child more aware, more alert. The theory was they were too distracted by the stimuli that were coming into their central nervous system. They overresponded, and the stimulant drugs apparently made it possible for them to concentrate. When it does work, it does slow them up to the point where they sit like mummies. Their activity is controlled, and they improve enough to follow instructions. Over the years, there have been varying hints in the literature—soft neurological signs, slight abnormalities, neurological reflexes, and so forth—that have been altered by drug therapy, meaning improved. I'm not overly convinced that this is true.

"But the schoolteachers are very impressed with drug therapy because here we have a kid who is climbing the walls and now suddenly he's sitting down so they can work with him. What's not convincing are several factors. One is the ultimate result of drug therapy leading to problems which we don't know about. And we talk about retardation of growth, doubly documented with Dexedrine. Does it cure them? This is the big argument. I don't think we have enough follow-up to know if we really cure anybody of so-called learning disorders, attention-span difficulty, hyperactivity with drug therapy. I think we go on to have hyperactive adults, too. We see them, and we know they're hyperactive. I'm sure you've seen executives who are constantly moving. I see them in my office. They're worse than the kids, fidgety kinds of personalities, bundles of energy. It is acceptable because it is controlled. The person has somehow learned to adapt and control his behavior. He's not pushing the kid next to him or running around the classroom. He fidgets with his feet or his hands constantly. I think this is what happens to some of these kids—they do eventually become fidgety adults."

Does he still get pressure from the schools to put problem children on drugs?

"I've been here so long I think they've started to listen. I've gone to the school board to talk to them. I've argued with psychologists, schoolteachers. We had a helluva session five years ago when I went up before the Patchogue-Medford school district's psychologists and teachers and told them what I thought of their referrals. They were referring my kids, my patients, without calling me, to the city to get drug therapy. So I said it was disrespectful to me. I told them it was a disservice to the child. They don't even know the background. They should have consulted with the physicians. And they in turn blasted me and physicians for not caring."

Not far from Dr. D'Agrosa's office is the office of Dr. Stephen Honor, a psychologist who specializes in treating hyperkinetic children and their families. Up until 1975 Dr. Honor "had been by and large using medication" to treat the hyperactive children sent to him by area physicians. "I was using both medication and behavioral therapy," Honor explained. "For the most part, it was Ritalin and Cylert. I think that combination of drugs and behavior modification, to my mind, is the most effective to this point, but I always opt for that last because I don't like to see kids on drugs, particularly for long periods of time."

Psychologist Barbara Johns is a member of the Smithtown school district's child study team, which also includes a social worker, a learning disability specialist in reading, and a speech language therapist. Dr. Johns's assignment is to meet and counsel parents and teachers of children in special education classes and to evaluate the progress of the children, many of whom are classed as being hyperactive or learning disabled. In her experience at the school district and previously as a psychologist in a private clinic, she prefers a more cautious and conservative approach to the use of drugs to treat hyperactivity. Dr. Johns believes that hyperactivity "can be a plus and that diminishing the child's level of productivity isn't the answer. The most effective method of working with hyperactive children is to channel the child's energy appropriately." Most successful people, in her view, are "hyperactive; otherwise, how could they get so much done?"

Of the 400 children in Smithtown's special education program, she said, "a great number" do receive medication but primarily only on schooldays and not on weekends or during the summer because "most parents don't seem to think it is necessary" when the children are at home.

In January 1975 Susan Martinez, an attorney for the Youth Law Center in San Francisco, received a call from the grandmother of Frank and Joe Montoya, elementary schoolchildren in Taft, a dusty California oil town not far from the Nevada line. Can a school force children to take drugs as a condition for staying in school? the woman wondered. Ms. Martinez answered vaguely, saying, "Basically, no," but asked for more information. The mother of the children, Diane Montoya, then called and "described the situation and said other children were in the same situation. They couldn't stay in school unless they took Ritalin."

Lawyer Martinez and Pauline Testler, another attorney for the youth center, had heard of isolated instances of children being forced to take drugs to remain in school but nothing of the magnitude described by Diane Montoya. They decided to make the long trip to Taft to have a look. "Mainly we felt we would go down there and find out it was greatly exaggerated," recalled Ms. Testler. "Instead, it turned out to be far worse than we could have imagined." Ms. Martinez, now an attorney for a congressional committee in Washington, recalled being shocked by the "blatant" wholesale drugging of Taft children with Ritalin by the school's physician. "From our experience," Testler explained, "it was not the parents who saw any need for medical intervention. The first they heard there was some need for medical intervention was from the school. They were told to go to a doctor . . . who prescribed it readily."

When the Montoyas and other parents whose children were placed on Ritalin tried to negotiate with school officials on the issue and presented a list of demands, including the right of full information about screening and test results, the school board refused to act. On September 8, 1975, the Youth Law Center attorneys filed a massive civil suit against the school district on behalf of eighteen children. The suit alleges the rights of the children and parents were violated by forced drugging as a condition for remaining in school and asks for $250,000 in damages for each child. More than three years after the suit was filed, it still had not come to trial, and attorneys for the children expected no early settlement. Ms. Testler, who replaced Ms. Martinez as the chief attorney in the case for the children, said in an interview in late 1978 that the parents, conscious of the legal ramifications for all children and parents in such a major test case, have not lost heart and are "very much determined to see the case through to the end."

As evidence in the case, the attorneys for the children have presented case histories of children who were misdiagnosed as hyperactive or as having MBD, of children being stigmatized as being mentally or educationally handicapped, of children suffering severe adverse reactions, and of children being placed on increasingly higher doses of Ritalin on demand of teachers.

Since the suit was filed, the Youth Law Center regularly gets calls, even today, from parents in other cities complaining about similar experiences. Ms. Testler believes the practice of forcing children onto drugs for behavioral purposes is widespread with regional differences. "In one community, there will be very little, and in a matched community it will be very high." Where there is a high incidence of children on Ritalin or other stimulant drugs, she said, "you can infer there is some organized promoting of use," and "you should look toward the school."

Dr. Nancy Durant, a child psychiatrist, said that the pressure from schools in the central New Jersey area where she practices sometimes is intense. "We have kids that come to the [Raritan Bay] Mental Health Center who are put out of school in Woodbridge, and we are told they cannot return until they are on medication and have been on it for ten days. You have that happen, and that's big pressure. There are a lot of pressures out there."

Sometimes the pressure to put a child on drugs to control behavior comes from the parents. Such was the case, as related by Dr. Durant, of a twenty-one-year-old mother of two children of her own and the legal guardian of four siblings.

The mother had been to a school conference with the teacher of her daughter, who had been classified as "perceptually impaired" by the school. "The teacher went through this litany of all the things this girl didn't and did do and how distractable she was. The mother had the child on Ritalin at the close of last year. The mother asked the teacher, 'Do you think she needs to go back on medication?' The teacher said, 'I wouldn't want to be responsible for a child being on medication.' The mother's reaction: 'You would just rather stigmatize and socially isolate her.' She said she was so angry she went directly to her pediatrician to get a prescription to put her back on the medication to see if that would improve her function in the classroom."

Dr. Durant prefers to work within the entire family system of a child "because it is a problem for the family, and sometimes there are problems in the family which exaggerate the problem" of the emotionally disturbed child. When she is unable to reach for treatment other family members who may, in fact, be the cause of the child's problems, she feels that sometimes she has no choice but to use psychoactive drugs to alter the child's behavior to be more acceptable to the others. She told of one young boy she put on Ritalin to keep him from being abused by his mother: "She was beating the life out of him without the medication. You have to think of the benefit ratio, what the whole picture is. This is a family with lots of problems, no question about that."

In another case, Dr. Durant thinks psychoactive drugs might save a nine-year-old neurologically impaired boy from being thrown out of a special education classroom in his home district. The boy got into a fight with another student at the school when he was called "a sissy." Big for his age, the youth "lost control," picked the other boy up, "and beat his head against a table," causing minor scars and bruises. The injured boy's parents complained, and his teacher wrote a letter to the teacher of the special education class demanding that the neurologically impaired boy be thrown out of school. Dr. Durant said the boy was not on drugs because "he happens to have a pediatrician who is very strongly opposed to any psychoactive medication for children, which means he will be educated in a more restrictive environment."

The boy is the oldest of five children in a "quite disorganized family," Dr. Durant explained, and many of his behavioral problems at school stem from his relationships with his parents and siblings. "He was telling me yesterday—I had asked him what he did after school—that he just watched television. He did not play outside anymore because, he said, his little brothers picked on him, and he's not allowed by his mother to hit back, which means he is displacing his aggression on the children at school. The tragic thing is that unless something happens in the immediate near term to render his behavior somewhat more acceptable to the teacher so she can see him as not a threat to the classroom itself, he is going to be educated in a more restrictive environment."

No issue is more sensitive to parents, teachers, doctors, and children than the involvement of the schools in the use of psychoactive drugs to treat children with MBD, hyperactivity, or various other disorders, whether correctly or incorrectly diagnosed, that adversely affect a student's ability to learn or, put another way, a teacher's ability to teach. "One need not be terribly creative to inflame passion with regard to stimulant drug therapy. The specter of 1984 or of the sinister scientist, hypodermic needle in hand, is easily conjured," lamented James Bosco, a professor of teacher education at Western Michigan University in Kalamazoo, who with sociologist Stanley S. Robin conducted the most extensive survey of stimulant drug use within a single school system. Using the western Michigan city of Grand Rapids as their model, they determined that less hyperactivity or MBD was being diagnosed and fewer drugs being prescribed than they expected. They concluded that only about 1 percent of the elementary school population was taking stimulant drugs in 1977. Estimates of drug use from 1970 to 1975 ranged from a conservative 2 or 3 percent to an absurdly high 50 percent with the consensus being that the national average probably was around 5 percent. The Bosco-Robin survey seems to confirm Ciba-Geigy's 1978 estimate of 212,000 children on drugs for MBD or hyperactivity, and it validates the impression that psychoactive drug therapy was on the decline by the late 1970s.

One reason for this trend was the growing evidence that while stimulants do help hyperactive children concentrate on menial tasks and rote learning assignments in the short term, they provide no positive benefits over the long term and can produce severe and damaging side effects, including stunted growth. The most devastating study was conducted at the Montreal Children's

Hospital by Dr. Gabrielle Weiss under a grant by Ciba-Geigy. To determine whether Ritalin had any long-term advantages, Dr. Weiss and her colleagues extensively tested three different groups of hyperactive children. Twenty-four were treated with Ritalin for three to five years, twenty-two with the powerful tranquilizer Thorazine, and twenty received no medication at all. After comparing results from extensive testing, they concluded that Ritalin "was helpful in making hyperactive children more manageable at home and at school but did not significantly affect their outcome after five years of treatment." The children in the Ritalin group originally were put on the drug in 1967 for an experimental study sponsored by Ciba-Geigy, and twelve of them were still on it five years later at the time of the follow-up in 1972. The researchers were clearly disappointed in the results and said they were surprised the Ritalin children had not done better in the follow-up testing. They said their "failure to demonstrate a better five-year outcome in adolescence" for the Ritalin children was "difficult to explain" and confessed they may have "expected too much from any one drug or from any one method of treatment of hyperactive children." The follow-up results showed "the three groups were not significantly different with respect to emotional adjustment, delinquency, mother-child relationship and mother's impression of change." Further, there was no "statistically significant difference" in academic performance. Dr. Weiss also reported that the twelve children who remained on Ritalin for the entire five years found it highly difficult to concentrate when taken off the drug for two weeks prior to the follow-up testing. Although these children said they liked being "off the pill," their teachers complained about their classroom behavior and the parents found the two-week drug vacation for their children "very difficult." Dr. Weiss, a psychiatrist, speculated that the parents may have "overreacted" to the two-week drug holiday and "their child's regression toward a more hyperkinetic behavior."

Although the Weiss study was first presented in 1973 and published in 1975, it was not included as late as 1978 on the lists of research papers on MBD and hyperactivity supplied by Ciba-Geigy to physicians and other interested parties. In addition, Felton Davis, the company's vice-president for marketing, said in an interview that he was unaware of the Montreal follow-up. The absence of the Weiss study, which Ciba-Geigy financed, in the general literature supplied to doctors lends a ring of truth to the charge that drug companies circulate only the literature that takes a benign view of drug therapy. (Ciba-Geigy did freely provide a copy of the study when it was specifically requested by one of the authors.)

Research at UCLA backs up the Weiss conclusions. Ritalin and other psychostimulants provide dramatic improvement in the attention span of hyperactive children at the outset of drug therapy, but "these dramatic effects tend to fade," explained Dr. Richard Schain, a pediatric neurologist. "There's no doubt the drugs produce effects immediately. They can be startling at times, and teachers and parents will be impressed. But tolerance builds up, higher doses need to be given, and such a dependence develops that the individual can no longer be tolerated by parents or teachers without the drugs. The original problems are still there." Dr. Schain, whose "basic philosophy is that physicians should not be in the business of altering personality through drugs," said that when children are taken off the stimulants, there is a "big rebound," and patience is necessary to permit the child's personality to reestablish itself. "We are inclined to taper it off rather than go cold turkey. It's not that the children can't tolerate it. Others won't. Parents and teachers find them intolerable." For Dr. Schain what it comes down to is that "if you're in the child business, you have to adapt . . . rather than change them with drugs."

Dr. Weiss's study of the effects of Ritalin in long-term use also suggested that when the drug is used for three years or longer, "it becomes increasingly less effective, and 'tolerance' slowly develops." In a research project at the Institute for Child Behavior and Development at the University of Illinois, Drs. Robert L. Sprague and Esther Sleator determined that keeping the dosage level low is critical in improving learning ability in the short term. They found that learning performance decreased as Ritalin dosage levels were increased while social behavior became more acceptable at higher levels and less acceptable at lower dosages. "Thus," they said, "a doctor seeking primarily to optimize the behavior of the child in school on a basis of reports by the teacher would be likely to prescribe a dose of medication well above the point of peak enhancement of learning. . . ."

From the studies showing that often the prime motivation for placing children on stimulant drugs comes from teachers and parents wanting to control behavior, we can only conclude that increasingly large doses of the drugs are needed—and much of the medical literature recommends this upward adjustment—to satisfy their needs rather than to help the children learn. In testimony before a congressional committee in September 1978, Dr. Daniel X. Freedman, who was chairman of the 1971 HEW panel that endorsed stimulants for MBD, speaking on behalf of the AMA, acknowledged the potential for abuse and "psychological dependence" in the use of amphetamines at high-dosage levels, citing the widespread abuse to control obesity. At the same time, however, Dr. Freedman said amphetamines in low total daily doses are "useful in selected cases of minimal brain dysfunction" with no evidence of tolerance or abuse.

"Drugging," says psychologist George Krebs, "is laziness." Krebs believes that by labeling a child "hyperactive" and, therefore, sick and in need of drugs, nobody—not the child, not the parents, not the siblings, and not the teacher—has to do any work to find and resolve the underlying problem. All drugs do, Krebs said, is mask symptoms. "If you give a hyperactive child a drug to stop his acting out, the result is further feelings of helplessness and the feeling of being victimized," he said in an interview. He believes, too, that when parents demand of physicians that they " 'do something for my kid quick,' they really are saying, 'Do something for me.' Parents want instant relief."

Like Krebs, the goal of Roland Ostrower, director of the Foundation for Child Mental Health, is to remove children from drugs and treat their emotional problems without drugs. Ostrower runs Public School 205 in Manhattan, a unique school that has been helping hyperactive and emotionally disturbed children basically with a "Freudian outlook" since 1970. The purpose of the program is to help a troubled child "develop his own personality, own controls, and own life" through psychotherapy, individualized counseling, and tailored educational and physical activities. The school takes about forty children between the ages of six and nine each year, many of them from economically disadvantaged families, and reports a 70 to 75 percent success rate in returning the children to regular classrooms after three years. "Unfortunately it is easier to use drugs and say, 'I'll see you in two months,' but drugs are not going to deal with the underlying problems. We don't think it is possible to survive without knowing what's going on, and that's why we take an approach directly opposite of giving drugs."

Child psychiatrist Roger D. Freeman, director of services for handicapped children at the University of British Columbia in Vancouver, runs an outpatient clinic for children, including those for whom there are complaints of hyperactivity. Dr. Freeman and the staff "spend six to eight hours on each case and sometimes more before we have a grip on what's going on." The staff makes school and home visits, spending hours with the parents and teachers of the children, and applies behavior modification and other nonchemical therapy to treat not just the child but the family as well. "It is a time-consuming approach . . . and we can only see a few hundred children a year," Dr. Freeman said in an interview, adding that this approach might only be practical because it is in a university setting. "I don't want to imply that this is the way to do things for millions of people in a huge city," he said. "Some of the California practitioners might see more than one thousand in a year, and most of those are on drugs." Dr. Freeman wanted to make it clear that he is "quite prepared to try a drug" and has used drugs for short-term therapy.

There are many other such nonchemical therapy programs throughout North America, but nonetheless, most children diagnosed as hyperactive have neither the opportunity nor the family resources for such treatment. There is, however, the approach taken by the Feingold Association. For $15 a year, children and their families can avail themselves of all the resources, including group therapy, of this rapidly growing approach to treating hyperactivity by removal of artificial additives from the family's diet. Preparing such a diet is not easy and demands the full involvement of every member of the family, which in itself provides positive benefits not only for the hyperactive child but for the others, too.

Probably the most active Feingold chapter in the United States is in Smithtown, the Long Island home of Vickie Giraldi, who took her child off drugs in 1974 to try, in desperation, Feingold's diet, found that it worked for her son, and began to spread the word with fervor among other parents with hyperactive children, doctors, teachers, grocers, in fact, anyone who would listen. What started out as a meeting of four or five parents in Mrs. Giraldi's living room in September 1975 mushroomed in three years into a nationwide association of nearly 150 local Feingold Association chapters and several thousand children and their parents working together to deal with a difficult, complex, and sensitive problem. "It's like a little dot of ink on paper that just gets bigger and bigger and bigger," Mrs. Giraldi, who served for two terms as the association's first national president, explained. In the beginning it was difficult because the Feingold diet was quickly attacked by the medical profession, the food and chemical industry, and the scientific community. "We received a lot of criticism, and they said it doesn't work," said Mrs. Giraldi, adding that favorable studies and positive results have muted much of the opposition. "Doctors that criticized us three years ago now are referring patients to us. Now they are handing out natural lollipops instead of red ones with dye." A few drug companies are even producing a few noncolored, nonflavored medications, and many school lunch programs have been modified to provide additive-free diets for hyperactive children in the Feingold program.

Opposition to the Feingold diet remains formidable. Felton Davis, Ciba-Geigy's marketing executive, grudgingly admitted that the growth of the additive-free diet as a way of treating hyperactivity has cut into Ritalin sales, saying it was "unfortunate" because patients "were taken off therapy, including drugs, who should not have been." Asked in an interview about reports from parents and some doctors that the Feingold diet works, Dr. Alphonso Strollo, a pediatrician for fifteen years before joining Ciba-Geigy as chief medical officer for pediatric medicine, replied in a manner indicative of the medical profession's reliance on easy solutions. "If I had to work that hard on something," he said, "it damn well better work."

The most powerful opposition to Feingold comes from the food, beverage, chemical, and drug industries, which have billions of dollars at stake in preserving the status quo in the processing, packaging, and marketing of foods, beverages, and drugs containing artificial chemicals to color, flavor, and preserve them. Leading the fight against the Feingolders, as they call themselves, is the Nutrition Foundation, an organization of high-sounding principles to match its euphonistic name, but in the opinion of some, in fact, a scientific front for the food and food-additive industry. With an annual budget of $1.6 million in 1978, the Nutrition Foundation includes such giants of the food industry as General Mills, Standard Brands, Dobbs-Life Savers, Campbell's Soup, Beatrice Foods, Procter & Gamble, Royal Crown Cola, Welch Foods, Del Monte, Amstar (sugar), and the Nestle Company.

Shortly after Dr. Feingold published his book *Why Your Child Is Hyperactive* in 1974, the Nutrition Foundation impaneled a National Advisory Committee on Hyperkinesis and Food Additives and called the group together for a two-day meeting on Long Island in January 1975. Although the scientists on the committee had agreed not to publicize its findings prematurely, until after more study and deliberations, the staff of the foundation issued a press release suggesting it had concluded that the Feingold diet for treatment of hyperactivity had no validity and could be nutritionally harmful. The committee's report issued five months later did indeed question the scientific testing procedures used by Dr. Feingold, but it also acknowledged that his "claims may prove valid, and, if so, may represent a major breakthrough in the treatment of this complex condition." The foundation subsequently funded a study by J. Preston Harley at the University of Wisconsin Food Research Institute, which has over the years received in excess of $600,000 from the food industry. The Wisconsin study showed no benefits from the Feingold diet generally and recommended drug treatment as more effective. But other studies funded by the foundation, including one at the University of Pittsburgh, failed either to prove or to disprove the Feingold thesis, although some positive results were recorded. Vickie Giraldi says there is reason for encouragement in these reports and other studies under way in 1978 but cautions followers that the Nutrition Foundation "will continue to disclaim Feingold's hypothesis. . . . Is it any wonder why they do this? The food industry is a multibillion-dollar-a-year business."

The food, drug, and chemical industries argue that Feingold's hypothesis was based on uncontrolled studies and was therefore unscientifically proved. At least three studies financed by the Nutrition Foundation sought to disprove Feingold's theory but only heightened the controversy because of the source of the funding, the methods used to conduct the tests, and the inconclusive and ambiguous results. An FDA-financed study at the Kaiser Research Institute and the University of California completed in February 1979 raised more questions than it provided answers. Out of twenty-two children aged one to seven who were identified as being hyperactive, only one child reacted adversely to the addition of artificial colorings to his diet. "The findings tend to support the conclusion that, while some behaviorally disturbed children may respond to some aspect of the Feingold diet, the elimination of synthetic food colors from the diet does not appear to be a major factor in the reported responses of a majority of these children," the FDA said in announcing the findings. The summary was substantially less conclusive, stating that more and better studies need to be conducted. Said the authors, "It should be re-emphasized that the findings in this experiment cannot be used to either negate or support the hypothesis on a statistical basis."

Whatever the scientific validity of the Feingold theory, it clearly works for many children. It may be that the Feingold diet works as a placebo that is positively reinforced by the active involvement of the entire family in the child's activities, by the self-help group therapy available to the children, parents, and siblings, and by the strong faith its adherents place in the diet's therapeutic value.

Many doctors have taken the position that the Feingold diet is at least worth a try. Some are even willing to try it before drug therapy, which is a welcome change. Smithtown pediatrician Joseph D'Agrosa, quoted earlier in this chapter, is one such physician who has seen enough results from the Feingold diet to try it before he prescribes drugs.

About the time Dr. Feingold first began to publicize his findings, Dr. D'Agrosa had begun to experiment with removal of candy, milk, and other foodstuffs from the diet of hyperactive children whom he had determined to be "reactors" to certain substances. "No real literature was available on the subject, and we just tried experimenting, and we saw something happening, whether we were imagining it or not, and then I heard about the Feingold Association." Dr. D'Agrosa called Vickie Giraldi, who invited him to her house and told him of her own experience with her son—how "she had a kid who climbed the walls. She took him off all these candies and things after she heard about Feingold, and the kid slept through the night and became a human being."

Dr. D'Agrosa got a copy of Dr. Feingold's book and began using the diet. At the time he and his partners had sixty-three children on Ritalin. Four years later, he had sixty children on the diet and fewer than a handful on Ritalin, other stimulants, or tranquilizers, but he looks on the diet as no more a panacea than are drugs. "If a kid has other problems, they should be solved, along with the diet," he explained. "I would be in favor of universal use of the diet, provided a kid has motivated parents willing to know its limitations and its use, who are willing to spend the time doing it, and then follow through on other suggestions the kid needs. I think it cannot be used as a crutch, nor can pills."

Still, Dr. D'Agrosa has seen enough positive results to try the diet first, and tacked on his wall next to his neatly framed and laminated medical licenses and degrees is a cheaply reproduced certificate of membership in the Feingold Association. In a verse entitled "I'm a Natural," it says:

> Congratulations.
> You can come to parties,
> You can join the fun,
> You can play the games,
> Of them, there is a ton.
> Chemicals are out for you,
> Your food is only pure.
> Never to cheat is the rule.
> You're a Feingold kid for sure.

Hyperactivity in children is an identifiable disorder, as any parent of a truly hyperactive child will testify; but drug therapy is not a panacea, and neither is the Feingold diet. Nor is behavior modification. What is clear, however, is that too often the easiest route is taken—stimulant medication over long periods—and often it is the only mode of treatment applied. Sadly, medical science only now, after more than a decade of widespread use of the amphetamines, is beginning to discover what Dr. Mark A. Stewart, an early proponent of the use of the drugs who changed his mind after seeing their effect after prolonged use, concluded in 1972.

Said Stewart, a child psychiatrist: "The drugs hid the child's real personality, often leading to a postpuberty identity crisis. By the time the child reaches puberty he is a child who does not know what his undrugged personality is. And worse, the child's family does not know how to accept his undrugged personality."

Although the link has not been firmly established, there is growing evidence that hyperactivity could be caused, at least in part, by the drugs administered to women during pregnancy and childbirth. As noted in the previous chapter, studies just being completed as this book was prepared showed that the powerful psychoactive sedatives and painkillers used to relieve the anxiety of the mother while carrying her baby and to relieve her of pain while delivering impair a child's motor skills and cognitive processes. Other studies also have shown that alcohol when used by a pregnant woman in excess may also cause hyperactivity in children.

If these conclusions are correct, then it is a tragic irony that drugs cause hyperactivity, are used in excess to treat it, and often result in even worse problems in adolescence and adulthood. It is, indeed, a vicious circle.

Chemical Solitary Confinement | 6

Solitary confinement is the dank, black, and rat-infested hole of medieval dungeons, the padded cell of mental institutions, the "tiger cage" in a Southeast Asian jungle, or the "time-out room" of a modern detention center. There is today what Kenneth Wooden, author of *Weeping in the Playtime of Others*, a frightening account about the mistreatment of incarcerated children, calls the new solitary confinement.

Although it has by no means replaced the old, this new solitary confinement results from the use of powerful tranquilizers to isolate and punish persons by placing them in their own space, mentally and emotionally apart but physically not alone. The motivation remains the same: punishment, control, and, in the rationale of the guardians, self-protection and protection of others.

Chemical solitary confinement is today the most common mode of treatment of the mentally ill and mentally retarded in American institutions, but its use is more economic than therapeutic. It is also used as a straitjacket for the sane and healthy children and adults in correctional facilities.

Wooden, who traveled the nation to find out why 50,000 children between the ages of five and sixteen are locked up and how they are being treated, found many correctional officers and administrators all too "thankful for the supportive custodial role psychotherapeutic drugs play" in keeping children in line and costs down. The phenothiazines, of which the tranquilizer Thorazine, or chlorpromazine, is the most common, were being used, Wooden found, not for the control of disturbed psychotic persons but, more often than not, to minimize fighting, running away, and general misbehaving, as well as for punishing and controlling. Many of the incarcerated children Wooden saw were forced "to endure not only the old methods of isolation but the new as well. Locked within four small walls behind metal doors, they find themselves in a frightening, bewildering state as medicine injected into their bodies takes hold of their minds. The evils of yesteryear, brutal punishment and solitary confinement, combine with the evils of modern drugs to further enure these children to their keepers."

Frank Borgerson was one such child. A middle-class boy from a broken home in the Minneapolis suburb of Roseville, Frank, whose court record shows a long history of petty crime, by the time he was sixteen had spent nearly three years in institutions. His younger brother Jeff, two years behind him in age, also had done time. Mostly they were jailed for running away in stolen cars, and as Frank later described it, "I'd run away because I didn't like a place, and they'd stick me in a worse place, and it kept getting worse and worse."

In the summer of 1976 both were on the run from Minnesota juvenile detention centers, Frank from Red Wing and Jeff from Totem Town. They were caught, and Frank was charged with car theft and running away. Jeff, then fourteen, was charged as a runaway. The Ramsey County Juvenile Court sent them both to a new and privately operated institution with the high-sounding name of the Center for Behavior Disorders. County officials had begun to use the center to place some of their hard-core juvenile offenders, and Frank qualified with his long history of car thefts and escapes. Although Jeff did not qualify, juvenile authorities thought it would be a good idea to keep the brothers together and sent Jeff to the center, too. Jeff later recalled, "They kind of wanted to put me in there with my brother just to see how we would act together in the same place."

On June 16, 1976, Frank was sent to the center to join Jeff, who had been committed ten days earlier. Located in a renovated building in Minneapolis, the Center for Behavior Disorders was a new facility, unique in Minnesota because it was privately owned and operated. A private entrepreneur, Rollind Collins, to secure a license to operate a juvenile detention center, had sufficiently convinced county judges that he could handle some of their tougher cases and take some pressure off public facilities as well.

As soon as he arrived, Frank resolved to run away. He told his story under blazing television lights at one of the most unusual hearings ever held in the nation's capital. The hearing was organized by the *Children's Express*, a magazine written for children by children, which folded after nearly two successful years when the organizers failed to persuade enough advertisers of children's goods to divert a small amount of their ad budgets from Saturday morning television. The hearings were the outgrowth of a series of articles on incarcerated children in the magazine. Held at the Children's Embassy of the Day Care and Child Development Council of America, March 28–30, 1978, the hearing was organized and conducted by reporters from the *Children's Express*, all of whom were between the ages of ten and fourteen. They questioned U.S. senators, doctors, juvenile justice experts, reporters such as Wooden, lawyers, and, most significantly, children who had been jailed. Frank was one of the witnesses, telling how he did indeed escape shortly after he arrived at the Center for Behavior Disorders because he saw other children being administered tranquilizers and he couldn't "handle . . . the way they changed when they was on the drugs." After a short period on the outside, Frank said he returned to the center and was put on Thorazine. "I didn't have no coordination with my hands, I couldn't see right, I couldn't control my saliva, I couldn't talk right, and I couldn't do anything right. I couldn't even walk. I was just a zombie, a walking robot, just really bad," he told the incredulous young questioners, who then asked him who had administered the drug.

"All the staff there administered it. I was given it orally. I just drank it. They'd go to the locked room, they'd get the drugs, and four times a day they'd give me two hundred milligrams of Thorazine, and if you didn't take it then, they'd shoot you with it.

"It's a scary thing," Frank continued. "You think you're losing everything 'cause you ain't got no control of yourself. You're too lazy to talk. You can't open your mouth; if you do, it's hard for people to understand you. You can't express yourself to people. You see other people doin' their own thing that ain't on drugs, and you feel like a loner, you know? You're over there in the corner, and you can't even lift your finger, you're so tired.

"Me, I was on a shadowing program, and I was just zonked out. Sometimes they'd say—you know, on files—'Frank ain't lookin' too good today; he's too perky or somethin'. He ain't zonked out enough.' That's what they think a person should be to help him, zonked out. You can't help somebody when they're zonked because you ain't dealin' with the real person. When I was on it, I would be real frustrated, which would get me in trouble because I couldn't handle being a loner and not being able to express myself. Like I thought I was goin' crazy on drugs. I was really scared."

The staff of the Center for Behavior Disorders had standing orders from a consulting psychiatrist to give Frank 200 milligrams of Thorazine four times a day. The orders were written after he briefly escaped and was identified as a potential runaway. Frank told the *Children's Express* hearing that the psychiatrist, identified in court testimony as Dr. Arlene Boutin, did not examine him prior to issuing the drugging orders. Nor did she make arrangements to monitor regularly his response for adverse reactions or to take routinely his blood pressure. (In some persons blood pressure has been known to fall to fatal levels upon administration of the drug.) Frank's daily dosage of 800 milligrams was well in excess of the 500-milligram dosage recommended as usually sufficient even for the most "acutely agitated, manic or disturbed" adult psychotic patients. The manufacturer, Smith Kline & French, says 500 milligrams is enough to control even these "exceptionally severe cases."

Frank did suffer a severe adverse reaction that almost killed him. His regular dosage was 800 milligrams a day, but it would be increased to 900 milligrams if he didn't appear "zonked enough." One day he was given 1,100 milligrams and "almost suffocated to death" as a result. "I was out in the back in the sun, and when you're on Thorazine, you ain't supposed to be in the sun 'cause your skin is too sensitive. Well, I went out there, and I didn't want to, but they made me. I couldn't do nothing about it, so when I was out there, my tongue swelled up, and then my body got . . . I fell down, and my body cramped up into a little ball, and I couldn't breathe. I was just barely getting out enough words, asking for help, and they thought I was joking. So finally, one staff member came and seen that I wasn't joking. They brought me in, gave me some water, and laid me down. They weren't supposed to give me water because if I had water, I could have went into a convulsion or a seizure or something, and I could have died. My blood pressure was really low."

Frank and Jeff were two of nineteen children being held at the center. Frank was one of three youths kept on a daily dosage of Thorazine. Of the others, one was considered a potential runaway and had some history of violence, according to Linda Miller, a St. Paul attorney appointed by the court to represent Frank after he finally succeeded in running away from the center. Ms. Miller ended up representing all nineteen in a federal civil suit. The third boy was drugged because "he was really a big boy, and people were scared of him. He was about six-one and very big; otherwise, he didn't have a bad record of running away." All three were kept on heavy doses of Thorazine, and all three subsequently suffered severe ill effects.

In the fall of 1976, three months after he had been committed, Frank escaped. Jeff was released in November. Frank was arrested again and complained, as had others, of the treatment at the Minneapolis center. "People would see me all doped up. Somebody eventually said, 'Hey, this can't be for real.'" State and county authorities checked it out, found it was "for real," and closed the Center for Behavior Disorders in December. Criminal charges were filed against Collins, the owner, and Angel Catania, a nurse. Catania pleaded guilty to mistreatment of prisoners. Collins was acquitted in a jury trial of charges of aggravated assault with drugs and other mistreatment offenses. Collins, who had come to Minnesota to establish the center after California authorities had closed a similar one there, moved to Calgary, Alberta, where he opened yet another one. Psychiatrist Boutin cooperated with the prosecution in the criminal proceedings against Collins and was not charged by the state. "They feel strongly that she was perhaps at the most negligent," said Ms. Miller, the attorney representing Frank and the others. "They feel she was deceived. She was just out of school. I feel more strongly that if she didn't know what was going on, she should have checked. The records show children were being administered drugs that weren't on the charts. If she didn't look at the charts, she showed negligence." Ms. Miller said Dr. Boutin knew of the incident when Frank suffered a near fatal reaction to Thorazine after being exposed to bright sunlight, and "incidents like that should have made her look and see again." The records also indicate the children were given dosages of Thorazine "significantly" in excess of the normal recommendation, and they proved to Ms. Miller's satisfaction that the drugged children had "very little contact with the psychiatrist who authorized the drugs. There was no proper follow-up at all, and these drugs are dangerous."

Although Collins was found innocent of criminal charges, his legal troubles were not over. Ms. Miller filed a massive class-action civil suit on behalf of all nineteen children in the U.S. district court. The suit names as defendants Collins, Catania, Boutin, the state of Minnesota, Hennepin County, and various state and county officials and agencies. The civil action, which alleges, among other violations, intentional harm with drugs, was in the pretrial stage as 1978 came to a close and was not expected to reach the trial stage until 1979 at the earliest.

Frank will carry the physical and psychological scars of his six years in jails and nice-sounding places like the Center for Behavior Disorders the rest of his life. He has been diagnosed as having tardive dyskinesia, a common reaction to consistently high doses of major tranquilizers for which there is no known remedy. It is estimated that 15 to 20 percent of all persons receiving the major tranquilizers for extended periods suffer from this drug-caused disability. According to Smith Kline & French, which makes Thorazine, tardive dyskinesia "is characterized by rhythmical involuntary movements of the tongue, face, mouth or jaw. . . ." Frank, for example, has no control over his saliva. His attorneys think he also suffered permanent brain damage.

It would comforting if we could report that the experience of Frank and the abuses of the Minneapolis center were isolated incidents. But there is mounting evidence that such abuses have existed in our public and private institutions, custodial or correctional, for years. In fact, wherever people are confined and drugs are used, there is the human inclination and the economic motivation to take the easiest, most efficient route for control, and that simple, inexpensive path is through sedation.

Until a lawsuit filed by relatives of inmates forced an end to the practice in 1975, every child sent to the Goshen State School in New York was automatically—without physical or psychiatric examination—given a standing order for 25 milligrams of Thorazine to be injected intermuscularly. Nurses were authorized to increase the dosage to fifty milligrams if they decided twenty-five was not enough. Because it is the most direct route to the central nervous system, muscular injection provides ten times the potency of orally administered tranquilizers.

Dr. Edward Kaufman, associate professor of psychiatry at the University of California and editor of the *American Journal of Drug and Alcohol Abuse*, has participated in the evaluation of more than twenty correctional and custodial institutions in six states as an expert witness in civil and criminal lawsuits brought by patients, inmates, relatives, and public interest groups. "Intermuscular Thorazine is used almost everywhere I go in very high doses and without proper precautions," Kaufman said. He has seen many "institutions that depend on medication as a major modality of treatment, yet the individual's dose is set on the first day and in sixty percent of the cases, it isn't changed thereafter." In addition to the common adverse reactions, such as drug-induced Parkinson's disease, Dr. Kaufman believes the drugs contribute to the high suicide rates in institutions. "In fact, when somebody is suicidal in these institutions, intermuscular Thorazine is the drug most frequently given to them, which may make them too tired to kill themselves but makes them so depressed that when they get the energy, they are very likely to do it."

Dr. Jerome Miller, former director of youth services for the states of Massachusetts and Illinois and now director of the National Center for Action on Institutions and Alternatives, tells about a reformatory for girls in Pennsylvania, where he found "every other kid was on tranquilizers." The drugs were prescribed for the girls, 75 to 80 percent of whom were there for such status offenses as running away, by a female psychiatrist whose records indicated that "any girl not in a classic nineteenth-century role was seen as ill."

Miller, who shocked the juvenile justice system in the early 1970s by closing all of Massachusetts's reform schools and by transferring thousands of offenders to community centers, says excessive use of tranquilizers was a "major issue" in many of the institutions he has inspected during a decade of involvement. "Our experience was that there is a lot of it," Miller said in an interview.

Lately Miller has grown concerned about the treatment of children in child care institutions. The system encourages deprived and neglected but otherwise healthy children to be sick in order for the institutions to qualify for maximum funding by state and federal agencies. The private institutions, which as a rule are the best run, are encouraged by the reimbursement formulas to take children who are physically, mentally, and emotionally healthy and diagnose them as "emotionally disturbed" or, to use a label in vogue today, "developmentally disabled." Once so labeled, a child qualifies for drug treatment. Miller finds that commonly the diagnosis follows the admission. The incentive is to take and keep over a long period of time the kids who are the least trouble but who are labeled with an emotional or mental illness. On the other hand, a truly troubled or disturbed child who is in need of maximum care and attention is dumped into the poorest facilities, usually the crowded, poorly staffed, and poorly equipped public ones. In short, the best treatment goes to those children in least need or who could manage without it, while the worst treatment is given to those most in need.

The potential for abuse—as well as the real and documented cases of abuse—for the inappropriate use of psychoactive drugs on children in institutions is enormous, considering the staggering numbers of incarcerated children. According to *Corrections* magazine, there were 26,000 juvenile offenders in public penal institutions in 1978, and an additional 20,000 were in private and equally secure facilities. In addition, on any given day there are an estimated 400,000 youths being held in detention centers for children, and another 600,000 in adult jails. Most of these are being held on status offenses, such as running away. The latest survey by the Law Enforcement Assistance Agency (LEAA) indicated that in 1975 there were an additional 49,000 children in public or private correctional training schools, ranches, camps, and farms.

Also being institutionalized are an estimated 100,000 mentally retarded children in public facilities. The Child Welfare League estimates that at least 10 percent, or 50,000, of the 500,000 children in foster care are in private institutions, and most of these are physically or mentally retarded, emotionally disturbed, or learning disabled.

By conservative estimates, the total number of incarcerated children in America reaches 1.3 million on any given day, some 300,000 in what can be considered long-term custodial or penal care and 1 million in juvenile or adult jails on short-term periods for status offenses. Miller estimates there are 3 to 4 million Americans of all ages in institutions of all kinds, ranging from prisons to nursing homes and from boys' camps like Boys Town to juvenile prisons. Miller believes his estimate is low and notes that institutionalization is a $35-to-$50-billion-a-year industry and that as many as 4 million Americans are living in institutions of some sort on any given day. *American Geriatrics* magazine says that one out of every four Americans will spend at least some time in an institution during the course of a lifetime. As we have seen, children to the age of sixteen or seventeen make up a substantial portion—more than a third—of the incarcerated population. Because of their age and legal status as minors and because they are in the critical stage of physiological, mental, emotional, and social development, incarcerated children are vulnerable to abuses of behavior control, social and legal manipulation, and medical indifference, ignorance, and misfeasance, including indiscriminate drugging and psychotherapeutic and psychosurgical experimentation.

Since 1970 John Rector has been involved in issues affecting children, first as a special assistant to Senator Birch Bayh of Indiana and then as the first administrator of the federal Office of Juvenile Justice and Delinquency Prevention. Rector was instrumental in drafting a 1974 law overhauling the juvenile justice system to put more emphasis on rehabilitation, community-based programs, and deinstitutionalization. As Bayh's assistant he organized a series of congressional hearings on the problems of incarcerated children and their possible solutions. One of the major findings was the widespread and inappropriate use of powerful psychoactive drugs not for any valid medical purpose but rather to control and manipulate behavior to the advantage not of the captive children but of the keepers. Says Rector: "Anyone intimately familiar with what goes on in the institutions of this country with regard to young people, whether they be dependent, neglected, abused, delinquent, retarded, or what have you, learns very quickly that drugging plays a major role in the modern way in which we overinstitutionalize and incarcerate young people."

One of the most mistreated and misunderstood segments of the population is the mentally retarded. In the United States, there are an estimated 6 million people, or 3 percent of the population, with mild to profound mental impairment, according to the President's Committee on Mental Retardation. The impairment almost always is irreversible and permanent and caused by some 200 known factors leading to some organic injury to the brain. The most common causes are genetic defects, biological diseases, birth injuries, and psychological or social deprivation.

It is important to draw a distinction between the mentally retarded and the mentally ill since the two are often incorrectly lumped together to the disadvantage of both. A mentally or emotionally disturbed person potentially can be cured. The mentally retarded person has permanent damage to the brain that in almost all instances cannot be reversed or cured. Mentally retarded persons do have mental illness problems, but to no greater degree as a general rule than the population at large, although they are more vulnerable to the pressures and frustrations of living because of their impairment than are nonhandicapped persons.

Nothing so angers Mickey Marlib, associate executive director of the Association for Children with Retarded Mental Development, than the classification of the mentally retarded and the mentally or emotionally ill under one tent. He bristles even at the mention of the two classifications in a conjunctive sentence. "The first thing we have to get straight is that an emotionally disturbed person has a potential for cure. A mentally retarded person often is born with brain damage and has definite damage that is a lifetime ailment. A retarded person is basically slow, but there are various degrees of slowness from mild to moderate to severe and to profound. There are functional degrees of mental retardation. He is not primarily one that goes off the wall. He is basically a very placid, warm person. An emotionally disturbed person goes off the walls for various reasons." Marlib is sensitive to the distinction because he runs into substantial public opposition and ignorance in the association's effort to remove mentally retarded persons from institutions and place them in group homes in residential neighborhoods of New York City. The common response is, "We don't want them," and Marlib and his colleagues "have to go out time after time and spell this out: 'Our kids are not emotionally disturbed. Our kids are basically warm and placid persons. All they want to do is live in humility and dignity.'"

Of the nation's 6 million mentally retarded, many function at levels that would be considered normal, and many are able to develop to a point above levels of definable mental impairment. Only a small minority require institutionalization. Fred J. Krause, executive director of the President's Committee on Mental Retardation, said as of 1978 there were 151,000 mentally retarded persons confined in public institutions and another estimated 45,000 in private facilities. The vast majority of those in the public institutions are judged to be either severely or profoundly retarded, while those in the private institutions, which have the prerogative of selection, represent a cross section from mild to profound. Some will be institutionalized for their entire lives, many for ten years or longer, and many will be released when they reach young adulthood, only to be reconfined when they are older and once again less able to cope on the outside.

The willful drugging of the incarcerated mentally retarded population is one of the worst ongoing scandals in American society. The most powerful tranquilizing drugs with the worst side effects are the ones commonly and consistently used on the most innocent, unprotected, and relatively emotionally stable groups of people. No responsible medical expert ever has argued that tranquilizers and other psychoactive drugs have any therapeutic value in the treatment of mental retardation, yet 55 percent of the mentally retarded in institutions regularly and for long periods receive psychoactive drugs. The two most commonly administered tranquilizers in mental retardation facilities are Mellaril, or thioridazine, and Thorazine, or chlorpromazine, both of which belong to the powerful and dangerous class of drugs known as the phenothiazines.

The phenothiazines were the psychoactive wonder drugs of the early 1950s and have been credited by mental health professionals as revolutionizing the way we treat severely psychotic patients. In its evaluation of psychoactive drugs, the President's Commission on Mental Health said in its 1978 report: "The discovery of chlorpromazine in 1952 profoundly altered the treatment of schizophrenia and, as a consequence of this and other discoveries, psychiatric treatment is radically different today than it was 20 years ago. Indeed, even our way of thinking about psychiatric illness is radically different."

Having so enthusiastically lauded the effectiveness of Thorazine, the commission briefly summarized the side effects, including tardive dyskinesia, the Parkinson-like disorder characterized by lip smacking, tongue protrusion, and movement of the extremities. The commission, which on the whole took a very favorable view toward drug therapy, said this involuntary muscle movement occurred in 5 to 40 percent of the patients under long-term treatment with Thorazine.

These are the drugs used daily and in large doses on the majority of the mentally retarded in institutions. The purpose is not to relieve symptoms of such severe disorders as schizophrenia but rather to control behavior through heavy sedation, putting otherwise emotionally healthy individuals, most of whom are children or adolescents, into a chemical solitary confinement. "If you have these kids floating around on cloud nine, you don't need fifty attendants but only ten," said Mickey Marlib, who is working to get kids "out of these damn institutions."

Dr. James Clements, director of the Georgia Retardation Center in Atlanta and a member of the President's Committee on Mental Retardation, runs a program for about 430 mentally retarded persons and never has more than 1 or 2 on psychoactive drugs at any time. But the Georgia center, which is a public facility, is rare in its approach. "It has been my experience that on the average about fifty-five percent of institutionalized retarded are getting one or more behavior-modifying drugs. The highest I've seen was about eighty percent in an institution in Minnesota," said Dr. Clements, who wrote new and tougher standards for the use of such drugs for the Joint Commission on Hospital Accreditation. "These drugs are not prescribed for the individual because he's psychotic but mainly to control his behavior, a lot of which is geared to the environment in which he resides. Much of it is given because they have not developed other programs to treat people."

Dr. Clements says he has seen a high percentage of mentally retarded persons being administered a combination of psychoactive drugs, five or six at a time in some cases. "Frequently one is prescribed but doesn't give the expected results, so another is used, and another. By that time you don't have the vaguest idea what the drugs are doing."

Usually, he said, the drugs are administered in high enough doses to sedate the individuals so that it "is not an uncommon thing to see children or adults who are sleepy most of the time." More serious adverse reactions are evident. Dr. Clements told of "one young man who had been able to walk, talk, and take care of himself. He developed tardive dyskinesia from phenothiazines, and the last time I saw him he was totally bedridden."

Because of their impairment, mentally retarded persons are slow to learn, but they can and do learn. The most commonly used drugs, Thorazine and Mellaril, however, repress learning ability, particularly at the high-dosage levels that are prevalent in institutions. As two of the widely recognized experts in psychopharmacotherapy in children, Dr. Robert Sprague and Dr. J. S. Werry, said in a review that concluded that psychotropic drugs are "used heavily" on the mentally retarded: "It is equally apparent that the main problem of the mentally retarded is slow learning and that their behavioral problems are all too often handled by administering large amounts of tranquilizing drugs which characteristically suppress learning. Thus, for treatment, the MR are often placed in institutions where social stimulation is reduced, where tranquilizing drugs which suppress learning are administered in large amounts, and where, ironically, it is expected that these combinations should produce new skills to enable the retarded to become rehabilitated members of the community."

Sprague, director of the Institute for Child Behavior and Development at the University of Illinois and chairman of the FDA's Pediatric Advisory Subcommittee, which was formed in 1974, reported in a paper for *Child Psychiatry* in 1977 that he found "deplorable conditions involving extensive use of psychotropic medication, often for long periods of time at high dosages" during an inspection of private facilities for the mentally retarded in Texas. In one facility Sprague found the average stay for patients was 7.8 years, and 66 percent of the patients regularly received anticonvulsant medication. "The physician supervising these patients had ordered only one laboratory test to monitor this medication in 184.3 patient years." (A patient year is the equivalent of one patient in a facility for one year.)

In another study, Sprague and a colleague, Dr. Esther K. Sleator, despaired of the lack of research and demonstration data on the use of psychoactive drugs on the mentally retarded needed to provide guidelines for their proper use. However, they presented five suggested rules: (1) Psychoactive drugs should be used only for severe behavioral problems that cannot be satisfactorily handled by other techniques; (2) the drugs should be continuously used for fixed periods of time, not longer than six months; (3) the dosages should be periodically reduced or the drugs completely withdrawn to determine whether the patient still needs them; (4) combinations of psychoactive drugs should never be used; and (5) the benefits of uses should be weighed against the risks with "potential learning suppression and possible dyskensias" entering the equation.

The evidence of indiscriminate warehousing of mentally retarded with chemical straitjackets has been before the FDA, other federal and state agencies, and Congress for twenty years, yet the practice continues unabated. The FDA in effect condoned the use of phenothiazines on the mentally retarded when it was challenged by the Mental Health Law Project, a Washington-based legal advocacy group. These young attorneys and others like them throughout the nation have won scores of landmark court decisions establishing the rights of patients to humane treatment and rational medical care, including the right to informed consent and the right to refuse treatment. These attorneys and judges have brought more reform to the system of institutionalized care than all the warnings and pious pronouncements of the medical profession and the government. In some instances, the courts have challenged the medical profession's most cherished underpinning—the "sacred right" of the doctor to prescribe and treat as he sees fit.

In July 1974 four young lawyers in the prestigious Washington law firm of Hogan & Hartson filed a petition with the FDA on behalf of the Mental Health Law Project, challenging the legality of using phenothiazines such as Thorazine to "treat" the mentally retarded. Citing the 1962 FDA regulations that require a drug company to prove that a drug is safe and effective for a prescribed use, the lawyers documented conclusively that the phenothiazines were widely and heavily used on the mentally retarded without an FDA-approved indication that they were either effective or safe for such use. Therefore, they argued, the use of these major tranquilizers for the mentally retarded was illegal. They asked the FDA in numerous petitions to order the drug companies to stop the sale to institutions for the mentally retarded and to discourage doctors from using the drugs, as well as to rewrite the labels of the drugs to note specifically that they had not been approved "for the control or management of resident behavior" unless a "specifically identified psychotic condition" was present.

Four years after the petition was filed, the issue had not been resolved, at least not to the satisfaction of the attorneys for the Mental Health Project, some of whom have since left Hogan & Hartson and joined the nonprofit organization as staff lawyers. After referring the matter to its Pediatric Advisory Panel, the FDA concluded that the major tranquilizers were effective in treating severe behavioral crises in mentally retarded patients but not in the treatment of mental retardation per se and ordered new wording on labeling of these drugs to reflect the distinction. As of late 1978, the wording was still in the drafting stage, with the drug companies seeking as wide a latitude in the wording as possible. The FDA's position of not restricting the use of phenothiazines to specific and identifiable cases of psychosis and of acknowledging the effectiveness for behavioral control, which ultimately is a subjective judgment, in effect endorses the continued and indiscriminate use of these dangerous drugs to manipulate and control behavior for the benefit of the staff, not the patients. When the FDA made known its intentions in 1975, the Mental Health Law Project protested that the FDA's action "on balance has been more damaging than helpful to the effort to control medication abuses of retarded citizens. It has gratuitously legitimized use of two drugs, Mellaril and Thorazine, for 'severe behavior problems,' thus singling out retarded persons as appropriate recipients of medication for behavior control while not approving the same medications for other persons for the control of similar behavior."

The potent tranquilizing drugs—Thorazine, Mellaril, Stelazine, Prolixin, Serentil, Triavil, Vesprin, and Haldol, to name the more common ones—unquestionably are effective in controlling behavior. When used on a large population of institutionalized persons, as they are, they can help keep the house in order with the minimum program of activities and rehabilitation and the minimum number of attendants, aides, nurses, and doctors.

David Ferleger, director of the mental patients' division for the Civil Liberties Project in Philadelphia, described in congressional testimony how one of his clients, Kenneth Souder, an inmate at Fairview State Hospital in Pennsylvania, first refused to take drugs and then voluntarily complied to avoid punishment. According to Souder's court complaint, the staff doctor "would enter the ward with a tray of hypodermic needles filled with Prolixin, line up the whole ward, or part of the ward, and administer the drug."

Typically, Ferleger said, "what we have are wards of thirty or forty people with two or three attendants who are supposed to take care of this enormous group of people sitting around, no activities, no programs, benches or chairs along the walls. It is not at all surprising that for the occasional patient who gets up and runs around or screams or causes a fuss and takes the time of these two or three attendants, . . . that patient is going to be, as patients say, 'zapped' with some drug to keep him or her quiet."

The nation's custodial and correctional institutions are, as a rule, not only understaffed but poorly staffed. Although most states prohibit the practice, it is common to have ward attendants administering the powerful antipsychotic medications on PRN orders—in other words, whenever it is thought to be necessary. Nor is it uncommon to have the drugs prescribed by poorly trained physicians who see the patients neither before issuing the orders nor after the drugs are administered. It is not uncommon to find the staff physicians in these hospitals to be foreign-born and foreign-trained doctors, who, in many cases, are not able to pass licensing examinations and have a communication problem with patients because of language barriers.

The powerful but dangerous psychoactive drugs developed since the 1950s have revolutionized mental health care and have enabled society to eliminate many of the past abuses of mental wards characterized by the "snake-pit" imagery. But these drugs are not a substitute for adequate programs of activities and re-habilitation and a properly trained and sufficient staff. When used as wholesale means of chemical straitjacketing, the drugs only replace an old abuse with a new one, equally dangerous.

In one of the more dramatic presentations of the hazards, a New York medical examiner has presented records of 203 autopsies from two state mental units in one county that support his claim that 30 percent of the patients died as a result of being overdrugged. The coroner, Dr. Frederick Zugibe of suburban Rockland County, said autopsies show that 30 percent of the deaths were caused by "aspiration of food and vomitous materials," which was in turn caused by the patients' being so sedated that their normal body reflexes malfunctioned. Zugibe notes that death by aspiration occurs among mental patients at a rate twenty times higher than that among patients from the noninstitutionalized population. "The only common denominator in the institution cases that was apparent was the use of tranquilizing and sedative drugs. If you look at it statistically, there is a causal relationship. This is not unique to Rockland County. This is going on in every institution in the state of New York and everywhere in the country. These deaths are not overdoses. The deaths are occurring at the therapeutic dosage levels." Zugibe cited extensive medical literature to support his assertion, including a report from the Detroit medical examiner that "food aspiration following suppression of the gag reflex by tranquilizing drugs is a common phenomenon in mental institutions."

In addition to the evidence linking psychoactive drugs to aspiration deaths, there is evidence that the drugs contribute to deaths from physical diseases by masking pain and other symptoms. Zugibe said autopsies reveal a "significant number of cases" of patients dying from physical ailments where the patients "revealed no reported complaints of the usual symptoms associated with these diseases and were either found dead or discovered in a terminal state."

When Zugibe raised the alarm in public, the New York mental health establishment reacted with anger. Even before his conclusions were investigated, Dr. James A. Prevost, commissioner of mental health, and Thomas A. Coughlin, commissioner of mental retardation, attacked Zugibe as "totally irresponsible." When the State Mental Hygiene Medical Review Board completed its investigation eight months later, it elected to attack Zugibe's personal integrity rather than address the issues he presented. Although the review board accepted the finding of aspiration death in twenty-nine cases presented by Zugibe and said it could not confirm or refute thirteen others because of inadequate microscopic slides, it dismissed the statistical link as comparing "apples and oranges" and demanded that Zugibe apologize to the mental health community. Zugibe refused to back away, and the review board exerted political pressure to have him removed from his job.

The link Zugibe made between aspiration deaths and the sedative effects of tranquilizers is not unlike the scientific connection made between cancer and cigarette smoking. That the review board could not see this connection is not surprising. The chairman of the Mental Hygiene Medical Review Board in New York is Dr. Sheldon C. Sommers, who also is chairman of the Scientific Advisory Committee of the Council for Tobacco Research, an industry-financed organization that vehemently fights the government's effort to restrict smoking because of its apparent link to lung cancer.

Until the past decade the medical profession, along with state and federal health and welfare officials, was left to its own devices in the manner in which it ministered to the mentally ill and mentally retarded. But in the past ten years the courts, responding to patients' lawsuits filed on their behalf by civil rights attorneys, have stepped in to correct common abuses and establish the constitutional and common-law rights of patients to appropriate treatment, informed consent, and, in certain instances where a person has been judged competent to make a decision, the right to refuse treatment. In some cases, large monetary awards have been given to persons forced to take psychoactive drugs in the absence of valid medical reasons, or to submit to unnecessary psychosurgery or even sterilization.

In a New York case, the State Supreme Court went to the heart of the process, awarding $750,000 in 1976 to Daniel Hoffman, then twenty-five, who had spent eleven years in classes for the mentally retarded as the result of inadequate testing and follow-up. In 1956, when Hoffman was in kindergarten, he scored one point below 75, the normal cutoff line, on an IQ test and spent the rest of his school years classified as mentally retarded, despite the fact that in subsequent testing he scored above the normal IQ level. Hoffmann, who has a severe speech impediment, submitted to the retarded label because, as psychiatrist Lawrence Kaplan testified, "if one is treated as mentally retarded . . . he assumes in the long run that that is the role he should play in life." In late 1978 the appellate division of the state court upheld the decisoin against the New York City Board of Education but reduced the award to $500,000.

In a far-reaching decision the United States Supreme Court ruled that a person cannot be committed to a mental institution and simply ignored. As Robert Plotkin of the Mental Health Law Project puts it, "When persons are committed for purposes of treatment, treatment must in fact be provided." The establishment of the "right to treatment" opened the way for an assault on the well-established but now-tenuous right of a doctor to determine the best means of treatment for a confined mental patient. An important case involving a mental patient's right to refuse treatment began working its way through the federal judicial system in 1978, when seven patients in a Massachusetts state mental hospital, with the assistance of the American Civil Liberties Union and the Greater Boston Legal Services Agency, claimed they were "assaulted" by psychoactive drugs and as-

serted their right to refuse to take them. The patients' legal
brief argues that they have a constitutional right to refuse a
physician's prescribed treatment and should be able to choose
among alternatives, including no treatment at all or even treatment the physician feels might do them more harm than good.
The civil rights attorneys won the initial skirmish in what is expected to be a prolonged legal battle when a U.S. district court
judge issued an injunction allowing the patients to refuse drugs
until the case is resolved. The state appealed the injunction, but
the U.S. court of appeals upheld it. In a friend of the court brief,
the Massachusetts Psychiatric Society argues that the major antipsychotic drugs often are the only rational treatment for severe
mental illness, and physicians who refuse to use them could be
held liable should more serious disintegration of the patient's
mental health result. Further, the psychiatrists contend the right
to refuse treatment could clash headlong with the legally established right to treatment. The psychiatrists' position is that under
the right to treatment the patient must be given the most appropriate treatment, be it drugs or not, whether the patient wants it
or not.

The activist attorneys' response to this is, as Plotkin stated it,
"that civilly committed mental patients should have the same
opportunity as other persons to weigh and consider treatment
alternatives. Competent patients should not be subjected to
forced psychiatric treatment, regardless of whether the treatment
is characterized as 'benign' or 'hazardous.' Persons properly ad-
judicated as incompetent should have treatment imposed upon
them in only the most limited circumstances." And Plotkin concludes, in a statement many doctors would find repugnant: "It is
the legal system, and not psychiatry, that has the moral and constitutional obligation to decide whether citizens may be treated
without their consent."

The Pacification of the Elderly | 7

Modern society does not know what to do with its old people. Children do not know where to house them and resent paying for their care or simply can't afford it. Now adults, they have their own lives to lead. Big Business does not know how to get them off the job, or when. Big Labor only hopes they'll go soon and worries that higher pensions will take a big piece of the negotiation pie. Politicians puzzle and debate over them, hold hearings, consult their polls, and get younger hairstyles. They stop by a nursing home in the morning and blast Social Security in a speech at night for busting the Treasury. Local bureaucrats stretch more red tape over fewer thin dollars, initiate a senior citizen discount for buses and subways, and call a press conference to say that's good but more needs to be done. Universities study subjects that attract more research dollars and find better use for scholarship money, but in the spring they make a big to-do about the grandmother who returned to earn her degree. Concerned homeowners fight zoning changes for apartment buildings for the elderly who no longer can afford to keep their homes and pay for food and health care, too.

Medical science calls a person over sixty-five a geriatric, which is like calling an infant a pediatric and largely ignores the aging process and the aged as subjects for study and research.

As late as 1978 not a single medical school in the United States taught geriatrics as a separate subject.

Doctors find the elderly unprofitable patients because they take up a lot of time, have a limited ability to pay, suffer from too many ailments, and are hard to cure. Too often, the old and the sick are pronounced senile and shipped off to an institution to die. In the youth-oriented cultures of Western society, the elderly are an irritant to be put out of sight and out of mind in nursing homes, geriatric wards, mental institutions, low-cost housing projects, back bedrooms, and, if they can afford it, the golden ghettos of the South and Southwest.

But the elderly just won't go away as American society rapidly turns gray. By 1978 persons sixty-five or older constituted more than 10 percent of the population, and by the year 2000 they will make up 20 percent. By the turn of the century the population of senior citizens will have grown by 35 percent, according to estimates by the U.S. Census Bureau. In contrast, preschoolers will increase in numbers by 17.6 percent, and those between five and nineteen by only 2.3 percent.

In a major upheaval for a society geared to the young, the percentage of elderly by the end of the twentieth century will have risen to 20 percent from an unnoticed 4 percent at the beginning. By that time life expectancy will have increased from seventy-seven years (in 1976) to eighty-one years for women and from sixty-nine years to seventy-two years for men.

Society should be able to accommodate this aging explosion, providing a productive and healthful environment, a dignified and useful social and political role, and the economic wherewithal to live and die with grace. But the record thus far in the United States is not encouraging, and unless fundamental changes are made in attitude and treatment, the outlook for the elderly is bleak.

To date, American society has responded by shunting the elderly aside, denying them social, political, and economic equality, and drugging them into submission. The chemical pacification of the elderly is so common and widespread that even an otherwise cautious public relations executive for a major drug firm remarked that she had seen nursing home patients "carrying their tranquilizers around in Baggies." A retired couple who opted for a small home in a mixed neighborhood after the salesman for a retirement complex lauded the community's ambulance and burial services, call St. Petersburg, Florida, the twentieth-century haven for the old, Valium City.

Here's the record:

Persons sixty-five or older constitute about 10 percent of the U.S. population but consume more than 25 percent of all prescription drugs and an even higher percentage of nonprescription drugs. More than 20 percent of the drugs used by these senior citizens are psychic mood changers—tranquilizers, antidepressants, hypnotics, painkillers, sedatives, sleeping potions of various strengths, and combination drugs that include hidden mood changers. A study by the National Institute of Drug Abuse in 1977 indicates that about two-thirds of all persons sixty-five or older reported using prescription drugs, and nearly 70 percent said they were users of over-the-counter products, chiefly analgesics or pain relievers. Not surprisingly, the drugs most commonly used by the elderly are those for cardiovascular conditions. The second most commonly used drugs are sedatives and tranquilizers, and the use of such drugs, NIDA reported, is "becoming more visible in our society—not only in nursing homes, but in the community as well."

The NIDA survey also indicated a widespread dependency on —or to use a stronger term, addiction to—the psychotropics. Of those questioned who reported using tranquilizers and sedatives, nearly 51 percent said they could not perform "their daily activities" without drugs. Almost all said they obtained their psychotropic drugs from physicians, and 90 percent said they had no difficulty getting the prescriptions from their doctors. Nearly three times as many women as men reported using tranquilizers, antidepressants, and sedatives.

The authors of the NIDA study were quick to point out that most of those using psychotropic drugs "understood what these drugs were supposed to do" and cited the fact that they obtained the drugs through legal prescriptions from their doctors, which presumes—falsely, we think—that their doctors knew what they were doing. Dr. Laurence T. Carroll, director of NIDA's Division of Resource Development, cited as evidence of proper consumption the 1977 conclusion in congressional testimony that since the elderly consulted with their doctors and received their prescriptions from them, the elderly "tend to be knowledgeable and responsible consumers of legal drugs." Carroll did, however, cite a separate study being conducted for the agency by the Stanford Research Institute which shows that "the elderly receive a disproportionately high number of prescriptions for the tranquilizers, sedatives, hypnotics and anti-depressants."

As the NIDA study, as well as others done by government and university researchers, shows, the problem of drug use among the elderly is not just with the psychotropic drugs but also with the fact that these powerful psychic mood changers are commonly taken in combination with many other prescription drugs and often with alcohol. In the NIDA survey, only 5 percent of those interviewed said they abstained from all drugs. More than a third said they used between two and four prescription drugs, and 5 percent said they used five to nine prescriptions. Almost all said they were prescribed these drugs by their doctors. About half said they used alcohol in combination with Rx and over-the-counter drugs. Nearly 20 percent admitted to being frequent users of alcohol.

Herein lies the danger. Taking a variety of drugs for a variety of ailments is a dangerous practice, posing high risks for a patient of any age. But the use of drugs in combination is particularly life-threatening for elderly persons. Because of the natural aging process, the elderly are less tolerant of drugs, and the tranquilizers, antidepressants, and sleeping potions are especially dangerous. When we get old, our body machinery is less capable of metabolizing, absorbing, and discharging most substances, including chemicals. In addition, the older one becomes, the more emotionally and mentally vulnerable one becomes because of the losses that occur—loss of loved ones, friends, jobs, homes, income, health—in a society that discards people and things when they have outlived their usefulness. Rather than help the elderly deal with their sorrow, drugs act to hide it.

Moreover, many doctors have virtually no medical training in caring for the aged, know very little about the changes in the body as the result of aging, generally know only what the drug companies tell them about the pharmacology of the drugs they prescribe, and take scant time to talk to their patients about their physical, emotional, and economic problems or to explore alternate nonchemical therapy. With the 1950s came the age of the tranquilizer, and with these chemicals a cure-all mentality, a panacea to resolve the problems of the elderly, not to mention the problems society had in dealing with its aged. Miltown, the first popular tranquilizer to become a part of the American lifestyle, was promoted by Wallace Laboratories, its maker, as the one drug that "belongs in every practice of geriatrics." Doctors were told that "virtually any of your patients, regardless of age or physical disorder, can be given the drug with confidence, either as a primary treatment—or as an adjunct to other therapy to relieve the anxiety and tension associated with the physical disorder." Wallace Labs also boasted that Miltown "is compatible with almost any other kind of drug therapy" and therefore would not "complicate treatment of patients seen in geriatric practice." This has been proved not to be true. In another advertisement in the *Journal of the American Geriatrics Society* for March 1974, Wallace promoted Deprol, a combination of Miltown (or meprobamate) and benactyzine hydrochloride in a 400 to 1 ratio, as being useful treatment in these "typical" situations: "fear of cancer or other life-threatening disease, pre- and post-operative fears, postpartum despondency, family problems, death of a loved one, loss of work, retirement problems, financial worries, and many other stressful situations." The brief fine-print summary of adverse reactions includes depression, especially when accompanied by anxiety, tension, agitation, rumination, or insomnia.

The "typical" situations for which Deprol and Miltown and their more popular successors, Librium and Valium, are prescribed are the typical situations that all elderly—and many younger—patients face. Who doesn't have "family problems" now and then? Who doesn't have "financial worries," and who hasn't lost a loved one? The chemical cure-all mentality displayed in the Miltown and Deprol advertisements reflects a frightening trend toward solving social problems with drugs.

Dr. Robert N. Butler, the first director of the National Institute on Aging and winner of the 1976 Pulitzer Prize for his book *Why Survive? Being Old in America,* calls it "pacification through drugs" and despairs of the systematic mistreatment of the elderly by his fellow physicians. "It just kind of happens," Butler said in an interview. "Say a woman, seventy, comes in and her seventy-three-year-old husband has died, and the doctor gives her a tranquilizer because she is agitated, which is understandable. Soon she is just not hungry, begins to suffer nutritional effects because she's not eating, and she just kind of sits, loses physical abilities. This is a woman adversely affected by her medication. The doctor doesn't do this out of malice. But by being too busy, the doctor doesn't sit down to unravel stage by stage the situation the person is in. The patient just stays on the tranquilizer and gets labeled as showing signs of senility."

Drugs of all kinds are given far too often to patients without consideration of their side effects and without proper instructions and follow-up. The negative side effects often are worse than the ailment they were prescribed to relieve. Because elderly persons are less tolerant of drugs and more susceptible to their adverse qualities, what might be therapeutically sound, helpful, and safe for a younger person is counterproductive and harmful for the elderly person. The side effects of many drugs—not just tranquilizers and other mood-changing chemicals—often produce the symptoms of senility and are wrongly diagnosed as irreversible senility and wrongly interpreted by the individual in question as senility. When a young person who has forgotten something casually says, "I must be getting senile," he or she does so knowing it's not so. But when an older person forgets or gets confused and says that, it can have frightful and very real implications, producing even worse anxiety, confusion, fear, and loss of interest that confirms for patient and doctor alike that senility is indeed the prognosis.

Sarah, seventy-two, is generally robust and active, living alone since the death of her husband three years ago in a comfortable Southern California apartment overlooking the Pacific Ocean. Her major medical problem for many years had been glaucoma, a disease of the eye which impaired her sight and caused her some pain. To reduce the pressure of fluids on the eye, her ophthalmologist prescribed Neptazane, a diuretic produced by Lederle Laboratories, a division of the American Cyanamid Company. Although not a tranquilizer, the side effects of Neptazane are psychoactive.

The woman was told by the doctor first to get a prescription of forty fifty-milligram tablets, and if they caused her no difficulty, to get a bottle of 100 tablets upon refill. There was no discussion of the possible adverse effects, and the woman "assumed the drug was harmless." About eighteen months later this woman, who had led an active professional and social life, closed herself in her apartment and isolated herself from friends. She became convinced that she was having "a nervous breakdown" and became increasingly depressed, anxious, and frightened. Finally, at the urging of her friends, she saw a psychiatrist, who admitted her to a psychiatric hospital. After a number of interviews and tests, the psychiatrist was satisfied that the woman was not chronically depressed or anxious and was not senile. The doctor then alertly asked about the woman's medications and called the ophthalmologist who had prescribed Neptazane. Ten days after checking into the hospital, the woman walked out. Neptazane had caused the symptoms that puzzled, confused, and frightened the woman. She had experienced all the possible adverse reactions to this common diuretic: fatigue, nausea, headaches, dizziness, confusion, depression, and tingling of the feet and hands.

Because the ophthalmologist told her that she could continue to take Neptazane if she felt no ill effects initially, this woman took the medication for more than a year and suffered the consequences of the drug's negative effects caused by prolonged use. The doctor who prescribed the medication did not tell her of the possible side effects, and neither did her druggist. Nor was she told to supplement her diet with potassium—for example, bananas—to help prevent the side effects. No one told her of the package insert of dosage instructions, contraindications, warnings, and adverse reactions that is available upon request. (The FDA wants to make it mandatory to include the instructions with each prescription.) The prescribing physician did not ask about the drug on subsequent visits, and the patient did not bring up the subject of her emotional and mental problems because she did not think it appropriate to discuss them with her eye doctor. But the inescapable conclusion this woman ultimately reached was that she'll never "take anything they prescribe for me on blind faith alone again." Had the ophthalmologist taken a few minutes to read and explain the adverse reactions that were possible with prolonged use of Neptazane, this woman could have been spared a personally agonizing time, unnecessary hospitalization, avoidable medical expenses, and the frightening thought that "I was losing my mind." Had she known what the possible side effects were, she could have identified them and associated them with the medication and consulted with the prescribing doctor.

This otherwise assertive woman had not thought it appropriate to question her doctor, to insist that he explain and, if necessary, write out the possible side effects, and to keep him posted on the unexplainable symptoms of depression she later experienced. She accepted her doctor's judgment and what he told her—as well as what he *didn't* tell her—on blind faith. This is a particularly serious problem for the elderly. "They take on faith what their doctors tell them and don't know, when something goes wrong with them, what to attribute it to," explained Betty Duskin, director of research for the National Council of Senior Citizens. "There is a classic tradition in this country to treat doctors as witch doctors. One doesn't question what he does when in fact, the physician is not a pharmacologist and doesn't understand the potential side effects of the drug he is prescribing."

Elderly people are liable to have a number of physical things wrong with them as a natural process of aging. Typically, a person sixty-five or older is taking three or four different drugs for as many different ailments. It's likely that this typical senior citizen is also a heavy user of over-the-counter medicines, from cold tablets to aspirin to laxatives. Those over sixty-five spend more than $2.5 billion a year for prescription drugs alone. More than a third of the drugs used by the elderly are mood changers, the psychotropics, and of the twenty most prescribed drugs for this class of patient, twelve have some sort of sedative effect. A recent government study in three states—Illinois, Ohio, and New Jersey—found that 35 to 40 percent of all prescriptions under Medicare, the assistance program for the elderly, were tranquilizers and sedatives. These drugs can be risky. "Physical speed and coordination may be impaired, and actual death can occur from slowing down the body's functions," according to Dr. Butler.

"Fear and depression can strike older people on drugs, when they equate such slowing of their responses with failing health and dying."

Even the drugs not specifically classed as psychotropics can have the same effect on older persons. We looked earlier at the diuretic that produced fatigue, nervousness, and depression in a woman being treated for glaucoma. The antihypertensives can produce a similar result. One of the most popular drugs used to control high blood pressure, Inderal, is sold in Europe as a tranquilizer, and Ayerst Laboratories expects FDA approval to promote it as a sedative in the United States.

Psychotropic drugs have a potential for habituation in and by themselves, but their use in combination with other prescription and over-the-counter drugs, alcohol, and even certain foods and nonalcoholic beverages can produce severe drug reactions, including death. For example, the heavily prescribed MAO (monamine oxidase) inhibitors, used to lower blood pressure and in the treatment of depression, adversely react in combination with such common foods and beverages as blue cheese, yogurt, sour cream, chicken livers, Chianti wine, salami, and bananas, to name just a few.

So it is just not the drugs you take that can be risky. It is how you take them, when you take them, and what you take them with. To protect yourself, you must tell your doctor what other drugs you are taking and for what purpose, and you must be candid with your doctor about your life-style, including the foods you eat and the beverages you drink, especially if you drink alcohol in any amount.

But the one cardinal rule to follow is to assume your doctor does not know much about the elderly and the changes that take place in the body with advancing age. Nor can one expect a physician to know much about the drugs he prescribes and how they work in the body and on the mind by themselves or in combination with other prescription or nonprescription drugs.

It is one of the medical tragedies and a blot on a society that prides itself on its health care system that the body of knowledge about gerontology is so thin today, having advanced hardly at all in the last 100 years. Until the late 1970s little or no attention was paid to the medical and health problems of the elderly by the medical schools, doctors, federal and state governments, or the vast social welfare system. Despite the fact that the elderly are their biggest customers, the drug companies have done little to study the effects of drugs on the elderly or to instruct them and their doctors in the judicious and proper use of prescription drugs.

The irony is that this generation of elderly citizens is living longer because of benefits reaped during early and middle years from advances in the treatment and prevention of the grim killers of an earlier age—influenza, pneumonia, tuberculosis, typhoid, diphtheria, smallpox, scarlet fever—and modest advances in the treatment of heart and vascular diseases and, to a lesser degree, in the treatment of cancer.

In a cruel hoax, medical science is able to bring us through early and middle years only to abandon, neglect, and ignore us when we reach what is romanticized as the "golden years." The medical ignorance of the aging process is called "medical senility" by one lay expert, Arthur S. Freese, author of several medical books, including *The End of Senility,* and contributing editor of *Modern Maturity* magazine. "The real problem with the medical care of the elderly is simply the fact that the medical profession is not familiar with the medical problems of those over sixty-five. The single biggest problem of those over sixty-five is their reaction to drugs," according to Freese. To compensate for their lack of knowledge and their inability to treat the elderly's physical, mental, and emotional problems, doctors respond by drugging them. "This," says Freese, "is one of the crimes of America. It is an absolute crime to sedate them and manipulate them so that they will not cause any problems. This certainly is not just a medical problem. It's a public problem. One of these days every one of us is going to pay for it when we get older and become too old and too weak to fight."

No less an expert than Dr. Butler, the Pulitzer Prize winner and the director of the National Institute on Aging, notes that not only is aging ignored as a topic for study in medical schools, but also medical students are exposed to the worst kind of stereotyping of the elderly and commonly refer to elderly patients as "crocks," "supertentorial" (meaning their illnesses are imaginary), "foggies," "floaters," "cruds," and "crap." Most of the elderly patients to which medical students are exposed are ward cases, brain-damaged alcoholics, and others with terminal and well-advanced conditions. "That's all he sees, sick and broken-down elderly patients, the really sick ones," says Freese. "One wonders, if all they saw were the sick and dying babies, whether any one of them would go into pediatrics." Geriatrics as a specialty simply does not exist in the United States. Out of the nearly 400,000 doctors in the United States, only 6,000 belong to the American Geriatrics Society, and only a handful are truly geriatric specialists. A study of University of California medical students showed that the attitude of the students toward the elderly worsened during the four-year course. Not only do they only see the worst cases, but medical students also get very little classroom or clinical training in the elderly and their diseases. As late as 1978, only one medical school, Cornell, had a chair, or a recognized position of authority, in geriatrics, and that position was not filled for lack of suitable candidates. In Great Britain there are ten funded chairs of geriatric medicine, and most Western European nations generally have much better training programs in health care for the elderly than the United States.

Dr. Butler, a psychiatrist who specialized in geriatric medicine because of the puzzlement and grief he felt as a seven-year-old upon the death of his grandfather, says the medical profession is indifferent to the elderly because doctors are not trained to deal with their ailments and find them "bothersome, cantankerous, and complaining" as patients, professionally frustrating because they have so many ailments that defy quick cures, financially unrewarding because they are least able to pay and take up the most time, and an office-management nightmare because of the tedious and endless paperwork involved in getting payment through Medicare, Medicaid, and private insurance.

Former U.S. Senator Frank E. Moss, who conducted four years of hearings on nursing homes and health care for the elderly and who now practices law in Washington, sums it up well: "One of the complaints made during the hearings was that medical schools did not teach a course in geriatrics. Very few doctors liked to practice it, and consequently there were relatively few doctors that specialized in the care of the elderly. The doctors we talked to indicated that it didn't seem very rewarding to a medical doctor because in long-term care the chances of recovery are almost nil. Simply to give continuing care over a period of time and make a person better able to care for himself—but in the end the person is going to have terminal degeneration and demise—is not what a doctor gets inspired to practice medicine for. He wants to get out and make people well."

Working within this indifferent attitude is the sincere desire of most doctors to provide relief, the less honorable but very real tendency to look for quick and easy solutions, the expectation of the patient to "get something" for his ailment, and the well-organized and heavily financed promotion and salesmanship of drugs as the cure-all. As a consequence, Dr. Butler notes, general practitioners and psychiatrists "find psychoactive agents an all-too-easy answer for the many complicated physical and emotional reactions of late life. It is much simpler to give a pill than to listen to complaints. Chemotherapy can often bring cessation of symptoms as the patient becomes benumbed and pacified."

The elderly also fall unwittingly into another human failing. Because they usually are seeing more than one doctor for different ailments, they sometimes get caught between conflicting professional judgments. Ron Gaetano, a pharmacologist who heads an upstate New York drug abuse program and who has done pioneering studies in the use and abuse of drugs among the elderly, tells of a man in his sixties who suffered the fatal consequences of conflicting treatment and no communication: "This man's doctor gave him Percodan, a painkilling opiate, because he had a congenital condition and was in pain. Because of his late stage of life, the doctor said they shouldn't operate. The patient did exactly what his doctor said, didn't take any more or less than what was prescribed. He functioned well for about three years, but then went to a second physician for an anxiety problem of some kind. This doctor said, 'You are addicted to Percodan.' It probably was an addiction, but he wasn't confused or dizzy.

"The second doctor put him on Valium. Within six months, the patient was more confused and disoriented, and the second doctor gave him higher doses of Valium. When he continued to experience problems, Doctor Number Two put him in a hospital and pulled him off Percodan without warning. What happened?

Within twenty-four hours, the man had chills, which were not treated, and then suffered shakes and diarrhea. He died of cardiac arrest within seventy-two hours.

"The interesting thing is this patient was completely healthy with the exception of the congenital condition and was functioning until he went to Doctor Number Two. He had no history of a heart condition. It was simply a case of one doctor going against another doctor with no communication at all."

Contrary to popular belief, most elderly persons are not living in nursing homes. In fact, only 5 percent of the 23 million Americans sixty-five or older are living in nursing care institutions at any one time. It perhaps seems as if more are in nursing homes because of the rapid growth of the nursing home industry since Medicare and Medicaid took over a large portion of the funding of long-term care in 1965 and the widespread abuses and scandals that followed this growth. Hardly a day passes without news of mistreatment, inhumane treatment, unsanitary conditions, kickbacks, fraud, and political skulduggery involving nursing home operations. It is beyond our scope and purpose to review this sad chapter in nursing home conditions except as it applies to the misuse and abuse of drugs, particularly the psychotropic chemicals, which in itself is often neglected as an area of investigation by state and federal health officials. The abuses in New York State's nursing home industry were so common that a special state prosecutor was appointed to ferret them out. But a spokesman said the prosecutor was concerned about physical beatings, along with political bribery and the defrauding of government agencies, not with chemical abuse, "because how do you get an indictment for drug abuse?" It is difficult to prove in a court of law, that's true, but the record of the chemical straitjacketing of elderly persons in nursing homes is clear.

The use of high-potency tranquilizers and antidepressants is so common—often persons are automatically put on these drugs upon admission, regardless of physical and emotional condition—that senility is chemically induced by medication in many instances, thus justifying the use of even more drugs. Case histories of such abuses abound in the files of federal, state, and local health and welfare agencies. Here's one:

An eighty-six-year-old woman, described by a social worker as a "lovely woman," functioned independently but was having memory lapses. She occasionally got lost while traveling to visit a friend but was able to call her friend for directions when this happened.

The woman, who had been living in a rooming house, applied for nursing home admission. At this time she became confused and disoriented by her new surroundings. Shortly after admission, she was started on twenty-five milligrams of Thorazine. She began to wander into other patients' rooms and was having difficulty controlling urine. The nursing staff said she became "combative" and had to be restrained. Part of the problem, the nursing home inspector who checked into the case said, was that the woman now persisted in using the French language of her childhood and was not understood by the staff, nor could she understand the staff.

On a visit to the nursing home, a state health department nurse found the woman tied up with a sheet so tightly that no movement at all was possible. The woman's hands were very cold. The nurse found the following note on the patient's chart: "Resident very lethargic and hard to rouse. Right hand cyanotic—wrist restraint removed." The circulation had been cut off completely on that occasion. It was not clear why a lethargic patient had to be restrained.

The woman's medications were changed. Both Mellaril and Haldol were tried several times. She fell and cut her head on one occasion, and finally she developed symptoms of Parkinson's disease from the drugs. Eventually, the woman, who had entered the nursing home with the ability to function independently, was drugged into senility and hospitalized in a psychiatric ward.

Often elderly patients get caught in a vicious circle of drug dependency and drug-induced conditions. In one typical case, a ninety-year-old woman resident of a nursing home had been on Thorazine for about eighteen months. Her son became concerned about a progressive deterioration of her mental faculties and had a psychiatrist examine her. The psychiatrist discovered that the woman had Parkinson's disease symptoms, and he determined that it was caused by the Thorazine, which is not an uncommon occurrence. To combat the Parkinson-like symptoms, he put her on Cogentin and stopped the Thorazine. The patient continued to be lethargic, and the dosage of Cogentin was increased. She then developed dehydration and vomiting, a side effect of Cogentin, and was admitted to a medical hospital acutely dehydrated and unresponsive. She died shortly thereafter.

The most commonly used psychotropics in nursing homes are the most powerful ones, first, because they are cheaper, and second, because they act faster and with greater effect. Thorazine, a product of Smith Kline & French generically known as chlorpromazine, and Mellaril, a product of Sandoz generically known as thioridazine, are the two most common tranquilizers used on nursing home residents. The FDA classes Thorazine and Mellaril as major tranquilizers, and they are more tightly controlled than the so-called minor tranquilizers such as Valium, Librium, Miltown, and Equanil.

According to the Special Committee on Aging of the U.S. Senate, Thorazine and Mellaril account for more than 50 percent of all tranquilizer purchases for nursing home patients. Of the twelve most-used drugs in nursing homes, eight are tranquilizers or sedatives. The other four are painkillers, with Darvon Compound, which can cause addiction, being the number two drug behind Thorazine. In total purchases, tranquilizers alone account for 20 percent of all nursing home drugs. Using 1970 figures compiled by the General Accounting Office, the Senate committee estimated the annual cost of tranquilizers in nursing homes to be $60 million per year. This works out to $60 for each of the 1 million persons residing in nursing homes at any given time. Sixty dollars will buy a lot of Thorazine. At the brand-name price of about $40 per 1,000 25-milligram tablets, that comes out to 25 milligrams four times a day for each elderly resident. More likely the institution is purchasing its drugs by the cheaper generic, or chemical, name, in which case it could purchase 1,000 25-milligram tablets of chlorpromazine for about $20, half the price of the trade name Thorazine. In this more likely purchase, $60 would buy 200 milligrams of the drug per day for each patient. The recommended adult dosage for severe cases in outpatients is 25 to 50 milligrams three times a day, or no more than 150 milligrams per day, and the recommended adult dosage for "acutely agitated, manic, or disturbed" patients in mental hospitals is 500 milligrams per day. These are recommended dosages for middle-aged adults, and the dosage for the elderly should be lower by one-third or one-half. What this means is that enough Thorazine and Mellaril is being used in nursing homes to provide each patient with a high enough daily dosage to keep him as sedated as an acutely disturbed forty-year-old patient in a mental institution.

Of course, this does not mean that every person in a nursing home is receiving that much tranquilization. Many may not be receiving any, or very little, and some are receiving more. What it does indicate is that an excessive amount of sedative drugs is being used, lending credence to the charge that the drugs are being used primarily not for the medical therapy of the residents but for the comfort of the staff. A "vivid memory" for Dr. Butler, the director of the National Institute on the Aging, is the "zombielike persons only dimly aware of the world around them" whom he has seen in nursing homes, mental hospitals, and psychiatric wards. A pharmacist who worked in a nursing home recalls the patients as being like "mummies in cages" and remembers dispensing tranquilizers, not because the patients needed them, but rather to control their behavior for the convenience of the staff.

Dr. Butler observes: "You see people treated more for the advantage of the provider—namely, the administrators, nurses, and physicians—than the patient. You can have a quieter atmosphere if you zonk people with medication." It is far cheaper to use psychotropic drugs to provide a "quieter atmosphere" than to provide adequate medical and support personnel, nonchemical therapy, social and vocational activities, proper diet, and friendly and comfortable physical surroundings.

The use of powerful drugs to control behavior is clearly shown in the case of a seventy-seven-year-old woman who had been in a nursing home for nearly two years with "mild confusion" her only mental problem. One day the woman had what the nursing home staff called a "paranoid episode" and accused her roommate of stealing some of her clothes. Rather than make even a minimal effort to help the woman work through her fears and sudden mistrust, the staff placed the woman on Haldol, a major tranquilizer, even though she had Parkinson's disease, for which Haldol is contraindicated. The patient became increasingly confused, and her speech became slurred. So she was taken off Haldol and put on Mellaril and Cogentin, a drug used to control the symptoms of Parkinson's. "Subsequently, she had difficulty finding her room and needed help in dressing and with personal hygiene, which she had not before," said the New York Health Department doctor who investigated the case. "She became more agitated and developed dryness of the mouth and increased urination due to the Cogentin." As the woman became more agitated, the staff increased the dosage of Mellaril. A psychiatrist who saw her a few weeks later noted that the woman "now had increased confusion, abdominal pain and distention, and other physical problems," and he canceled both the Mellaril and the Cogentin, which he felt were "probably responsible" for her worsened condition. But by that time her condition had deteriorated so far that she was transferred to a hospital for medical and psychiatric evaluation.

Within a few weeks a patient who had lived and functioned independently in a nursing home for two years with only mild instances of confusion was chemically turned into a highly agitated and confused patient in need of psychiatric evaluation as the result of a single episode of paranoia. (This case, as well as others cited in this chapter, was documented by medical authorities.)

With the assistance of the Minneapolis Age and Opportunity Center, the Senate Committee on Aging held hearings in Minnesota and took fifty sworn affidavits from nursing home personnel to determine whether tranquilizers were indeed being used to control patient behavior for the comfort and economic well-being of the state and home. The Senate committee in its final report to Congress said the testimony "proved conclusively that unlicensed aides and orderlies have ready access to the medications and narcotics in many nursing homes . . . [and that there was] indiscriminate tranquilization to keep them [patients] quiet."

One nurse testified that patients would be awakened in the middle of the night to be given a tranquilizer to make sure they would "stay out of their hair." An orderly said if a patient "moved a muscle," he was given a tranquilizer. "You could have dropped some of these people off of the building and they wouldn't have blinked their eyes," the orderly said.

Mrs. Daphne Krause, executive director of the Minnesota center, said the group's six-year investigation proved "indiscriminate tranquilization" was a common practice, and she offered this explanation: "For the beleaguered nurse's aide, tranquilizers are a happy solution. If patients are sedated, they cause the staff few problems. The administrator is happy, too, because bedbound patients bring the highest rate of reimbursement."

Val Halamandaris, the attorney who directed the nursing home investigation for the Senate committee and subsequently directed studies on problems of the aging for a House committee, said in an interview that not much has changed since the scathing report was issued by the Senate in late 1974. "I have contended all along that you can manufacture the ideal nursing home patient," he said. "You take someone who is well and give them a tranquilizer and sit them in bed all day. If a patient is bedbound and develops bed sores, you can qualify for maximum funding. You get the highest rate of reimbursement [under Medicaid and Medicare], and the patient costs you the least amount of money to take care of. You can easily manufacture these with Thorazine."

Senator Charles Percy, an Illinois Republican, explained how the system works in his state, where nursing homes are reimbursed on the basis of points assigned to each patient according to his disability. The more points assigned to the patient, the higher the payment to the home. With each point worth $6, a patient who is a behavior problem is worth eight points, or $48 in additional funding. Those with behavior problems require daily injections of a tranquilizer, and this is worth another six points, or $36 per month. Since a resident on heavy doses of tranquilizers will be bedridden, the patient will need expensive ointments for bed sores, qualifying the home for another eight points, or $45. The incentive then for the operator of a nursing home is to keep the patients sedated and in bed rather than to provide the type of care and activities to keep them out of bed, rehabilitate them, and return them to society with productive and satisfying roles to play—or, at the very least, to provide them with a comfortable environment free of all but the necessary medications in which to spend their remaining years.

The drug companies have to share a major portion of the responsibility for the chemical pacification of the elderly. The advertisements in medical journals, particularly in the magazines specializing in geriatric medicine and in nursing home management, appeal directly to the instinct to use drugs to control patient behavior as a means of making life easier and more financially rewarding for nursing home operators and their staffs, as well as for the families of the elderly. Take this one for Thorazine:

"'She's driving us crazy. Sits around and complains all day, then wanders around the house all night.'"

"'It has to be her way all the time . . .'"

"'We don't want to send Mom away, but we can't take much more of this.'"

Smith Kline & French presented these complaints heard by physicians from "harried children of elderly patients" in a 1964 advertisement in the *Journal of the American Geriatrics Society*. Ignoring the admission of the children that they are the ones who are going "crazy," Smith Kline & French recommended Thorazine for Mom and promised that once the tranquilizer calms her, "life becomes easier for her and her family."

As noted in the chapter on advertising and promotion practices, Abbott Labs went so far as to create a new disease called institutional anxiety caused by the "institutional setting itself" and recommended that new nursing home patients be treated with Tranxene, a tranquilizer, not to make them feel better but to make things easier for the staff. There is no mention in the Tranxene ad copy about nonchemical ways to make it easier for the elderly to adjust to their new environment and feel a bit easier about being institutionalized.

Roche advertised Valium "to help promote patient comfort and ease patient care," and Sandoz boasts that nursing home personnel like Mellaril because "they find their work load greatly lightened as patient demands are replaced by a spirit of self-help and self-interest." Sandoz also says the family of the patient likes Mellaril because their visits are typically "more cheerful, pleasurable meetings" and they go away with a more comfortable feeling for the home. McNeil Laboratories promotes Haldol as a "good choice for successful management of the disturbed elderly patient." The key words, directed to the staff, are "successful management of. . . ." There is too much "management of" the elderly and not enough "care of."

Within this atmosphere of accepting pills as a panacea, it is okay to use drugs indiscriminately for control rather than as just one tool in a total health care program that includes a proper diet, physical, vocational, and social activities, psychological and group therapy, and friendly, safe, and comfortable living conditions. The pill-popping mentality of the twentieth century makes it socially acceptable and economically realistic to sedate the elderly nursing home patient into pacification until death.

The nursing home industry exploded with the enactment by Congress in 1965 of federally financed Medicare and Medicaid programs for the elderly. Suddenly the government had agreed to reimburse facilities for "reasonable costs" of extended care. The legislation encouraged private commercial operators by guaranteeing a fixed return equal to Treasury bond interest. The industry skyrocketed and became a hot Wall Street investment venture and means for quick profits. Care facilities more than doubled by 1973, and nursing home beds were added at the rate of 169 each day. Patients were actively recruited through mass advertising appeals. Another interesting development occurred. States, which had the responsibility of paying for the care of elderly patients in mental institutions, saw an opportunity to shift the financial burden to the federal government by transfering mental patients to nursing homes. Between 1969 and 1973 the number of elderly patients in mental hospitals declined by 40 percent. The decrease was partly brought about through better community care programs, but tens of thousands were dumped into nursing homes, few of which had the professional staff or facilities to handle these mentally ill patients, many of whom had been diagnosed as "senile," not as mentally disturbed, in the first place. But the new nursing home entrepreneurs were anxious to fill their growing number of beds, and if they lacked the staff and program for proper psychotherapy, they had an abundance of psychotropic drugs. Dr. Jack Weinberg, a psychiatrist who directed a program to transfer mental hospital patients to nursing homes in Illinois, told the Senate Committee on Aging that he was offered $100 per head by a nursing home operator for every patient he could direct to the man's facility. Dr. Weinberg was "appalled" and rejected the bribe. Dr. Weinberg also testified that he was reluctant to move these patients because many were suffering from chronic brain syndrome or senility and needed twenty-four-hour coverage, and this was not available in most nursing facilities.

Anna Cappola was one of these mental hospital patients moved to a nursing home. For thirty years she had been a patient at Manhattan State Hospital in New York, but on June 21, 1973, Mrs. Cappola, then only sixty-eight and the mother of three grown children, was transferred to the Bayview Convalescent Center in Ocean County, New Jersey, because, as her daughter tells it, "it would cover her under Medicaid and because she would be closer to her family."

Upon admission at Bayview, Anna Cappola was said to be suffering from diabetes, pneumonia, and senile dementia. There was no mention of her being "schizophrenic catatonic," a diagnosis that had kept her hospitalized in a mental institution since the age of thirty-eight.

Mrs. Cappola seemed to adjust well to her new surroundings. She displayed no evidence of returning to the stupefied mental state of unreality for which she has been committed to the psychiatric hospital many years before. The Bayview nursing staff found her "pleasant, cooperative, and alert," and Mrs. Cappola would tell her family that the aides, nurses, and doctors "were good to her."

Her medical chart showed she was given one milligram of the powerful tranquilizer Haldol twice a day, which is in the middle range of the recommended dosage for "geriatric or debilitated patients." She was taking Lanoxin, a digitalis used for heart congestion; Dyazide, a diuretic for hypertension; Benadryl, a potent antihistamine with sedative properties; extra-strength Tylenol, a painkiller; and insulin for diabetes. The nursing home classed Mrs. Cappola as a patient "who needed supervision with activities of daily living" but who could get around without assistance. At times she "would become agitated and attempt to leave the facility," but otherwise she was "cooperative and alert." She attended Bayview's resident council meetings on a regular basis, sometimes wishing that she could see her husband and three adult children more often. Her fellow patients "suggested she get Social Service to have the family visit more often."

The last time Mrs. Cappola had been out of Bayview was for a week at the end of March 1978, when she visited her daughter. Five and a half months later, on Saturday, August 19, Anna Cappola packed her suitcase and headed out the front door. "I'm going to check on my children," she told the nurse. She was taken back to her room, given a glass of milk, and put to bed.

The next day, Sunday, was visitors' day, and if Mrs. Cappola had thoughts of leaving, they were not apparent to the staff. She went about her usual activities. Between three and four that afternoon, she sat at the receptionist's desk, greeting visitors and having them sign the guest book. Later, after supper, she told the staff nurse she wanted to retire early. It was about six-twenty when Anna made her way unassisted to her room on the fifth floor. Ten minutes later she opened the window of Room 519, her home for several years, threw her pocketbook and packed valise out to the ground below, and then stepped out, to fall to her death on the pavement five floors down.

The medical director, Dr. William Jones, speculated that Mrs. Cappola, who had no record of suicide attempts, thought she was on the first floor, not the fifth, and was trying to sneak out. Officer Edward J. Hays, the local detective who investigated, filed this report: "It is this officer's opinion that the victim, in attempting to escape from the confines of the center, mistakenly judged the distance from her room to the ground due to her senile condition. This action was rational to her. Investigation complete."

The New Jersey Health Department investigated routinely, and a spokesman said the department concluded that "the death was accidental. There was adequate staff at the time. The death does not reflect slackening or poor procedures on the part of the institution."

The case was closed. The federal government counted her among those "discharged," a statistical description used whether a patient goes out alive or dead.

Anna Cappola's long journey that began as a "schizophrenic catatonic" in a New York mental hospital ended thirty-five years later as a "discharge by death" because she wanted to leave a nursing home to visit her children.

Why was Anna Cappola never returned to society? She had been diagnosed as being out of contact with reality to the point of stupor. But she became well enough to be discharged to a nursing home where she needed some assistance to function but was "pleasant, cooperative, and alert," and could get around on her own without assistance. In thirty-five years as an institution-alized patient, Anna Cappola got better, but she never got re-habilitated.

Unfortunately rehabilitation is not the function of the nursing home system. As Dr. Butler of the Institute on Aging found, "Often drugs represent the only form of treatment given to older persons. An overall treatment plan that includes attention to diet, physical and social activities, psychotherapy, and correction of living problems may be totally ignored." To be sure, there are many homes where efforts are being made to return elderly per-sons to their families and society with productive, satisfying, and comfortable roles to play. But because of several social and eco-nomic factors, including the profit motive, which operates in the long-term care facilities that are commercial, privately owned enterprises, it is easier just to house them with minimal care and in minimal surroundings and keep them under control with drugs until they die.

The outlook for treating the elderly, whether in institutions or in the community, in a humane and rational way as opposed to the indifferent warehouse and chemical straitjacketing approach of the last twenty-five years is not as bleak as it might seem by this review. There is hope. As the elderly grow in numbers and in awareness of their potential to live fruitful lives, they are be-coming more assertive of their social, economic, political, and medical rights. There is a growing concern within the medical profession about the way the elderly have been pushed aside by the health care system. Medical scientists and some doctors are at least aware today that they know very little about the aging process and the way drugs work in the bodies and minds of older persons. Even some drug companies, most notably Hoffmann-La Roche, are paying more attention to the problem. Some old-fashioned values and ethics concerning the use of medication —understanding the risks and limitations of drugs as well as the benefits in more rational balance—seem to be returning, if only incipiently, to a profession and society grown dependent on chemistry to make everyone feel better, to cure all ills, and to solve difficult social and economic problems.

One of the first things being done in quality-care nursing homes is to reduce the number of medications being taken. Dr. Michael McGarvey, deputy director of New York State's Division of Health Facilities Standards and Surveillance, tells how the medical director and the head of nursing at one home substantially reduced the number of drugs being taken. When they began their coordinated approach, each patient was taking five or more different drugs on the average. They discontinued all medications in a blanket order, conducted complete medical work-ups on each patient, and issued new prescription orders for conditions for which drugs were "explicitly indicated." As a result of this zero-based approach, they cut the average number of drugs per patient from five or more to three or fewer.

Betsy Todd, a registered nurse who conducts workshops for health professionals on the care of the elderly, knows of a pharmacist at a Florida nursing home who cut the use of sleeping pills by 80 percent by merely changing the nurses' rounds from 9:00 P.M. to 11:00 P.M.: "The nurses would go through the rooms around nine, asking, 'Who's awake?' and give a pill to anyone who was. Who goes to sleep by nine? By eleven most of them were asleep naturally."

Studies show that this simple act of reducing daily drug consumption by eliminating all but those absolutely necessary can improve the physical and mental health of elderly patients by reducing the risks of adverse reaction and by negating or potentiating the effects of necessary medication and by lessening the potential for physical or psychological addiction. Moreover, cutting the number of medications has the obvious benefit of reducing the drug bill of these fixed-income citizens who pay an average of $300 a year for drugs in nursing homes and about $100 for those purchased in the community.

Nursing home patients, whose average age is eighty-two, take five to seven different drugs each day on the average. Some take as many as ten to twenty. The average person sixty-five or over will take thirteen different drugs in a year's time. The risks are high.

Statistically, a person taking five different drugs has a 5 percent chance of an adverse reaction. The risk increases to 45 percent if twenty are being taken. Studies in the United States and Great Britain show that 25 percent of the hospital population over eighty will suffer adverse reactions to drugs. Of 177 patients admitted to the University of Florida hospital for drug-induced illnesses, 41 percent were over the age of sixty.

There are some exciting programs being developed and used to reduce the number of psychotropic drugs on elderly persons. Dr. James C. Folsom, a psychiatrist who directs ICD Rehabilitation Center in New York, successfully has pioneered chemical-free treatment programs not only for the elderly but for mentally disturbed patients of all ages. He is particularly concerned about the widespread use of tranquilizers and other psychotropic drugs on the elderly, and he and his colleagues at ICD have proved that patients can get better and have a better chance of returning to society as functioning members in a drug-free treatment program.

"What we depend on is developing meaningful human relationships—bringing people back to the reality of who they are, where they are, and what is going on," Dr. Folsom explained in an interview. "Confusion, fear, anger, and frustration are roles other people cast the elderly in. We're brainwashed into believing when we get old, we are going to get senile. As we get older, in a system that expects us to grow old that way, we accept it. But what is commonly known as senility can be stopped and reversed." And often a kind of "instant senility" can be brought about in the elderly when they experience a crisis and become momentarily confused, disoriented, hostile, fearful, and anxious. Once an elderly person displays these symptoms, it is automatically assumed that senility has set in, and there is no recourse except the use of drugs to control behavior.

Dr. Folsom tells about his father, an active and alert, independent and self-reliant octogenarian, in an episode that had a profound influence on his professional career. On his eighty-first birthday, Dr. Folsom's father underwent surgery for a fractured hip. Awakening from anesthesia, he found himself in a strange and darkened room. He was alone and unsure of where he was or what had happened. A nurse entered and without speaking gave him another injection of a sedative. She silently left and he fell asleep again. When he awakened next, he found himself in another strange room with blank walls and drapes pulled. Someone was standing over him with a pillow. The person did not speak, and the elderly Folsom feared he was going to be smothered. He fought back but was restrained, tied down, and given another sedative. When he became conscious, he was highly confused and out of touch with reality. He confused the names of his sons and spoke of loved ones who had died or long ago passed out of his life as if they were a part of his life at that time.

"In this crisis situation, he reverted to an earlier, more comfortable time," explained his son. "At another age he would have quickly put all of what happened through his thought process. The typical solution for these situations is drugs, and I think they compound the problem. In my experience they do."

But in this case, Dr. Folsom and other family members intervened and successfully reversed the "instant senility" of their father. By being constantly reminded of who he was, when it was, where he was, what happened, and who he was with, and simply by being treated as a human being, his father regained his sense of reality.

Dr. Folsom and his colleagues at ICD are using just such an approach to help rehabilitate others. Called Reality Orientation (RO), it is an approach to problems of mental illness first tried at a Veterans Administration Hospital in Topeka, Kansas, in 1958 under Dr. Folsom's direction. The central idea was simply to help the staff overcome prejudices about the elderly and train them to work with these "senile" and apparently helpless patients as if they expected improvement. The program worked so well that Dr. Folsom took it to a large state mental hospital at Mount Pleasant, Iowa, where a more refined and systematic Reality Orientation program was tried on a larger population of elderly senile patients. Prior to the Reality Orientation, only 3 percent of the patients sixty-five or older "had been able to leave any way other than by death." In the first six months of RO, 49 percent of those patients in the test program were discharged, and at the end of the year, the percentage had risen to 57 percent.

"Orientation to reality was taken at its most basic meaning," Dr. Folsom explains. "If the patient did not know his own name, he was first taught his own name. If he did not know where he was or where he was from, these facts were taught next. He was then taught such things as the day, week, month, year, his age, and so on. Once a patient was able to grasp any bit of information, he then began to recall and be able to use increasing amounts of material previously known but seemingly forgotten as he became 'senile.'"

Everybody—family, doctors, nurses, aides, cafeteria workers—who comes into contact with the patient is involved in the treatment. Psychoactive drugs are not used.

Encouraged by the results in Iowa, Dr. Folsom in 1965 took Reality Orientation to a 964-bed VA Hospital in Tuscaloosa, Alabama, where sixty-four patients were assigned to an even more comprehensive program. They had been considered "hopeless" cases, but within a year, five patients were discharged, two were transferred to VA facilities requiring more self-care, eight remained at the Tuscaloosa hospital but were able to accept and handle privileges, one was on a trial visit at home, and one was awaiting foster care placement. Twenty-nine remained in the program. Of the others, nine were removed because of severe physical conditions, four showed regression, two were unable to cooperate, and three died.

It worked so well that Dr. Folsom was asked by the VA to carry the technique to other VA hospitals. Now he and his ICD team are carrying the program to nursing homes, showing how a drug-free program can produce better results.

Kenneth Pommerenck, the social worker who directs ICD educational programs in Reality Orientation, says he had to overcome his own prejudices and fears before he could begin to help nursing home staffs and other health professionals overcome theirs. "I came genuinely to feel that senile patients were my people, and the people we had to help and change were the staff and family." Dr. Folsom and Pommerenck approach the problem of overmedication of nursing home patients as if the staff and system were crazy and the patient were sane. Predictably, they encounter resentment and resistance at first, but once they demonstrate results, the staff members, particularly the nurses and aides in closest contact with the patient, become enthusiastic and cooperative. "Once you quit treating a patient like a log in a bed, you begin to see that person like a person. Then you change and they change," Pommerenck said.

The first thing the RO people do when they go into a nursing home is to educate the doctors and nurses on a nonchemical approach to therapy. They go slowly in the reduction of psychotropic drug use, not because the patients can't tolerate a faster withdrawal but because the staff can't. All mood changers are withdrawn, says Pommerenck, "just as soon as the staff can handle it." Once the psychotropic medication is reduced or eliminated, they work with the staff to develop a meaningful program that treats these "senile" patients as human beings. "There's not much we can do when they are heavily sedated," Pommerenck explains. "Not until we free them from medication can we tell what kind of individual we're dealing with. Once the medication is withdrawn, we can ask, 'Where is that human being!?' "

That's the key—finding the human being. Once we can look at elderly persons as human beings to whom we can relate our own human experience, we can expect them to relate to us, and we will be able to discard our notion that they are somehow separate and unnecessary. But first we must get over our fear of growing old. It is important not only for those of us who are elderly but also for those of us who are not. For unless we do, we run the grave risk of being treated as we treat the elderly today. If we continue to deny aging, we will not overcome our fear and ignorance and we, too, will be shunted aside and chemically pacified into accepting a self-fulfilling prophecy of irreversible senility.

Selling the Chemical Solution   8

"The point of a physician's pen in that critical freeze-frame of time before it touches his prescription blank. This is when promotional efforts succeed or fail. The moment that marketers spend millions of dollars to influence."
—Healthmark Communications

"We are an agency that knows that health care marketing is a vital force. We apply it vigorously to identify and create markets. To develop products and services. *Build. Promote. And Sell* [emphasis added.]"
—Marshall Smith & Associates

"Writing a pharmaceutical ad is no more frustrating than writing an ad for Jell-O or toilet paper."
—John Lally, vice-president, Sudler & Hennessey

"We can introduce you to the single most affluent (and influential) group around. The healers, movers and shakers in the huge health care industry."
. . .

"The Verbal Prescription is obviously the most powerful sales producing testimonial a product could have. That's why doctors should know your OTC story. . . . Medical Economics. It's the most effective way to reach the high prescription writers. Even when they're not writing."
—*Medical Economics*

Healthmark, Marshall Smith, John Lally, Sudler & Hennessey, and *Medical Economics* are hardly household names. Although little known outside a small professional circle, they are part of the traditionally low-profile business that significantly influences the health care of every citizen. They are the Madison Avenue of the health care market, operating behind the scenes in what *Medical Economics* calls "the richest market in the world." They are the hidden persuaders behind the prescription drug market expected to exceed $9 billion in 1979.[1] They play a critical role in determining what drugs doctors prescribe for their patients. Although doctors discount it, the role of Madison Avenue and the marketing practices of the drug companies are as ingrained in the medical care of society as is the practicing physician. As Marshall Smith, the advertising agency quoted earlier, brags, "We are a . . . vital force. We apply it vigorously to identify and *create markets. To develop products and services. Build. Promote. And Sell* [emphasis added]."

The name of the game is selling, and as John Lally puts it, the approach is "no more frustrating than writing an ad for Jell-O or toilet paper." The stakes are high. To capture a share of the profitable prescription drug market that rapidly is approaching $10 billion a year, drug companies spend an estimated $1.5 billion a year in advertising and promotion. If you include advertising and promotion for over-the-counter drugs, the total easily exceeds $2 billion.[2] To influence the prescription habits of doctors, the drug companies are willing to spend 25 cents of each revenue dollar for sales promotion. By contrast, only about 15 cents of each revenue dollar goes back into research. The thrust of the advertising and promotion effort is to encourage the mistaken belief that drugs "offer effective cures across the whole range of human problems," Leonard G. Schifrin, professor of economics at William and Mary, told the House Committee on Narcotics Abuse and Control in testimony on August 10, 1978. "The industry, quick to nurture this belief and to capitalize on its

[1] The Pharmaceutical Manufacturers Association's estimate of 1978 U.S. sales of prescription drugs. The PMA estimated that global sales of U.S. manufacturers totaled $16.7 billion in 1978. Domestic sales in 1977 were $8.2 billion. These are wholesale figures. The price consumers actually paid would be substantially higher.
[2] The $1.5 billion figure for advertising, promotion, and sales of prescription drugs is an estimate. The PMA says it is high, estimating that U.S. drug firms spend $1 billion on marketing, promotion, and advertising, including continuing education programs for doctors. Senator Gaylord Nelson's Subcommittee on Monopoly has since the early 1970s estimated that drug companies spend 25 percent of gross revenue on advertising and promotion. At least two major drug companies, Ciba-Geigy and Roche, accept this estimate, but the industry as a whole probably spends a lesser percentage. We think $1.5 billion is conservative.

development, spends upwards of $2 billion a year to influence physicians (in the case of prescription drugs) and consumers (in the case of nonprescription drugs) toward the use of drugs to alleviate all sorts of symptoms of distress and to gain the selection of their labels in the marketplace. Price competition rarely occurs; competition in differentiation, novelty, claims and promotion is the cutting edge of market rivalry."

Unlike consumer advertising for OTC drugs, breakfast cereal, or hair spray, in the "ethical advertising" business, as it is called, the "buyers" are middlemen: doctors, pharmacists, nurses, hospital administrators, and, increasingly so in modern society, government bureaucrats involved in federal and state health programs.[3]

The consumer is the patient who takes the pill and pays the bill but does not see the ad. In a free-market society, the excess of mass advertising is the price most consumers are willing to accept to have choices of price and quality. The buyer accepts responsibility for his purchase whether he is aware or unaware of the persuasive advertising forces at work. But when a consumer purchases a prescription drug, there is little or no opportunity to be aware of the promotional influencing behind the physician's decision to choose the class or even the brand. Except for a few states where the option of generic substitution is required, even the price the consumer pays for the drug is determined by the doctor.

Without question, the key figure in the pharmaceutical marketing equation is the doctor. On your behalf, he is the most targeted individual for advertising in society, for the doctor decides what you, the patient, will purchase "in that critical freeze-frame of time before [his pen] touches his prescription blank." It is that instant that drug companies spend $1.5 billion a year to influence. Billions are at stake. With the accidental discovery of the sedative qualities of Librium and the subsequent development of its sister tranquilizer, Valium, Hoffmann-La Roche, a privately owned Swiss company, grew from relative obscurity as

[3] Although government agencies purchase some 20 percent of all prescription drugs for such agencies as the Indian Health Service and the Defense Department, no one in Washington seems to know exactly what is purchased and for what reason.

a manufacturer primarily of vitamins in the late 1950s to one of the largest and most profitable drug companies in the world. Today Hoffmann-La Roche virtually has cornered the world market for minor tranquilizers, having conducted the slickest and most effective marketing campaign in the history of pharmaceuticals first to capture a piece of the tranquilizer market held by Miltown, then to seize it, and finally to expand it by making normal anxiety a sickness in need of a chemical cure.

Relative to the billions of dollars at stake, the market of doctors is small. Not only is it the "single most affluent (and influential) group around," it is one of the most concentrated and oddly, considering the degree of education of doctors, one of the most susceptible to influence. Of the more than 370,000 active physicians in the United States in 1978, only about 200,000 were in office-based practices and considered "prescribers" by the industry. Less than half that total are considered "high prescribers" by the drug industry. To influence the 200,000 or so doctors who routinely prescribe drugs, the drug companies and their Madison Avenue agencies spend approximately $7,500 a year on the average for each doctor who uses the Rx pad.

The millions of dollars drug companies spend annually to influence prescribing habits and increase sales results in overmedication for many, raises the costs of health care significantly, and gives drug manufacturers substantial economic power in the health care system. The influence wielded by drug companies raises serious questions about the quality of health care. For several years the Subcommittee on Health of the U.S. Senate Committee on Labor and Public Welfare held lengthy hearings, compiled several volumes of testimony, and finally in 1978 proposed new regulations to bring more control to the marketing practices of pharmaceutical companies.

Citing the high mortality rate from adverse drug reactions (for which there are no precise records but which are estimated from a low of 30,000 deaths a year to a high of 170,000), Senator Edward Kennedy said the question is "to what extent do the advertising, marketing and the promotional activities of the pharmaceutical companies contribute to this problem." The evidence presented to Congress, he added, indicates the drug companies' influence on the physician's decision-making process has a "substantial impact, and one that may not be in the public interest." He described the way it works:

"We have a system of the hard sell, rather than a system of objective information dissemination; we have salesmen instead of analysts; we have the tools of selling—gimmicks, gifts, bonus deals—rather than the tools of science and medicine—comparative information, analysis of risks, and benefits of competing products. When scientific information is distributed it is usually favorable to the product. Negative comments are rarely distributed."

The reason drug manufacturers have such a "substantial impact" on the health care of every American is really simple. The job of educating doctors in drug therapy traditionally has been left almost entirely to drug suppliers. As late as 1978 only about half of the nation's 123 medical schools had clinical pharmacologists on their faculties. Dr. Kenneth L. Melmon, chief of clinical pharmacology at the University of California Medical Center, testified before the Senate committee in 1974 that fewer than 10 percent of the medical schools had courses in drug therapeutics, leaving a vacuum filled by an industry bent on "hustling drugs." Although drug therapy is the most common form of treatment in today's health system, the average doctor receives only six to ten hours of training in pharmacology in medical school.

"It's kind of a bizarre situation, but it is perfectly true," said Peter Rheinstein, a medical doctor and attorney who heads the Food and Drug Administration's advertising section. "In the field, the drug industry plays an important role for the education of their product." Rheinstein supervises a professional staff of four charged with the responsibility of monitoring the billion-dollar advertising campaigns of the drug industry.

Using the word *education* relative to the materials provided by the drug industry on drugs is stretching it to its broadest application. At best, it is biased information; at worst, it is misleading, inaccurate, and incomplete.

The fact that the medical profession relies on the pharmaceutical companies for its "education" in drugs and their proper use is a blatant case of conflict of interest that would not be tolerated in any other profession. Who, for example, would take the advice of a stock analyst who got all his information from a corporation representative whose livelihood depended upon selling his company's shares?

This is not to say that conflict of interest does not exist in other areas of society. It does, but significantly the abuses are recognized by all parties as abuses, and when they are exposed, generally something is done about it. But in the medical profession, the heavy involvement of the drug manufacturers in the information and education processes is accepted, expected, and cherished not only by doctors but also by researchers, educators, and administrators. When Dr. John Colaizzi became dean of the Rutgers University College of Pharmacy in New Jersey, home of such major drug houses as Roche Laboratories, Warner-Chilcott, Ciba-Geigy, Wallace Laboratories, and Sandoz, he publicly promised the drug companies that Rutgers would be "industry-oriented." Colaizzi openly solicited financial support from the drug industry for research and graduate programs.

It is this open acceptance and expectation of financial support from the drug companies, whose business self-interest is motivated by increasing drug sales, that worry a small minority of doctors fighting vainly against the tide. "What frightens me," says Dr. Robert Seidenberg, a psychoanalyst and professor of psychiatry at the State University of New York at Syracuse, "is not just the tremendous presence of drug companies but the sad and self-serving lack of recognition of the conflict of interest. The prevailing attitude is that the whole thing is innocent. Practically every major lecture is underwritten by drug companies at professional meetings. If you attend, you get credit in continuing medical education. If a guy wants a cup of coffee at a meeting, it is paid for by a drug company. Our publications are almost entirely supported by the industry. We get gifts of expensive books, cassette recorders to play their tapes, FM radios to listen to their ads, leatherette cases, plants for our offices, reprints of monographs, expensive pen sets; even the symphony music at one meeting was paid for by a drug company. Thousands of dollars in free gifts are there for the taking, even free drug samples. Often we get free samples even if we don't want them."

Most doctors and drug company executives do not think such underwriting either is inappropriate or in any way compromises the medical profession. The attitude of one officer of a drug company interviewed by the authors is typical. The firm, which markets a minor tranquilizer, had sponsored an educational symposium on the "proper use of antianxiety agents." More than 1,000 doctors attended, earning valuable free credits for continuing education certification required by their professional association. Asked if it was ethical for his company to pay for the education of doctors, the executive said: "The question [implies] something is insidious about it. I don't see it. I don't see it as a question of compromising ethics. I think there is certainly nothing wrong with it. We are providing a service that might not be easily provided in another manner. It was educational material to improve their ability to practice medicine. Is the company doing something that is selling its products? Are we compromising the education of physicians? Are the physicians in cahoots with the drug companies? I don't see that. There was no promotion about our drug. I don't even recall our product being mentioned, and I wouldn't personally take the position of trying to promote that. One of the panelists even talked about using psychotherapy as opposed to ethical drugs. But there's no question about their talking about the use of drugs. These were the top people in that field, fellows who really know what's going on."

If your product was not mentioned, was it clear who paid for the program? he was asked. "Look," he said, "there was a substantial investment involved. This is a commercial company. This is not a foundation, and I think if you do something like this, somebody should know who is doing it. I wouldn't have done it unless the company got credit for promoting this service." (The executive asked that neither he nor his company be identified by name. "There's no doubt about it, I'd get fired," he said.)

It was true that out of five members of the panel discussed above, one doctor did advocate taking a nondrug approach to treating anxiety, but the others generally favored drug therapy. Typically, while one or possibly two members of these seminar panels take a stand for alternative nonchemical approaches, the majority favor the use of psychoactive drugs, and it is not uncommon for the lecturers to make frequent mention of the drugs of the sponsoring company. As Dr. J. Richard Crout, the FDA's director of the Bureau of Drugs, puts it, "The system simply hires the person who agrees with it."

Although Dr. Crout, as we show in the next chapter, is considered by some to be soft toward the industry in new drug approvals, he is outspoken in his fear that the "growing influence of the pharmaceutical industry on medical education is a long-term threat to the integrity of my chosen profession." As he told the Senate Committee on Monopoly in 1976, "It has long been recognized that the industry-supported detail man is an important and influential system. I don't think the money changes their view. The system simply hires the person who agrees with it."

It should be noted that not just physicians in private practice avail themselves of free education from the drug industry. Doctors employed by the federal government, including the FDA and other health agencies, receive continuing medical education credits by taking audiovisual courses sponsored by Hoffmann-La Roche. The FDA, however, is applying for accreditation from the American Medical Association to offer continuing medical education programs, which presumably would be less biased.

What the heavy involvement of the drug industry in the education of doctors means, Seidenberg believes, "is that in thinking of therapy, it becomes almost a reflex to think of using drugs as the first weapon in your armamentarium. The consumer pays for it through prescriptions and is unnecessarily exposed to the potential of adverse drug reaction and, in the case of tranquilizers, addiction. It adds to the cost of medical care, something the medical profession should be upset about but isn't."

The marketing of prescription drugs traditionally had taken three distinct but integrated forms. Detail men—salesmen who call on doctors, hospitals, and pharmacists—are the centerpiece of the sales effort. In 1976 drug companies spent $800 million on their detail force, which numbered about 20,000. The second largest item in the traditional promotion budget is for medical journal advertising. The drug industry spends more than $125 million a year to support the 1,000 medical publications in the United States. The average general practitioner receives about sixty medical publications each month. All but a very few are free of charge and are supported entirely by drug company advertising. These free publications are called controlled circulation journals in the trade. The third largest share of promotion budgets is for direct-mail circulars. Health care suppliers spent

$65 million in 1976 on direct-mail promotion, about $39 million of that for pushing prescription drugs.[4]

To the three traditional methods of sales promotion—detail men, journal advertising, and direct mail—the pharmaceutical industry has added a fourth that has grown rapidly in the past decade. Under the headline "Education—New Drug Promoter," *Advertising Age* in its 1978 health care issue reported that the "outlook for education programs as a promotional tool is excellent, according to those involved in producing the programs. Most believe they will continue to account for a greater and greater percentage of the total promotional budget." One reason for the growth in this area was cited by Harold Mehling, vice-president of Science & Medicine, a company specializing in educational programs for the medical profession. "There are a lot of problems in getting a doctor's attention," Mehling told *Advertising Age*. "Coming to him in a scientific study with credible information and with advertising unopposed by competitors in that setting has evidently been recognized as a valuable thing for drug companies to do." The growth of continuing medical education programs as a sales tool clearly has eliminated the pretense behind the "education" offered by the drug industry to the nation's doctors. Continuing Medical Education (CME) is the outgrowth from the meritorious effort to help doctors keep up with advances in medical science following their graduation from medical school by continually updating their medical knowledge for as long as they practice. By 1979 several states had required doctors to acquire CME credits as a condition for licensing or as a condition for maintaining membership in medical societies or specialty associations. All medical societies now require doctors to be enrolled in a CME program as a condition for membership, and most hospitals require it to continue on staff. The object is to "improve the health care of the patients," says Richard Myers of the AMA's CME staff. "Everything done in putting on a CME course should be geared to this objective, not just giving information to fill up the doctor's head." To qualify for the AMA's Physi-

---

[4] *Advertising Age*, February 13, 1978. The advertising and sales promotion figures are provided by IMS International and based on self-reporting by the drug companies. They are believed to be conservative.

cian Recognition Award (PRA), which is accepted as the standard for required CME, a doctor must acquire 150 hours of educational credits over a three-year period. Of that total, doctors must earn a minimum of sixty hours from Category 1, programs that have been reviewed and accredited by the AMA or an accredited association or institution. The remaining ninety hours can be accumulated through programs under five other categories of diminishing value. CME has spawned a postgraduate educational industry estimated at between $1.5 billion and $2 billion a year. How much of this tab is picked up by the drug industry is impossible to determine with any degree of accuracy. Harold Mehling of Science & Medicine estimated that educational programs have grown from 3 percent of promotional budgets of drug houses to 20 percent in the last several years.

At its June convention in St. Louis in 1978, the AMA sponsored sixty courses in all areas of medicine that earned Category 1 credits. According to Myers, "The drug industry had no input in these whatsoever in any shape or form. They were physicians putting on courses for other physicians." Doctors were charged $10 per hour for the AMA-sponsored courses. The various medical specialty associations also conduct CME courses at various prices and quality, and many of these are free of industry influence. But many CME courses, including those for Category 1, are financed by drug companies, usually in cooperation with an accredited medical college or teaching hospital. At the American Psychiatric Association's annual convention in Atlanta in May 1978, two Category 1 courses were conducted on the treatment of anxiety. Both were sponsored by drug companies that market tranquilizers. Wyeth Laboratories, which recently had introduced a new tranquilizer called Ativan, funded a four-hour symposium conducted by McLean Hospital of Belmont, Massachusetts. Warner-Chilcott, which also had introduced a new tranquilizer called Verstran, sponsored a three-hour course. Both programs were announced in advance of the convention with large display advertisements in the APA's weekly newspaper, *Psychiatric News*. Warner-Chilcott claimed its symposium was cosponsored by the APA, which a spokesman for the APA denied when asked about the apparent conflict of interest. Both the Wyeth and Warner-Chilcott courses met AMA criteria for Category 1 credit. In both instances, the majority of the lecturers generally took a benign view of using drugs for treating anxiety.

In early 1979 Roche Laboratories, the world's largest tranquilizer manufacturer, launched one of the most ambitious "educational" sales campaigns ever. Called the "Consequences of Stress," it is described as a "nationwide three-year program to educate physicians and the public on the diagnosis and management of stress." Early indications suggested the program was a highly sophisticated sales campaign to sell Valium not only to doctors but directly to the public, which would violate FDA regulations, by expanding the market to make stress—defined as "both the ordinary and extraordinary pressures of life that confront every individual"—an illness treatable with Valium. The campaign is an excellent example of how closely integrated are the drug industry ties with Madison Avenue, respected medical schools, professional medical associations, health foundations, and federal health agencies. The program also demonstrates how drug companies hide their sponsorship, if not their motivation, behind presumably respected and unbiased institutions. The promotional literature for the "Consequences of Stress" claims it is sponsored by the Cornell University Medical College "in cooperation with the American Cancer Society, the American Heart Association, the Epilepsy Foundation of America, the National Institute of Mental Health, and the National Kidney Foundation." The physician education portion of the program is accredited by the AMA, the American Academy of Family Physicians, the American Osteopathic Association, and the American College of Obstetricians and Gynecologists. Roche also claimed the endorsement of the American Psychiatric Association, but the APA later denied it had given its approval.

Cornell's involvement also is ambiguous. All the literature and educational material being circulated to both doctors and lay people carries the Cornell University seal and lists Cornell as a sponsor, and the director of the program is Dr. Theodore Cooper, dean of the medical college. But Cornell spokesmen said the university is neither a sponsor nor a developer of the program and serves only as the accrediting institution for the physician education portion of the "Consequences of Stress." The program was,

in fact, developed by Health Learning Systems, a highly successful developer of continuing educational programs operated by two
former detail men for Roche. Health Learning Systems contracted
to do the three-year campaign for Roche. Neither Health Learning nor Roche would say how much Roche is paying, but on the
basis of public statements by Edward Saltzman, Health Learning
vice-president, that the usual program running two or three years
costs $2.5 million to $3 million, it is safe to assume the Roche
promotion is costing at least $3 million. The educational materials
doctors are asked to complete and return to Cornell University, in
fact, go to a post office box rented by Health Learning Systems
in Fairfield, New Jersey.

Even more intriguing is the endorsement of the program by
two federal agencies of the Department of Health, Education
and Welfare—the National Institute of Mental Health and the
Alcohol, Drug Abuse and Mental Health Administration. The
stamp of approval of the latter agency is provided by the par-
ticipation of Dr. Gerald R. Klerman, administrator of the agency,
as a "special consultant." Klerman said there is no conflict of
interest since he is not being paid. With two government agencies
endorsing the program—Mental Health and the Alcohol and Drug
Abuse agency—a third agency of HEW, the FDA, was investigating it to determine whether there were violations of federal laws
prohibiting the promotion of prescription drugs directly to the
public or whether the physician education program was more
sales promotion than education. FDA Commissioner Donald Kennedy said the FDA "is concerned about the program because the
early materials focused heavily on Valium . . . to the exclusion
of other drugs and therapies." He said the FDA would be "watch-
ful" as the program continues, and he promised that "if it becomes
apparent that it is nothing more than a sophisticated advertising
campaign for Roche products, FDA will undertake appropriate
regulatory action under the law." Edward Saltzman of Health
Learning Systems said the stress campaign does not fall under
FDA regulatory rules requiring inclusion of warning labels because Health Learning, not Roche, developed and directed the
program and also because the materials being circulated are not
being used by Roche's detail men in their sales calls on doctors.
On June 14, 1977, the FDA ordered a similar program developed

by Health Learning for the University of California under a grant from Ortho Pharmaceuticals withdrawn from the company's marketing kits provided doctors but allowed continuation of the CME program. This was the first regulatory FDA action in the "gray area" of programs developed by an intermediary for a drug company. In this instance, the FDA found the Ortho materials for oral contraceptives constituted misbranding and were promotional.

Under FDA regulations, all materials that mention a specific drug product by name are considered promotional in nature and therefore must also include the label providing approved indications, dosage instructions, adverse reactions, warnings, and contraindications. Saltzman defends the frequent mention of Valium in the stress campaign on the ground that "Valium has become the street name for all tranquilizers."

The "public education" portion of the Roche program is even more self-serving. The public segment also was developed and directed by Health Learning, although the materials give the appearance of being conceived and developed by Cornell. The public promotion is being coordinated by Dudley-Anderson-Yutzy, a high-powered New York public relations firm, which mailed more than 2,000 press kits to newspapers and radio and television stations around the country. The firm also has "scheduled doctors on panels on local TV shows and on network shows," according to Barbara Hunter of Dudley. "We do this by trying to bring doctors to the attention of producers." In addition to convincing the public that the "ordinary and extraordinary pressures of life" felt by every citizen constitute an illness and to promoting Valium as the "fastest and most effective" treatment, the public campaign clearly was designed to counter the bad publicity given Valium by Betty Ford's account of addiction to Valium and alcohol. Dr. Cooper, who was an undersecretary for HEW before he joined Cornell as dean, makes prominent mention of Mrs. Ford's addiction and then quickly offers a defense of Valium, saying, "When you hear of a person who has gotten into trouble with tranquilizers, you'll most often find that alcohol is the villain."

The stress campaign does have some laudable aspects, particularly the portions that warn of the use of tranquilizers in combination with alcohol and other drugs and the portions that acknowledge there are nonchemical therapies useful in handling stress. But as is the case in all industry-sponsored "educational" programs, the bottom line is the emphasis on drug therapy and the expansion of the market by finding new emotional and mental disorders—in this case, "the extraordinary and *ordinary* pressures of life"—for which psychoactive drugs can be prescribed. Furthermore, the Roche program once again proves the rule articulated by Dr. Crout of the Bureau of Drugs: "The system hires the person who agrees with it." Although there are two or three doctors on the program who advocate nonchemical approaches to handling stress, the majority are decidedly pro-drug. Dr. Cooper, who is a member of the Upjohn board of directors, is, for example, enthusiastic about Valium.

The Roche program also illustrates another rapidly growing aspect of industry-sponsored "educational" programs—the use of modern electronic technology. The introductory seminar for CME credit was delivered to doctors in twenty-six cities by closed-circuit television. More than 12,000 doctors signed up for the program in response to a letter from Cooper on his letterhead as dean of the Cornell Medical School. Cooper's letter stresses that "there is no fee for this valuable 30-month program."

Closed-circuit television and radio have enabled drug companies to carry their oral and graphic messages directly to doctors in their homes and offices. One of the fastest-growing businesses in drug industry communications is the Physicians Radio Network (PRN). PRN, which began in 1974 with 1,000 doctors in two cities, had expanded its network by 1979 to more than thirty-five cities and more than 80,000 doctors, who receive on small FM radio sets specialized medical, general, and financial news and "product information." PRN also provides CME programs sponsored by drug companies. It claims a "significantly higher 'share of mind' among radio holders" than can be gained by advertisers in medical journals or through direct mail. Lest there be any doubt about the commercial objectives, we note that the initial lists of doctors provided free radio sets were furnished by advertising drug companies from their lists of "high prescribers." PRN is owned by Visual Information Services, a division of Republic Corporation, which also offers videotape CME courses for more than 700 hospitals and 115,000 physicians and 25,000 nurses and other hospital workers. These programs are almost entirely supported by Roche and are again provided free. In many hospitals, physicians are required or "strongly urged," as one doctor put it, to attend the programs as a condition for remaining on the hospital staff, providing Roche a captive audience. Once again, while the editorial content may be meritorious and unbiased, it is clear who is paying the bill and even the most sophisticated audience will be influenced. "Some companies feel a trailer is as much mileage as they can get out of it," said Richard Myers of the AMA. "Some others are more aggressive."

In what might be described as an "aggressive" promotion, Pfizer Labs sponsored a video discussion on depression with a panel of doctors. The program opens with the statement that 4 to 8 million Americans suffer from depression, but as the program progresses, the number expands to 20 million. Depression is loosely defined as the "absence of joy" and is said to affect, among others, housewives, underachievers, psychosomatics, insomniacs, and persons who experience inadequate sexual performance. The panel concludes its discussion with a plug for antidepressant drugs, particularly Sinequan, which is manufactured by Pfizer and which is one of the most heavily promoted psychoactive drugs on the market. According to the FDA's Crout, the message of the video lecture is "quite clear":

"—Depression is everywhere and being underdiagnosed;

"—Patients need not be actually depressed. Insufficient joy, psychosomatic complaints, or underachieving may be the only signs of symptoms and may be enough to make a diagnosis of depression;

"—Sinequan is the best of a good group of drugs, whose use, fortunately for the American public, is finally increasing to high levels;

"—The physician should join this welcome trend and use drugs more."

Crout does not doubt the integrity of the physicians on the panel and believes they were expressing honest medical opinions. "It is also likely, however, that the drug firm knew what each physician would say before they invited him and thus assured the emergence of a particular point of view in its educational production," Crout said. The Pfizer videotape was endorsed by the American Psychiatric Association and was distributed as an educational tool to doctors by Pfizer's detail men, the salesmen who are the first source of information on drugs for the majority of doctors and are the front line of the marketing effort.

The approximately 20,000 detail men who make up the sales forces of drug and surgical equipment companies in the United States constitute a vast and influential—but largely hidden from the public—force in the health care system. Detail men probably are second only to practicing physicians in their influence on every patient's medical care. In a basic training course for detail men, Merck, Sharp & Dohme's new salesmen were instructed to "become involved in the physician's decision-making process." The detail men were told to "personalize the patients treated by the doctors you visit. You will see them every day. In the offices, hospital corridors and in the waiting rooms. Take a good look at them. Remember, your efforts may affect *them personally* more than most people in their lives. *And they don't even know who you are.*"

The salesmen were told, however, not to get too sentimental about these patients because "this business of ours isn't all sentiment and personal relationships, no matter how grand and true and noble they may be. It is also a *business.* . . ."

The job of the detail man is to sell doctors on his company's line of drugs, but unlike most salesmen, the detail man does not himself take orders. Rather, the trick is to persuade the doctor to prescribe drugs for his or her patients. Each detail man is assigned anywhere from 100 to 150 doctors and, in addition, makes sales calls on hospitals and drugstores in his territory. They concentrate, however, on general practitioners and other doctors regarded as "high prescribers."

Considering their influence on health care, detail men receive only limited training in pharmacology from their employers. The drug industry has successfully defeated every legislative attempt to require licensing and formal training for detail men. Once on the road, the only thing that counts is performance, and performance is measured by sales. As one former detail man, Bennett J. Wasserman, told a Senate committee in 1974: "There is a gospel to be spread; there is a mission to fulfill. It can be achieved by increasing the number of prescriptions to be written for the products being promoted, and that means that the rallying cry is 'sell, sell, sell.' To too many detail men, 'all is fair' in their daily war with competition."

Four years later Charles Brannan, a detail man for Hoffmann-La Roche, told the House Committee on Narcotics Abuse and Control about the "tremendous pressures that were exerted on me by the company's high pressure artists called divisional sales managers and regional managers. These pressures were exerted purely for profit and can eventually destroy the salesman and his family." Brannan, whose territory included portions of Southern California and Arizona, said his "sole purpose was to get him [the doctor] to prescribe Roche products instead of the competitors' by any means I could. We were taught that after mentioning the first drug, the next two would not be recalled, so Valium was presented first." The Roche detail men were graded as "excellent, good, and poor" by doctors who sent report cards back to Roche, which would send the doctor's medical school $10 for each report. Brannan said Roche also did telephone spot checks to determine the last time doctors saw a Roche salesman "and what drugs they talked about." The pressure to sell is so great that many detail men crack under the strain, Brannan told the committee. He told of one detail man who broke down in a doctor's office "and started crying because the pressure was too great." This man had been on two Librax four times a day. Librax is a combination of Librium and a substance for ulcers. He told of another Roche colleague who "would receive shock therapy on an outpatient basis at Encinitas Hospital at 8 o'clock in the morning and [his sales manager] would pick him up at the hospital, and at 10 o'clock [he] would be working a display for Roche pushing Valium, Librium and Dalmane."

After seven years, Brannan said he became "totally depressed and could no longer push Roche products." He took medical leave and in 1978 left the company. In closing his testimony before the House committee on August 10, 1978, Brannan left the committee members with this troubling question: "How many more dedicated professional pharmaceutical salesmen will be destroyed by the master manipulators whose only motive is profits at the expense of many unsuspecting patients who think they can find happiness in a pure white, yellow or pale blue pill called Valium?"

Former detail men such as Wasserman and Brannan say the drug company salesman is caught between pressure to sell to get ahead and the conflicting moral obligation to warn physicians of the dangers attendant to the use of drugs, which would discourage prescribing of their products. Wasserman, now an attorney specializing in medical malpractice, found that the detail man "is given more tools by the company with which to discharge his duty to sell than he is given to carry out his duty to warn." The "tools to sell" include everything from free drug samples to color television sets, engraved desk nameplates to free trips to luxury hotels for continuing education programs, scripts for playacting a sales pitch to a reluctant doctor to instructions for negating adverse studies in medical journals and bad publicity in the lay press. During the heyday of drug growth during the 1960s and early 1970s, drug companies distributed gift catalogs not unlike Green Stamp gift books from which doctors and pharmacists could order presents for prescribing or selling drugs. The more you sold or prescribed, the more valuable the gift earned. Parke, Davis had a "Christmas Gift Book Awards" in 1973 through which doctors could accumulate prescription points for everything from a door knocker for 1,010 points to a silver necklace for 21,805.

Smith Kline & French, anxious to get a piece of Eli Lilly's $66 million-a-year market in Darvon, the widely abused and dangerous narcotic painkiller, gave walnut desk pieces with a gold nameplate to doctors who were "true SK-Line" friends and prescribed its chemical equivalent, SK-65, instead of Darvon. Smith Kline told the detail men that such an expensive gift should be given judiciously. "You're going to have to weed out the SK&F supporters and the nice guys from the true 'SK-Line' backers—those who regularly use 'SK-Line' pre-printed Rx pads, for instance, or other known high prescribers," the company said in a confidential memo disclosed at a Senate hearing. (By 1977, Lilly still held the market, realizing $140 million in U.S. sales from Darvon.)

Despite FDA regulations requiring drug companies to present the adverse as well as the positive effects of their drugs, whether in journal ads or in verbal pitches by salesmen, there are numerous examples of instances in which salesmen were instructed to avoid negative issues. In a January 8, 1973, article in the *Journal of the American Medical Association,* three air force doctors reported a 3.5 percent incidence of thrombophlebitis (blood clotting in the veins of legs) as the result of intravenous use of Valium. Within three weeks, Roche had a sales memo out to detail men instructing them not to initiate a discussion with doctors about the article. If the doctor mentioned the article, the salesmen were told to "clarify the question, obtain his reaction to the article (did he read, see the headline, or did a competitive salesman mention it to him), determine the reason for his question or his concern and get the physician to discuss his own clinical experience with injectable Valium."

In Senate hearings in 1974, Robert B. Clark, president of Roche, was questioned by Senator Edward Kennedy about this memo and a similar one that advised detail men to avoid dicussing a negative article on Bactrim, an antibiotic, in the *Medical Letter,* the most objective medical publication on drugs available. "Should the companies themselves be the ones who make the final decision, or should not the physicians, at least, be alerted to material that is raised in either *JAMA* or the *Medical Letter?* Ought not your company policy be to present the side effects as well as the good points?" Kennedy asked Clark. Clark agreed that "probably our representatives should not only be aware of that but be prepared to present it." Under questioning, he also agreed that Roche's policy should be to present adverse as well as positive information. Brannan, the former Roche detail man, told the House committee in 1978 that he was "never told to exaggerate claims on Valium, but if a confrontation came up about lay publicity, I was to be able to handle it by showing reprints by physicians to dispute the other opinion or have Roche's professional services department send a folder of information on the area in dispute." There's no practical way for the FDA or any regulatory agency to monitor the activities of detail men to determine whether they are indeed presenting the bad along with the good in their sales pitches, and in the high-pressure climate of drug salesmanship, it is not likely that a balanced presentation is made in the privacy of the doctors' offices.

Some of the flagrant abuses of the past have been eliminated, but as long as the detail man remains the cornerstone of the promotional marketing effort, the hard sell continues unchecked, if more subtle. One reason is that the medical profession continues to rely heavily on the salesman for information about drugs and how to use them. A survey by the Pharmaceutical Manufacturers Association showed that 53 percent of the nation's physicians consider the detail man "very important" in learning about new drugs. Another 31 percent consider the information from detail men "somewhat important," and only 16 percent consider this source "not very important or unimportant." In the same survey, 38 percent said advertising in medical journals was "very important," 35 percent said it was "somewhat important," and 27 percent felt it was "not very important" or "unimportant." Direct-mail promotion from drug companies was viewed as "very important" by 28 percent, "somewhat important" by 44 percent, and "not very important" or "unimportant" by 28 percent.

A survey commissioned by the FDA showed a similar pattern of heavy reliance on detail men, particularly by general practitioners and obstetricians and gynecologists. Of all physicians surveyed, 74 percent said they conferred with other doctors for drug information on an average of 2.2 times a week, and 61 percent said they consulted with detail men an average of 1.6 times a week. GP's indicated they relied less on peers and more on detail men than did the entire survey group, which included all specialties. Eighty percent of the GP's said they consulted with detail men 2.8 times per week. The survey also showed that GP's felt information provided by detail men was "most useful" more commonly than physicians as a whole. GP's also said they consult with colleagues less frequently and feel such consultations less important than specialists do.

What this suggests is that those doctors who prescribe the most drugs are the ones most receptive to drug industry information. Indeed, there is a correlation between the number of visits by detail men and the number of prescriptions written. According to a study by Hugh D. Walker, *Market Power and Price Levels in the Ethical Drug Industry*, published by the Indiana University Press, the more visits your doctor gets from detail men, the more drugs he prescribes. The survey also shows that the more your doctor relies on industry sources for drug information, the more drugs he will prescribe.

According to Walker, doctors who write 10 or fewer prescriptions a week are seen on a mean average of 2.8 times a week by a detail man and rely on industry sources 40 percent of the time and professional sources 60 percent of the time. Doctors who write 51 to 100 prescriptions a week are visited 4.13 times a week by detail men and get 75 percent of their information on new drugs from industry sources and only 25 percent from professional sources. Doctors who write more than 150 prescriptions per week are seen an average of 8 times a week by detail men and get 100 percent of their drug information from the industry.

The vast majority of all drugs are prescribed by general practitioners, internists, and obstetricians/gynecologists, so it should come as no surprise that drug companies zero in on these groups.

In today's specialized world, Madison Avenue has stepped in to integrate the promotional activities of the drug companies, coordinating entire campaigns from the detail man to journal advertising and from direct-mail solicitation to educational programs. It's all built around the detail man. "If it doesn't happen with the salesman in interaction with the doctor, it's not too likely nonpersonal media will save the day," explained Robert Dempsey, president of Medcom, a health care communications corporation. "Every time a doctor sees an ad with creative signals used, he is reminded of his experience in his office where he was favorably influenced by the salesman. If the salesman left a negative influence, the negative will be enforced."

In portraying people in medical advertisements, ad men create a patient type in the doctor's mind "so that when a patient comes in his office, he can say, 'Hey, that's the patient that fits.' The picture painted for him helps him see that patient as at least a candidate for that drug." In reaching for that "patient type," Dempsey acknowledges that "maybe we kind of go into stereotypes more than we realize."

The stereotypical anxiety patient is invariably a woman, unless it is anxiety associated with stomach disorders or heart trouble, in which case it's a male. We have seen in previous chapters how the drug companies reinforce the male-dominated medical profession's perception of women as anxious, nervous, distraught, depressed, down, uptight, frustrated, and irrational and, therefore, in need of tranquilizers to calm down or stimulants to pick up. Let's take a look at some of the other stereotypes.

The elderly: no group consumes more drugs than the elderly. Persons over sixty-five years of age constitute 10 percent of the U.S. population but consume 25 percent of all prescription drugs and are users of a correspondingly disproportionate share of over-the-counter medications. Thus, the elderly, older women especially, are a major target of drug company promotion. Typically, advertisers in medical journals depict elderly women as being institutionalized in nursing homes and geriatric wards.

The thrust of these advertisements is the promotion of drugs to sedate them, to arouse them, to supplement their diets, to assist in their body discharges, to control their blood pressure, to settle their stomachs, and often to control their behavior. More often than not the advertisements for the psychotropic drugs are aimed not at the elderly patient but rather at the institution's staff, promoting control, not care.

In one outrageous example, McNeil Labs promotes Haldol, a powerful tranquilizer, as a means of controlling "disruptive behavior in nursing home patients with minimal risk of sedation and hypotension." In a three-page ad that ran in many journals in 1978, McNeil pictures a smiling, alert, and wrinkled woman holding a cloth flower under the headline "I made a flower today." On the facing page, McNeil touts Haldol's effectiveness in keeping nursing home patients under control. The message is that not only can a nursing home keep patients under control with this powerful drug, but it can also make them creative and able to perform delicate tasks at the same time. In fine print in the corner, McNeil admits that the woman pictured made the flower as part of a vocational group therapy project "and is not a patient receiving Haldol." On the third page of the ad, McNeil reprints the FDA-required warnings that include "impairment of mental and physical abilities."

It is noteworthy that in the November 1977 issue of the *Journal of the American Geriatrics Society* in which this particular ad appeared, the magazine published an article reporting that a five-year study of one nursing home showed "that excessive numbers of drugs were being prescribed . . . [and that] the overall quality of prescribing practices was not of high quality."

Another stereotype is that of the angry, withdrawn, and unsociable elderly male. In a long-running campaign for Mellaril, a powerful tranquilizer, Sandoz Pharmaceuticals pictures an elderly man pushing away his wife. It is, the ad declares, "a family problem that belongs in the hands of the family physician." The ad reminds doctors that changes brought about by aging include "agitation, depressed mood, and anxiety" and that this is a primary concern of the physician who "knows the hurtful effect of these symptoms on the patient and their splitting effect on family relationships." To treat the man's "organic mental" disorder and heal the relationship, the Sandoz ad recommends "an old friend like Mellaril."

Sandoz does not mention alternative nonchemical therapy, not even counseling, as a future course of help or in conjunction with chemical therapy in the short term. Nor is there any mention in the text, even in the warnings section, that the National Academy of Sciences finds Mellaril effective only for "short-term treatment of moderate to marked depression with variable degrees of anxiety in patients with depressive neurosis."

The same drug Sandoz promotes to help heal the relationship problem between an elderly couple also is heavily promoted for the really angry man whose "senile psychosis" manifests itself in dangerous tantrums. In these ads, Sandoz pictures a fist-clenching, teeth-grinding elderly man approaching as if to strike. The recommended course of treatment for this "agitated geriatric with senile psychosis" is the same as for the more mildly agitated senior citizen—Mellaril. Sandoz also has promoted Mellaril for hyperactive children, for which it has not been proved effective.

Chief candidates for chemical treatment of hypertension, heart trouble, and stomach disorders are men in middle to late years. Men almost always are pictured in advertisements for drugs directly indicated for these disorders but also for psychotropic drugs to treat anxiety or depression that is presumed to accompany the primary difficulty. Since men infrequently see doctors for emotional problems, drug companies promote tranquilizers as adjunct therapy for the more typical male complaints of the heart and stomach. Hoffmann-La Roche has been particularly active in this area, pushing both Librium and Valium for the cardiac patient. In one ad, Roche told doctors that while they may be able to get their cardiac patient to give up fatty foods and cigarettes, they may have more trouble getting him to give up the anxiety he feels about having heart trouble. Valium is recommended not for heart trouble but rather for the normal anxiety the patient might feel upon learning of heart trouble.

Roche has so successfully promoted Valium and Librium as "adjunct" drugs that tranquilizers, most especially the two Roche products, are closely associated with the treatment of every conceivable illness.

In general, people pictured in drug advertisements in medical journals are white, middle-class Americans. Interestingly, blacks are rarely portrayed as either patients or medical professionals. The heavy users of the services of office-based physicians are those in the best position to pay, and the most lucrative practice is the one that treats middle-class patients, particularly white women. It is this class of patient that drug companies portray.

In recent years combination drugs have become fashionable. In taking combination chemical therapy to an extreme, Roche developed a drug that combines Librium (chlordiazepoxide) with Quarzan (clidinium bromide), a chemical that relaxes stomach muscles. Called Librax, this combination was first promoted as a secondary drug for ulcers and later for "the lower G.I. tract [that is] organically sound but oversensitive to emotional stress." This latter use was promoted in Roche ads with an asterisk reference to a fine-print warning that Librax "has been evaluated as possibly effective" by the FDA only for what Roche called an "irritable bowel syndrome." In terms of your health care, it means simply that Librax or any other drug classed as being "possibly effective" in a particular treatment has not been proved to do any good. Measured against the known risks, the benefits are doubtful.

In 1978 great emphasis was being placed in drug promotion on depression. The promotion corresponded with an increase in articles in medical journals and in the mass media on the problems caused by depression for millions of Americans. In an editorial in the November 17, 1978, *Journal of the American Medical Association,* Dr. Nathan S. Kline of the Rockland Research Institute in Orangeburg, New York, an institute heavily involved in drug research and experimentation, estimated there are "12 million to 20 million patients with depression presently in need of treatment." Kline said because these are too many patients for psychiatrists using drugs to handle, "this places the responsibility for dealing with depressed patients squarely on the family physicians, the general practitioner, and the internist," and he recommends that every medical practitioner "should be familiar with at least one or two antidepressants." Kline lamented that antidepressant drugs "that produce relief of depression in days or even minutes" may not be available for years, and he said medicine also badly needs "an antidepressant that is long-acting so that we can ensure patient compliance." Robert Seidenberg, the Syracuse psychiatrist, wrote a letter to the editor of the *Journal* saying the Kline editorial "sounds like a sales pitch given to detail men before they embark on their appointed rounds."

Among those drug companies jumping on the depression bandwagon were Roche, which introduced a new product combining a tranquilizer (Librium) and an antidepressant (Endep), and Schering, which increased its promotion for Etrafon, a combination of a powerful phenothiazine tranquilizer and an amitriptyline hydrochloride antidepressant. The combination of a tranquilizer, which depresses the central nervous system, and an antidepressant, which elevates it, is promoted on the rationale that if a patient feels depressed, he or she is going to feel anxiety about being depressed. In an apparent attempt to create the impression in doctors' minds that depression is everywhere, Schering's medical journal advertisements for Etrafon called depression-anxiety "a plague in our time" and broadened the application to include insomnia. Not content with the already-exaggerated figure of 20 million Americans in need of chemical treatment for depression, Schering said the total worldwide was 100 million people and "that number is expected to increase."

Unfortunately such exaggerated and distorted advertisements influence the diagnosis and prescribing patterns of the nation's doctors. A study made to measure physician perceptions of misleading advertising by the Institute for Survey Research at Temple University for the FDA showed that doctors who viewed misleading claims of efficacy of drugs would be influenced by advertising. "These results suggest that the expansion of claimed indications and efficacy might encourage excessive prescribing of this product," said the authors of the "Study of Features of Prescription Drug Advertising Using Physician Perception." "Speculating well beyond the obtained data, at least two lines of rationalization might be employed by physicians in justifying over-usage of this product as a result of exposure to misleading promotional claims," the authors said. "First, physicians may directly apply the expanded claims clinically, and thus prescribe the product for those patients with disease states for which the product is not actually approved by the FDA. Second, physicians who are misled by the expanded claims may feel that, since the product can be prescribed for serious chronic disease states such as cardiovascular disease and thyrotoxicosis, the product must be relatively safe, i.e., minimal side effects and contraindications. The result of this line of reasoning could be a lessening of inhibition to prescribe and a concomitant increase in prescriptions for an increased range of 'patient presenting problems.'"

The study also showed that GP's "are more likely to be influenced in the direction of the advertised message than" internists. This finding supports other studies showing that GP's, who are the heaviest prescribers of psychoactive drugs, also are the most dependent on industry sources of information about drugs.

The Temple study, which was dated August 1978, was based on the perceptions of 150 practicing physicians of misleading and nonmisleading advertisements developed by the FDA for the tranquilizer Tranxene and the antibiotic Vibramycin. The FDA altered a Tranxene brochure for the study because it "is typical of the tranquilizer material which FDA considers as capable of misleading physicians to believe that in addition to relieving anxiety, the drug has . . . been shown to be effective in the treatment of underlying disease."

Under FDA regulations, all ads for new drugs must be reviewed, and promotional material for old drugs is monitored periodically. In the case of a new drug, the clinical data presented in the company's New Drug Application are compared against the advertising claims to verify that the drug is being promoted only for conditions for which the FDA determined it to be safe and effective.

It was not until 1970, well after the drug explosion and the subsequent glut of medical publications and advertising pages, that a separate Division of Drug Advertising was created in the FDA. It began as a shoestring operation and remains so in a David-and-Goliath battle with the pharmaceutical giants. It is headed by Peter Rheinstein, who is uniquely qualified for the job as both a medical doctor and an attorney. Under his direction, a staff of four assisted by four secretaries and clerks and a budget of $200,000 a year attempts to monitor the continuing advertising and promotion activities of established drugs on the market, plus make in-depth studies of the advertising claims of new drugs. "I was asked the other day how we keep track of a billion-dollar-plus business, and I said, 'Very carefully,'" said William Purvis, a pharmacist on the staff. With an average of 800 packages of material submitted each month by the drug companies, either in compliance with the law or voluntarily, the department is overwhelmed. "This is just the tip of the iceberg. Each submission could have one to twenty-five different elements —ads, reprints, cassettes, films, booklets, videotapes, learning systems," Purvis explained. "We're only able to scratch the surface. But we change our priorities and really take a good look at certain things. It's like going over fifty-five on the parkway. The companies don't know when we're going to be around the corner."

The division gets some help from what Purvis calls "the fairy godmother," who sends detailed medical and clinical studies of advertising claims in "unsigned brown envelopes from competitors."

In addition to reviewing ad claims, the division monitors exhibits at medical conventions but is able to hit only a few on its travel budget of $3,000 a year. Furthermore, the growth of industry sponsorship of continuing educational programs has given the division added responsibilities. The FDA has enough trouble keeping up with the medical journals. As of 1978, more than 1,200 medical publications, including scores of slick magazines, circulated among doctors in the United States. Most of them are free, paid for by advertising from drug companies anxious to influence prescription and supply sales. During 1978 drug companies spent nearly $130 million in journal advertising alone. The only major medical publication in the United States that functions without drug company advertising is the *Medical Letter*, which was founded in 1958 by Arthur Kallet and Dr. Harold Aaron. Concerned about the lack of unbiased drug information, Kallet and Aaron, both of whom had been associated with Consumers' Union, borrowed $25,000 to establish a nonprofit publication supported entirely by subscriptions. The *Medical Letter* publishes brief, critical appraisals of new drugs that reflect a consensus of clinical trials and personal experience of experts who have no ties with drug companies. As an example of its approach, the *Medical Letter* asked a panel of experts not associated in any way with Hoffmann-La Roche to review the safety and effectiveness of the company's new antidepressant and antianxiety agent, Limbitrol. The *Medical Letter* consultants also reviewed other fixed combination antidepressants and antianxiety drugs, including the more powerful ones containing phenothiazine and tricyclics. The consultants concluded that there "is no good evidence that products combining small doses of phenothiazine with a tricyclic offer any advantage over the tricyclic alone." Similarly, most *Medical Letter* consultants doubt whether a combination of a tricyclic antidepressant with a benzodiazepine offers any advantage over adequate doses of a tricyclic alone. In contrast, Roche's ads boasted that "new Limbitrol achieved greater improvement more rapidly than amitriptyline or chlordiazepoxide alone" in its company-financed studies. Amitriptyline is an antidepressant and chlordiazepoxide is the tranquilizer Librium.

Dr. Ingrid Waldron of the University of Pennsylvania found a similar disparity between the evaluations for Librium and Valium by industry sources and by independent sources, chiefly the *Medical Letter* and articles in the *New England Journal of Medicine*. She compared the recommendations over a fifteen-year period, from 1960 to 1975, and found the industry evaluations much more favorable than the independent ones. "Aside from the obvious factor of motivation to sell, this reflects the difference between reliance on uncontrolled studies, in which apparent efficacy is inflated by placebo effects and spontaneous recovery, as compared to reliance on controlled studies," Dr. Waldron explained.

Another finding was that industry information on Valium and Librium minimized the significance of adverse effects "by emphasizing that they can be eliminated by adjusting dosage in most cases and/or are uncommon."

As an example of the more favorable recommendations from the manufacturer, Roche for more than ten years recommended use of Valium and Librium for the treatment of chronic alcoholism. The *Medical Letter* consultants, however, found both drugs "not effective" for treating alcoholism. The evidence then and now clearly establishes that alcohol and tranquilizers are cross-addictive and can be fatal when used together.

In another example, Roche recommends Valium and Librium for treating an irritable colon or peptic ulcer accompanied by anxiety. The *Medical Letter* finds such therapy "not effective." Roche recommends Valium and Librium for a whole variety of everyday kinds of stress, whereas the *Medical Letter* finds the drugs effective in relieving anxiety but overused and urges more caution.

The only readily available reference book for drug information is the *Physicians' Desk Reference (PDR)*, published by the Medical Economics Company, a subsidiary of Litton Industries. In its 1978 edition, the *PDR* included the "latest available information" on some 2,500 drug products. The information that is published in the *PDR*, the doctor's Bible on drugs, is provided by the drug companies which pay to have it printed. The product summaries are paid advertisements. But the editorial content of each description pretty much follows the summary data required by the FDA —the so-called labeling data—for inclusion with all drug advertisements. The data include a brief description of the drug's action, approved indications for use, side effects, warnings, contraindications, adverse reactions, and dosage and administration instructions. Price information is not included. Generally, the manufacturers print what is required, no more, no less. Until the new labeling regulations went into effect in 1964, the adverse effects were not required and normally not included. Fourteen years after the new regulations went into effect, the FDA still had not completed its updating of many drug labels, and the 1978 edition of the *PDR* contained descriptions that the FDA considered incomplete, inadequate, and misleading. The book is distributed free to 340,000 physicians and illustrates once again how economically dependent physicians are on the promotional dollars of the drug manufacturers. Their primary source of "objective" information about drugs—doctors refer to the *PDR* an average of seven or eight times a week—is written and paid for by manufacturers.

The hundreds of millions the drug companies spend on promotion and advertising gives them tremendous influence and clout, as the *New York Times* sadly discovered in January 1976, when it printed a series of articles on medical incompetence, including the misuse of prescription drugs. It is said that pharmaceutical companies in retaliation canceled advertising worth $500,000 in *Modern Medicine,* a medical journal based in Minneapolis that was owned by the *Times* company but operated independently of the newspaper. The newspaper quoted an officer of the medical journal as saying that the companies canceled their ads because they felt "you don't feed people who beat you up." The *Times* subsequently sold *Modern Medicine* and seven other medical publications to Harcourt Brace Jovanovich, Inc. The *Times* attorney who handled the sale said the uproar over the series of articles and the cancellation of the advertising in *Modern Medicine* was not a factor in the *Times's* decision to sell. Harcourt Brace Jovanovich, Inc., has confirmed that negotiations had begun before the incident.

One of the biggest medical publishers is the American Medical Association, which publishes the popular *Journal of the American Medical Association,* a weekly magazine; *American Medical News,* a weekly newspaper; and nine monthly magazines covering specific medical specialties. Each member of the AMA gets the *Journal,* the *News,* and one specialty publication free. The eleven AMA journals carried more than $12 million in advertising in 1977, about 10 percent of the total spent on space in all journals published in the United States.

Periodically, proposals are made from within the AMA to eliminate drug company advertising on the ground that it creates the impression of bias, if not bias in fact. The alternative to accepting advertising is to charge doctors a subscription fee, and each time this is suggested, it is rejected. When Dr. William R. Barclay became editor of the AMA *Journal,* he persuaded the board of trustees that it should be published without ads, and one advertisement-free edition was printed. "Much to my embarrassment," Barclay later recalled, "I got exactly forty subscriptions to that *Journal,* including libraries, academia, and government, and I had to go back to the trustees and tell them I was going to shred several thousand dollars' worth of *Journal* that we had stocked and could not sell." Barclay added that he was surprised to find that the scientific community "does place some value on ads." Had Barclay looked a little deeper, he might also have found a pocketbook issue: doctors have become so accustomed to getting things free from drug companies that they would not willingly pay $15 or $20 a year for a magazine they expect for free.

The AMA has another motive in maintaining the status quo. Since advertising revenue accounts for up to 30 percent of the association's total income, the monies are used to help fund other AMA activities, including its heavy political contributions and the Washington lobbying efforts in protecting the special interests of organized medicine and not incidentally those of the drug companies.

By most standards, the scientific editorial content of the *Journal* and the other AMA publications is of the highest quality. It is the advertising content, which constitutes about 45 percent of the *Journal* and 30 to 40 percent of the specialty magazines, which raises eyebrows. Senator Gaylord Nelson, a Wisconsin Democrat, zeroed in on inaccurate and misleading ads in questioning Dr. James H. Sammons, executive vice-president of the AMA, during Senate hearings on the advertising and promotion of prescription drugs in late 1973. There occurred this exchange:

"Sen. Nelson: It would be nice if the AMA would review the ads they run for accuracy . . . because you run ads in the AMA *Journal* that are disgracefully inaccurate and the history of it is clear as a bell.

"Dr. Sammons: Senator, every single one of the words in those ads [has] to have FDA approval and if there is a long history of inaccuracy, I submit to you the FDA will have to share that responsibility with whoever is responsible.

"Sen. Nelson: They see the ad after it runs. Do not try to shift it to the FDA. You complain that they interfered in the medical practice and you throw the blame on them when they do not deserve it. The fact of the matter is, doctor, you have run ads for years that promoted very bad use of drugs and we have volumes that will prove that. [Nelson then cited ads in the *Journal* promoting Parke Davis's antibiotic Chloromycetin for general upper respiratory illness. Nelson noted that it was "well known among leaders of the profession" that Chloromycetin was being misused 90 to 99 percent of the time.]

"Dr. Sammons: Let me point out to you that the AMA was one of the first people to point out the potential harmful effects of Chloromycetin.

"Sen. Nelson: But the disgraceful part is, you pointed it out and continued to take the ads that promoted improper use of the drug, and I can demonstrate that to you.

"Dr. Sammons: Senator, Chloromycetin still has a place in the armamentarium in the practice of medicine.

"Sen. Nelson: That is kind of a nonstatement; but it is misused 90 to 99 percent of the time, and you took ads that promoted the misuse and I think it is disgraceful.

"Dr. Sammons: Hindsight is better than foresight."

However, it was not hindsight, as Nelson said, because the AMA had noted the dangers and misuse of the drug in editorial content and still continued to run the ads. The practice continues, and as one critic, Robert Seidenberg, charges, "Even *Good Housekeeping* and *Parents* magazine do better in protecting their reader-consumers from false and misleading advertising."

The American Psychiatric Association, like the AMA, is another organization heavily dependent on the drug companies for income. The APA, with 25,000 members, publishes two journals, the *American Journal of Psychiatry*, a scientific magazine, and *Psychiatric News*, a newspaper. In the fiscal year that ended March 30, 1976, the two grossed $994,000 in drug company advertising. After cost of publication, overhead, postage, and staff, the APA earned about $30,000 in profit. According to an APA survey, only about 15,000 of its 25,000 psychiatrist members are in full-time private practice, and 30 percent of them prescribe drugs only "in rare instances," leaving about 10,500 who regularly prescribe drugs. That means the drug companies are spending about $100 a year for ads in the APA journals for each psychiatrist who prescribes drugs in his practice. Either those 10,000 or so psychiatrists are writing a lot of prescriptions or the drug companies aren't getting their money's worth.

The APA created a committee to look into the possibility of eliminating ads in its professional journals at the urging of its California chapter, the largest in the APA. A spokesman estimated that the net loss to the association would be $500,000 a year if all drug support were eliminated, including the drug ads and the $70,000 a year the APA gets from drug companies in the form of direct grants and contributions to annual meetings. He said that 50 percent of the pages in the two journals would be eliminated.

California psychiatrists banned drug ads in their publications, outgoing president Melvin Lipsett said, because "ads in journals influence the doctor's attitudes, and we want to be as objective as possible in deciding what's best for our patients. It also was the use of gifts by the manufacturers that we felt had some influence on the doctors." This view, as we have demonstrated, is decidedly in the minority in the medical profession.

Dr. Donald Farnsworth, the retired director of health services at Harvard and a member of the 1974 presidential Commission on Marijuana and Drug Abuse, thinks the California APA approach "carries things farther than they need go." Farnsworth, a psychiatrist, finds it "only reasonable" that drug companies in their advertising put their best impression forward. "When any particular advertising becomes offensive or quite obviously inaccurate or dishonest, then I think it should be settled on its own merits rather than condemning companies per se."

Led by Hoffmann-La Roche, maker of Valium and Librium, ten companies account for about two-thirds of the dollar volume of journal advertising. Roche is by far the biggest advertiser of the lot, spending nearly twice as much as the second largest advertiser, Merck, Sharp & Dohme. According to IMS International, an auditing and survey firm that works for the drug industry, Roche spent $13,797,000 for journal advertising in 1977. The figure is believed to be conservative. Merck spent $7,432,000, and Ayerst spent $7,235,000. Without question, the most heavily advertised drug is Valium. It's a rare medical publication that does not include a two- or three-page ad for the popular Roche tranquilizer.

As the *New York Times*'s experience with its sister medical publications demonstrates, the concentration of economic power gives a handful of companies an effective weapon should they choose to use it. Publishers of the major medical journals said, however, that they have not felt any drug company pressure to alter or slant editorial content. But all were aware that economic sanctions were a weapon that hangs over their heads.

"It's the old story," said Thomas Hannon, publisher of the AMA's journals and an AMA vice-president. "You've got your eggs in a very few baskets in this business, and that can be mighty risky." Hannon, who joined the AMA after a career in industrial publications, was quick to add that the AMA has not been subjected to editorial pressure from the drug companies in his experience. "The fact is, there is less of that in this field, in my view, than in any field I've been associated with before."

The *New England Journal of Medicine,* the oldest and most prestigious of U.S. medical journals, is not bothered by advertising pressure, but Milton Page, its longtime business manager, knows it exists. The *New England Journal of Medicine* receives about 50 percent of its income from display drug ads but keeps the ads physically separated from editorial content. A reader who does not want to see the ads can yank the middle section from any edition and have a complete magazine with all editorial content intact but free of drug pitches. "Advertisers want ads scattered throughout editorial material for better visibility, but we won't do this, despite some pressure from advertisers. We have lost some space but prefer to maintain our policy," Page explained. The practice of keeping ads completely separate from editorial content, once the rule in medical publications, now is the rare exception.

Page said that while economic pressure from drug advertisers may not be a problem for the *Journal of Medicine* and other respected journals, "it can be a real problem for some of the smaller publications. They have to kowtow to advertisers."

A publisher of an independent and respected scientific journal who was moderately critical of some drug company ads thought better of his remarks and asked not to be quoted or named for publication. He said he had a wife and children to support.

Dr. Charlotte H. Kerr, president of the American Medical Women's Association, expressed concern in an interview about the way women are portrayed in ads—never as doctors and always as patients or nurses—and then added, "We don't want to knock pharmaceutical houses because we can't afford to lose their support."

Another example of the powerful influence of the drug companies is that doctors do not even pay for their own conventions. The AMA, which holds two meetings a year, relies on drug companies and other medical suppliers to underwrite the cost of its week-long gatherings. According to the Convention Guide for the Health Exhibits Association, the AMA receives about $2 million from these suppliers from exhibit rental space at each convention. Drug companies are the biggest purchasers. "We have not been particularly successful in securing any support from other health suppliers," according to Thomas Carroll, director of the AMA convention marketing department. "It takes all our time to maintain a liaison with the pharmaceutical industry, and that's where the big bucks are."

Carroll said that despite the fact that exhibit space income does not offset the entire cost of a typical AMA convention, doctor members still are not charged a registration fee. To charge doctors would, he said, be "inappropriate. If they pay dues to the AMA, the last thing they want is to pay registration. It would cut registration drastically if the AMA charged its members."

The 1978 AMA summer convention in St. Louis, which most doctors attending recall notably because President Carter delivered a speech questioning their commitment to health care as a group, was typical in many ways. Of the fifty-five continuing education courses, not one program offered a refresher course in pharmacology. However, "public speaking" and "effective medical writing" were offered.

Across a foyer from the conference rooms where medical experts conducted seminars, pharmaceutical information was readily available in the exhibition hall, all paid for by drug companies: Eli Lilly, Pfizer, Parke, Davis, A. H. Robins, Abbott, Ayerst, Upjohn, Squibb, Searle, Sandoz, Ortho, and many others.

Many of the 2,200 doctors and 5,000 other health care professionals attending the convention strolled through the exhibition hall past the costly and eye-catching displays that carried out with consistency the advertising themes in print and broadcast media.

Standing at the Pfizer display for Sinequan, detail man Mike Kraft said his presence at the convention was "an ego trip. Back in my district I have to go to the doctor and hope he'll take a minute or two to see me. That's if I can get past his nurse. Here the doctor comes to me. And I might get four or five minutes with him."

A person identified with an *M.D.* on his name tag could hardly pass by a medical salesman who sought customers with the enthusiasm of a carnival huckster. "Doc, you look like a man who could use a new stethoscope," the salesman said, approaching a man with an *M.D.* on his tag. The doctor shyly agreed to try on the instrument.

A young drug salesman at the A. H. Robins booth watched the scene and scorned the stethoscope peddler's approach. "Dignity is important with doctors," he said. "Even if they are at a convention, doctors are a serious bunch. We don't act like car salesmen."

The Robins salesman had just filled out an order card for drug samples. The doctor, who asked that the samples be sent to her office, had walked a few steps before she turned and called back, "I almost forgot. Would you add some Robitussin?"

The salesman assured her he would. "We must give away barrels and tons of the stuff," the man said of the request for Robitussin, a cough syrup.

Often doctors hustle drug companies. This is especially true in the case of free samples. Despite the fact that since the congressional hearings most companies have stopped the practice of handing out free pills except upon written request, the drug companies still give away some 2 billion pills annually to physicians. Hoffmann-La Roche was the first major drug company to prohibit the wholesale distribution of free samples, although it has made exceptions for competitive reasons. Roche will provide samples upon written request, and Alfred Zobel, the company's public relations director, said the company will supply a request even though it knows a doctor is using them for himself or members of his family. "A doctor has considerable influence over our future. If a doctor gets really mad at us, he can crucify us," Zobel explained. He said Roche would support a "complete legal prohibition" against free samples and other giveaways but is afraid to do it unilaterally because "all our competitors would cream us. We would be much happier if we didn't have to do these things."

The company is so flooded with requests for financing of gifts, medical conventions, medical programs, educational seminars, and the like that it has printed standard refusal cards to send back to the doctors. It's not unusual for a local medical society to call asking Roche to support some nonmedical function. "Some of the requests are, should I say, aggressive. They'll say, 'We're having a golf tournament, will you contribute the door prize?'" Zobel said. "We do draw the line."

But what's happened is that the line between doctor and drug supplier is so obscured by mutual self-interest that both sides use their clout over the other to the disadvantage of patients.

The financial dependence of the medical profession on the suppliers of drugs is unhealthy for patients, for doctors, and for society. The consumer pays through higher health care costs but, more important, through inadequate treatment, overmedication, and increased exposure to adverse reactions to drugs. For tens of thousands each year, the price will be prolonged and unnecessary hospitalization. For tens of thousands more, the price will be death. For millions, it will be drug addiction or habituation. The doctor pays the price for forfeiting his best medical judgment to the influence of his suppliers. The doctor gives the appearance of being bought and liking it. From medical school through retirement, the doctor accepts the financial support of his suppliers for everything from office trinkets to postgraduate education. With a median income of about $70,000 a year in the United States, should not doctors be expected to pay for some of the things they now so willingly accept from the drug companies? When asked in surveys if they would like to have more sources of objective information free of the systematic bias of manufacturers, doctors overwhelmingly say yes. When asked to pay for it out of their own pockets, they say no.

Drug companies give away black bags to medical students and color television sets to physicians in private practice, pay for medical conventions, buy advertising to support the journals, hand out billions of sample pills, underwrite research in universities, fund educational seminars and radio shows, and send thousands of salesmen into the field because they want to sell more drugs, increase their profit for stockholders, and have the resources to develop new drugs. No matter how noble and pious their intent, profit is the motive. Profit is not bad. In the free enterprise system it is good. What is bad is the excess that results from the unchecked hard sell, the blatant conflict of interest in which organized medicine places itself, and the pervasive influence of the makers of drugs in our health care. The medical profession has been oversold on the chemical solution, which is not to say drugs might not be the right treatment for many for a short time or for a few for a long time. The problem is that too many people are taking too many drugs for too long. This is particularly true of the drugs that change the mood or alter the mind.

There is no opportunity in the system for the other side. Drug companies do not buy ads to tell doctors *not* to prescribe drugs. They do not buy ads to push a nonchemical approach. No one buys ads or sends out salesmen to extol the virtues of marriage counseling for marital problems, family therapy for problems with the kids, group therapy for the lonely, church for the unfulfilled, music for the tense, a good diet for the tired, a long talk for the fearful, a walk for the restless, a run for the overweight, a new hobby for the retired, a vocation for the widow. . . .

The chemical solution is what's sold, and it's been bought.

The FDA: Your Friend or the Drug Industry's? 9

As we have shown, the prescription drug problem in the United States is widespread. We have seen drugs become the number one method of treatment for the number one ailment—mood changers for mood problems. From the delivery room to the classroom and from the doctor's office to the nursing home, we have seen psychoactive drugs provided to treat not the medical problems of the takers but rather the management problems of the givers. We have seen creation of a new class of addict—the prescription junkie—and we have seen poly addiction become commonplace. In our overmedicated society, we have seen the creation of a new health crisis, what scientists call iatrogenic illness, which simply is illness caused by doctors. We have shown how the medical profession's heavy reliance on psychoactive drugs has contributed to this problem, and we have shown how the drug industry has encouraged this medical dependence. Blame also must fall on the FDA, the government agency charged with the responsibility of protecting the public's health against unsafe and ineffective drugs but whose record shows instead a greater concern for the welfare of the drug industry.

This proindustry bias comes not out of malice but from an attitude that places more emphasis on friendly cooperation with the industry than on public advocacy. The effect of this within the agency itself is to make the public the adversary and the industry the friend. This friendly working relationship between the FDA and the drug companies works well for the industry, as the following statement by C. Joseph Stetler, president of the Pharmaceutical Manufacturers Association, testifies: "As I look back over three or four years, we have commented on 60 different proposed regulations. At least a third were never published in final form. And every one, without exception, picked up a significant part of our suggestions."

Stetler, who made the statement in an interview with the editors of *Advertising Age* in 1978, also told of a series of private meetings between representatives of the drug companies and FDA officials to discuss mutual problems. Stetler said the meetings "attract a lot of people from the FDA. But they are not open to the press." Stetler added that the FDA personnel within "the confines of those meetings" will admit that the drug companies "probably understand them better than anyone else and are a big help to them."

Unfortunately the public does not have an equal voice in the FDA. On the contrary, we will show how the professionals within and without the agency who attempt to take an advocacy position in favor of the public and a more adversarial position in their dealings with the industry are systematically silenced.

Dr. Frances Norris was one such voice. At a Senate hearing in 1977, Dr. Norris blew the whistle on the FDA's manipulation of an advisory panel to get it to take a less restrictive position on OTC daytime sedatives and sleep aids. Although still listed as a member of the panel, Dr. Norris hasn't been asked to participate in any of its activities since she disclosed the FDA pressure to allow the drugs to remain on the market for further study rather than ban them immediately as the majority of the panel recommended. "Why haven't I been asked to participate?" she asks rhetorically. "Very likely I am considered inconsonant with the FDA's point of view." At the time of her public criticism of the FDA, Dr. Norris was also a member of an advisory panel on medical and neurological devices. The FDA sent her a letter saying that the committee had been disbanded, a favorite tactic used by the agency to get rid of disagreeable members.

Dr. Mary Howell is another public advocate who has been

silenced. In 1973 she was appointed to the FDA's key Neuropharmacology Advisory Committee, the group of outside experts whose recommendations on tranquilizers and other psychoactive drugs are influential in determining what drugs are approved, how they are used, and how they are controlled. Dr. Howell argued strongly for a highly restrictive warning on Valium and other tranquilizers, which she considers a "public health menace." Dr. Howell ran up against two powerful biases. She recalls the experience:

"As far as I could figure out, there were a lot of people on that committee that I would call drug company people—that is, people who received a lot of money from drug companies for research. Also, because I was the only woman, I think I viewed the whole problem differently—because women are the real victims of these drugs—than the men on the committee. So the committee did what almost any committee does when it really does not want to face an issue: they formed a subcommittee to study my suggestion, and that's the last I heard of it." Dr. Mary Howell did hear from the FDA, however. About a year after being asked to join the committee and while her proposal still was before the committee, she received a letter from the agency "thanking me very much for my service. I remember getting the letter and being utterly astonished because I had this memorandum pending. My feeling was that I was appointed in the first place as the token pediatrician and the token woman, and they had no further need for me and were particularly offended by my point of view." When she asked Dr. Tom Hayes, chief of the Neuropharmacology Division of the FDA, why she had been dropped from the panel, Hayes told her that members serve for only one year, which is not true of most FDA advisory panels and committees.

In addition to being concerned about Valium and other tranquilizers, Dr. Howell was one of the few members of the neuropharmacology committee to express skepticism about an application to market Cylert, a new drug developed by Abbott Laboratories for hyperactive children. Also a member of the committee at the time was Dr. Donald Klein, a New York psychiatrist who was on Abbott's payroll as a consultant for Cylert. Klein remained a member of the committee as a member or consultant long after Dr. Howell was told her services were no longer needed.

The controversy over Cylert, a stimulant, also resulted in the FDA's dismissal of the entire panel of outside experts hired by the agency to review the safety and effectiveness of the new drug and the forced resignation of a highly qualified FDA staff drug reviewer, Dr. Carol S. Kennedy, who was responsible for the examination of all psychoactive drugs proposed for use in children. A child psychiatrist, Dr. Kennedy had a reputation as a meticulous researcher and as a physician deeply sensitive to health issues and drugs affecting children. Dr. Kennedy and the panel of outside experts assigned to Cylert found serious flaws in Abbott's main supporting study and recommended that the application to market the drug be denied.

During 1970–73, the peak period for the diagnosis of hyperactivity and the meaningless ailment referred to as minimal brain dysfunction, Abbott was anxious to get its drug on the market to cash in on the boom being enjoyed by Ritalin. Under pressure from Abbott, the FDA dismissed the panel of outside experts and appointed a new one composed of doctors more sympathetic to Cylert and drug therapy in general. Dr. Kennedy was summarily taken off the Cylert case and assigned to review soft contact lenses, despite her argument that it made no sense to have a child psychiatrist whose specialty was psychoactive drugs evaluating contact lenses.

After four months, Dr. Kennedy applied under Civil Service rules to return to the Neuropharmacological Division and was reluctantly taken back. Once again she was assigned outside her specialty, being asked to review drugs for nausea, vertigo, and migraine headaches. A day after her return to neuropharmacology, Dr. Alice Campbell, another psychiatrist, who was a friend of Dr. Kennedy's and who also took a firm show-me approach to drug applications, was transferred without prior notice to the Methadone Monitoring Division, where she reported making "no decision or recommendation which required specialized psychiatric knowledge or abilities" in the year she was there.

In the spring of 1974 Dr. Kennedy resigned from the FDA and joined the Social Security Administration. Although she had been officially evaluated by FDA superiors as an "excellent" or "superior" drug reviewer, she was told by her new superior at Social Security that she had been labeled a "troublemaker" in an evaluation that followed her to the new job. The memorandum transferring her to Social Security, which presumably carried the negative rating, mysteriously disappeared from the files after the matter was turned over to independent investigators.

The drug industry was cheered by the transfers of Drs. Kennedy and Campbell and others who shared their views from key drug-reviewing positions. The two psychiatrists were called "problem children" in a drug-industry newsletter, the *Pink Sheet*, which circulates in Washington. The *Pink Sheet* also derisively referred to them and other drug reviewers who took an adversarial approach to the industry as "conscientious objectors." Within the agency itself, Drs. Kennedy and Campbell and other "conscientious objectors" were referred to by their superiors, including Dr. J. Richard Crout, the director of the Bureau of Drugs, as "hypercritical" or "nit-picking" of drug applications and the industry. Dr. Kennedy prefers to refer to herself as "guarded," "formal," or "at arm's length" in her approach to the industry, and Dr. Eric Denhoff, described as probably "the most pro-medication member" of the first Cylert review panel, has high words of praise for her dedication. "It became evident that I was working with one of the last Joan of Arcs, and I say that with respect," Dr. Denhoff said of Dr. Kennedy. "She went into everything meticulously, into the records in great detail. . . . She's just the kind of person you need in Washington, obstreperous as she might have been."

Dr. Kennedy is still in Washington, but she was driven out of her position with the FDA, where she performed as a watchdog to prevent unsafe or ineffective drugs from reaching the market for use on children. On July 26, 1974, a few months after she left the FDA, the agency approved Cylert, which studies showed was only minimally better than a placebo in the treatment of hyperactivity. It is on the market today.

Many like-minded FDA doctors and drug reviewers also have been hounded out of the agency by an administration that takes a more benign or "cooperative" view toward the drug industry than the "guarded" or "arm's length" approach favored by Dr. Kennedy and the others. On August 15, 1974, eleven professional FDA drug reviewers testified before a Senate subcommittee hearing conducted by Senator Edward Kennedy about pressure and harassment from superiors whenever they challenged a drug company, a drug application, and the supporting studies. The thrust of their allegations was that FDA's top management had a pro-industry bias, to the public's harm. Senator Kennedy summed up the "startling, alarming" testimony of the eleven witnesses this way:

"That their recommendations to approve new drugs have never been questioned, but their recommendations to disapprove drugs were almost always questioned.

"That their efforts to disapprove drugs resulted in repeated harassment from FDA officials—that files were altered or modified.

"That industry pressure apparently influenced the drug review process.

"That they were all, at one time or another, removed from the review process after recommending disapproval.

"That they were all transferred out of their divisions, pursuant to efforts to get specific drugs approved."

One of those drug reviewers who testified was Dr. Robert Knox, who joined the FDA in 1963 and quickly established himself as a highly competent authority on diet pills but also as a member "of the school which is critical of industry and its submissions." Dr. Knox was transferred from the review panel of anorectic, or antiobesity, drugs as the result of pressure from the A. H. Robins Company, which alleged that he was blocking its application for approval of a new drug, Pondimin, the brand name for fenfluramine. Unlike most diet pills, Pondimin is a depressant rather than a stimulant, and the company submitted its data for approval on March 3, 1967. Robins was anxious for quick approval to take maximum advantage of the profitable business in weight-reducing drugs, but Dr. Knox felt the supporting studies offered by the company were flawed, and he was instrumental in having the drug application denied. Although Pondimin was being recommended as an anorectic, Dr. Knox could not find anything in the studies about weight loss. "This was a drug for obesity, and I felt this was a glaring requirement that had been overlooked," he told the Kennedy committee. "I believe subsequently the review was altered to include something about weight loss." A subsequent investigation of the Pondimin affair substantiated that A. H. Robins complained to Dr. Knox's superiors after he denied the drug application a second time. According to the record, the drug company officials either directly or indirectly asked that Knox be removed from the review. Dr. Knox was removed, and a more sympathetic officer assigned to the drug ultimately approved it without examining the raw clinical data. In the meantime, Dr. Knox had disapproved an application for Voranil, a stimulant antiobesity drug developed by Ciba-Geigy and now marketed by USV Laboratories. He also was overruled on this application, and the drug was approved. Dr. Knox was transferred out of the division after being overruled on the second drug. The transfer also effectively got him out of the way of a general FDA review of all anorectic drugs because, as he later told independent investigators, "I was considered a potential obstacle to a plan to appease industry, which was to be implemented by being unduly lenient in approving anorectic drugs." Whether Dr. Knox's allegation is true or false, the scenario did, in fact, occur as he said it did.

Despite the general consensus that amphetamines were of little or no value in weight reduction and were potentially highly dangerous, as the medical literature clearly showed, the advisory panel on anorectics approved them for use as diet pills. The panel did so despite its own finding that the weight loss in short-term clinical tests was "only a fraction of a point a week"—or "clinically trivial." The panel also noted their potential for abuse and their addictive character. The amphetamines are known as speed on the streets and long have been a drug of heavy abuse.

Dr. Charles Edwards, FDA commissioner at the time of approval of the diet pills in 1972, later defended his action even though he himself felt the "harm done was greater than the benefit."

Despite the evidence of their dangers and ineffectiveness and without long-term studies as to their effects, the FDA found the drugs of value in the treatment of obesity. The FDA did, however, require labeling, noting that the effectiveness was "clinically limited." The wording on the label was changed at the last minute from "clinically trivial" to "clinically limited" because the FDA felt the latter was less humiliating. Whether this wording change was for the benefit of the FDA or the makers of diet pills is not clear, although it is apparent the FDA has been embarrassed by its kid-glove treatment of the manufacturers of the highly abused amphetamines. With tacit approval of the FDA that use of diet pills was valid, pill-pushing doctors throughout the nation charged ahead with fat factories that were little more than assembly lines for speed. In one case in New York, two doctors, Martin Turetsky and Philip Datlof, supplied 700 patients a week with liquid amphetamines without medical supervision, according to a suit filed by the Justice Department. Because of widespread abuses, the states of Maryland, New Jersey, and Wisconsin have banned the use of amphetamines for weight control.

Dr. Crout, the director of the Bureau of Drugs, defends the approval of the anorectics on the ground that the 1962 amendments to the Food, Drug and Cosmetic Act obligate the agency to approve drugs even though their effectiveness is only "statistically different from placebo." To that line of reasoning, critics of the FDA, such as Dr. Mary Howell, say not entirely without seriousness that when the difference in efficacy between a drug and a placebo is only slightly in favor of the drug, the public interest would be served by rejecting the drug and approving the placebo.

The debate over safety and effectiveness standards focuses, better than any other issue, the division between the FDA and its critics. The Cylert case is a good example. Aside from flaws in the study on the drug, Dr. Carol S. Kennedy, the FDA reviewer in charge of the application to market the drug for treatment of hyperactivity in children, was concerned about putting another psychoactive drug for hyperactivity in use in the absence of any substantial proof that it was significantly effective. Dr. Howell, as a member of the Neuropharmacology Advisory Committee when the drug came before it for evaluation, shared this concern.

"One of the things I learned on that committee was the really sloppy jobs drug companies do with their research," Dr. Howell remembers. "We were constantly sending research back to the drug companies, telling them that their methodology was wrong, that their studies really were inconclusive. Yet the FDA accepts a lot of this research and approves a drug for marketing when it really has not been shown to do the job very well.

"A prime case of this is the research behind Cylert. We had a lot of research that showed that in a lot of cases Cylert was, say, sixty percent effective in treating X number of cases, while a placebo was fifty percent effective. Now, if there is that small bit of difference between a drug which has a lot of potentially harmful side effects and a placebo, which has none, why does the FDA allow the drug on the market? In my view, if the placebo did that good a job, we probably should have approved the placebo as a drug to treat that particular disorder."

Dr. Roger D. Freeman, a child psychiatrist at the University of British Columbia, also remembers the Cylert case. He was one of three members of an outside panel asked by the FDA to review Abbott Laboratories' application to market the drug in the lucrative hyperactivity therapy business. In addition to having reservations about the effectiveness of Cylert, the panel found a serious discrepancy in the major supporting study submitted by Abbott. The study had been done by Keith Connors, a psychologist who has specialized in testing drugs in children. The panel found that some of the test results for children being tested on the drug were listed in the raw data as having been performed during the summer but in the company summaries as being done during the school term. The test results would have been "impossible to obtain because school was out for the holiday," Dr. Freeman and the other two panelists pointed out to the FDA. To Freeman, it was a shocking experience. "I thought I was in sort of the middle of a Watergate thing," he later recalled in an interview. "It was a very different experience to review raw data and then read the papers based on [those] data."

What particularly alarmed Freeman and the others was that after the discrepancy, which Connors said was caused by clerical error, was brought to the attention of the FDA, it was disregarded, and subsequently the FDA dismissed the panel without explanation, created a new one, took Dr. Carol S. Kennedy off Cylert and put her on contact lenses, assigned a different reviewer to the drug, and ultimately gave its approval for marketing Cylert. As the Senate hearing record and a later FDA investigation show, Abbott was putting heavy and direct pressure on the FDA for quick approval. What the FDA did was change the reviewer, change the panel, and invite Abbott to try again. This time the FDA did not give the second panel the raw data which contained what Dr. Freeman later described as "a lot of things that disquieted" the first panel. Freeman also says the FDA told the panel that if it wanted a higher standard of research for new drug applications, "there wouldn't be any study." Freeman, for one, does not ever "wish to repeat" his experience with the FDA. Another member of the disbanded Cylert panel, Dr. Gerald Solomons, director of child development at the University of Iowa, calls it "one of the most frustrating, embarrassing, and depressing experiences I have ever had in my medical career."

In testimony before Senator Kennedy's committee in 1974, Dr. Solomons summed up the case against the FDA: "I believe that in cases where the disease or entity being treated is life-threatening, that these considerations should be weighed and perhaps be a little bit more flexible [in approving drugs].

"But in a case like this [Cylert] in which there was, first of all, controversy about the syndrome existing in scientific circles, and secondly the fact that long-term evaluation of the drug had not been really delineated and proved safe, that there was no great rush to get in on the market, because there were at least two other drugs that had been proved to some extent—and not completely—relatively safe, and relatively efficacious in certain circumstances.

"But the need here to rush it into marketing, if you like, or approval, to me seemed to serve the interests of the company rather than the interests of the children."

Originally, Dr. Solomons, Dr. Freeman, and the third member of the panel, Dr. Eric Denhoff, were asked by the FDA to draw up guidelines for clinical trials of psychoactive drugs for use on children. The panel wrote the guidelines, submitted them to the FDA, but never heard anything more about them, perhaps because of the strong cautionary statement in the preface: "The climate of times, the demands of the public and the potential for abuses of psychoactive drugs necessitate a protective and objective attitude on the part of the FDA in order to safeguard the development of children and youth in the United States."

The FDA, incidentally, also asked the American Academy of

Pediatrics to draw up guidelines for testing drugs in children, and the FDA has yet formally to accept and issue those, although the assignment was given in the early 1970s.

The FDA ignored the guidelines written by Freeman, Solomons, and Denhoff and refused even to discuss their draft with them. This is not an unusual method used by the FDA when confronted with sentiment or fact that goes against the pro-drug mood. Dr. Howell had a similar experience when she urged the FDA to adopt a tough new policy regarding the use of antidepressant and tranquilizing drugs.

Looking back on the warning she suggested to the FDA in a memorandum in 1974, while she was a member of its advisory panel on psychoactive drugs, Dr. Howell said, "At the time I was concerned that the long-term use of these drugs could lead to long-term health problems. I was—and still am—concerned that a lot of medical practitioners, as well as their patients, believe that anxiety and stress can be resolved by taking a pill."

Although conceding that short-term use of tranquilizers could be considered to combat "situationally induced psychic distress, when the drugs in question are known to be safe and effective," Dr. Howell believes frequent and long-term use of drugs like Valium mask the root underlying emotional problems and also "hide real physical problems." Arguing that the kind of treatment people really need "is the help of other people, not drugs," and warning that the tranquilizing of America had become "a public health menace," Dr. Howell urged the FDA to approve a new warning label for all tranquilizing and antidepressant drugs. Dr. Howell's proposed label read: "Long-term use of [this drug], in the absence of adjunctive measures to assist the patient to overcome the symptoms for which the drug is prescribed, is rarely in the best interests of the patient's optimal mental health. Adjunctive measures may be designed to help the patient cope with the situations causing psychic distress, or to change those situations, or both. They might include psychotherapy; occupational, educational, or marital counseling; self-help, peer counseling—or direct change in occupational, educational, or marital status."

This warning label, Dr. Howell contends, would have gone a long way toward changing the prescribing habits of the nation's physicians if only out of fear of being sued. "The prevailing standard of what constitutes malpractice in the prescribing of a drug is how closely a physician adheres to drug labeling," she explains. "Such a label would force the doctor to recommend the adjunctive treatment a person suffering from stress, depression, or anxiety really needs."

While Dr. Howell's proposed label was pending before the Neuropharmacological Advisory Committee, she was told without advance warning that her one-year term on the committee had expired and her services were no longer needed. She was surprised at being removed from the committee but not that her proposed warning was not given serious consideration by the FDA or other members of the committee. "I really did not expect this suggestion to be adopted by the committee. I think there is a lot of politics involved in the FDA and a lot of pressure from the drug companies." The committee, she said, was dominated by people who were there "representing not the public interest but rather the interest of the drug companies."

Dr. Thomas Hayes, chief of the psychopharmacology unit of the FDA, remembers Dr. Howell and her suggested warning and credits her with being the impetus behind the warning put on all the minor tranquilizers that their effectiveness in long-term use—beyond four months—had not been assessed. This bland warning added to the labels by the FDA to tranquilizers in 1977 is a far cry from the tougher, more restrictive one suggested by Dr. Howell. Dr. Hayes agrees that "there is plenty of evidence these drugs have been overprescribed and that their use should be controlled," but he does not believe Dr. Howell's suggestion for exploring changes in life situations is appropriate. "I don't think the Food and Drug Administration should be put into a position of requiring a drug company to propose divorce as a possible solution to the problems of life on a drug label," he said, missing the point that these are only "adjunctive" measures that can be and should be considered.

Pressure from women and consumer groups to get the FDA to control the prescription of tranquilizers more tightly heightened in early 1978, when Betty Ford entered a drug rehabilitation center for dual addition to alcohol and Valium, which doctors had prescribed for her pinched nerve. As one FDA insider remarked after the former first lady's disclosure, "the number of network camera crews crawling around the Parklawn Building [FDA headquarters in Rockville, Maryland] definitely has raised our consciousness."

On June 28, 1978, FDA Commissioner Donald Kennedy met with Ann Harrison Clark, legislative counsel for the National Consumers League, and promised, as Clark recalls it, swift and strong action to curtail the prescription of tranquilizers. "Don Kennedy sat down with me and promised me a professional bulletin would be sent out to all doctors warning them about the abuse potential of the tranquilizing drugs," Clark said in an interview. "Further, he assured me that the new labeling would go into effect—at the next printing of the *PDR* [*Physicians' Desk Reference*]—that would warn doctors that Valium and some of the other tranquilizing drugs were addictive." Clark came away from the meeting with the impression Kennedy was "genuinely concerned about the problems associated with tranquilizers, and this time I finally expected action."

But as 1978 closed, there was no further action by the FDA to restrict the prescription of tranquilizers or to warn doctors of their addictive nature. Clark views the delay in what she felt was a promise by the FDA to take swift action as another example of the powerful influence the drug companies have over the FDA. According to the nonverbatim minutes kept by the FDA of the meeting, "Commissioner Kennedy stated FDA shares her [Clark's] concern about the prescribing of minor tranquilizers, especially Valium and Librium," but cautioned her that the "regulatory handles on the problem aren't as clear as they might be and that sometimes one has to be a little thoughtful about the choice of which one to use." The minutes also show that "Dr. Kennedy reiterated the fact that there [are] scientific data showing that Valium produces physical and psychological dependence and that the label could be revised to make the warning more apparent and stronger if necessary. Another way would be to provide the health professionals with more information and perhaps remedial advertising, which would correct any false impression gathered from previous advertising."

Kennedy further promised the FDA "will look at any data about people getting hooked on lower dosages, thus causing an increase to higher dosages which leads to dependence and the withdrawal phenomena."

The labeling in effect in 1978 regarding the addiction question carefully skirts the issue of physical and psychological dependence on Valium, reflecting Hoffmann-La Roche's position that withdrawal is "limited to those patients who had received excessive doses over an extended period of time." Clark and others contend that dependence can occur at the therapeutic dose. If its past performance is a guide, the FDA could take several years to "inform physicians and others about possible side effects and the addictive potential of these drugs," as Kennedy promised the FDA would do through patient education and by "moving to revise physician labeling."

Although Miltown has been on the market since the mid-1950s and Librium and Valium since the early 1960s, it was not until 1976 that the FDA put a warning on these tranquilizers and others cautioning against their use by pregnant women. According to an internal FDA memorandum obtained by the authors, the FDA was aware as early as 1962 that Roche had not submitted evidence that Valium was safe and effective for use by pregnant women. In a document dated August 9, 1962, staff physician Matthew Ellenhorn noted that Roche had "inadequate data or laboratory work performed on pregnant women, effects on babies born or time of administration during pregnancy." Yet not until July 7, 1976, did the FDA finally issue a warning against the use of minor tranquilizers by pregnant women.

The FDA's Hayes defends the slow action, saying, "We have limitations in terms of statistical confidence. We have to look at relative degrees of risk; we have to see more information before we act. We have to have a certain kind of proof before we can take an action, and it took awhile to get that kind of proof linking these drugs with birth defects." Hayes also said that "some of that delay may have been due to the time it took to get the notice published in the *Federal Register*."

To this explanation, Dr. Mary Howell replied, "That's ridiculous. What Hayes is saying is that the population should be the test case for these drugs, and only when they have been proved dangerous in general use should the FDA act." Dr. Howell and many other physicians note that the delay was inexcusable since the use of tranquilizers by pregnant women is unnecessary, and therefore, any risk at all is a high price to pay. The FDA does acknowledge this point, and the warning required for Valium and other tranquilizers states: "Because use of these drugs is rarely a matter of urgency, their use during this period [first trimester of pregnancy] should almost always be avoided." But it took the FDA two decades to recognize this simple high-risk, low-benefit concept regarding drugs during pregnancy. For many thousands of children the warning comes too late, as the chapter on psychoactive drugs and birth defects of the body and mind demonstrates.

After the eleven FDA medical officers and the three members of the Cylert review panel testified before Senator Edward Kennedy in August 1974, Dr. Alexander Schmidt, then FDA commissioner, investigated the allegations of bias toward the drug industry and mistreatment of employees who complained of this pro-drug, pro-industry slant. In a long and defensive report, Schmidt gave the FDA a clean bill of health, saying he found no improper drug approvals, no bias toward drug approvals, no industry domination, no pattern of harassment, no pressure to approve drugs, no arbitrary reversal of anyone by anyone, no secret meetings, and no improper alteration of records. The investigation was repudiated by the eleven medical officers and a review panel from HEW, and in May 1976, over the objections of the chairman of the HEW review group a reinvestigation of the allegations was begun by an independent investigative panel led by Norman Dorsen, chairman of the New York University Law School. The investigation itself was conducted by Frank E. Schwelb, a former member of Richard Nixon's New York law firm of Mudge, Rose, Guthrie & Alexander, the firm that also represents Warner-Lambert. This disclosure was made by Schwelb himself at the outset, and his report gives every appearance of objectivity, although principals disagree.

Nonetheless, the Dorsen report goes out of its way to clear the FDA of pro-industry bias while providing ample evidence to the contrary, proving rather a pro-industry prejudice. The report states: "We found no industry domination of the Bureau of Drugs, or industry protection by the Bureau of the Agency." The report quickly adds, however, that the investigators "did find individual cases of improper dealings with drug companies."

On the question of transferring medical officers who took a more adversarial approach to the drug industry, the Dorsen report substantiates the charges made against the FDA by its critics, concluding: "We found a systematic pattern of involuntary transfers and other unfavorable actions against employees who were more adversarial towards industry than management was." The investigators said, "The evidence is more consistent with the conclusion that these employees and consultants were harassed than with the conclusion that they were not."

On the question of a bias toward drug approvals, the Dorsen panel said, "We found no bias towards drug approvals *as such* [emphasis added]. We found conduct in several cases from which a reviewer could reasonably infer that he should be more lenient towards drug applications."

The investigators, looking into the allegations of secret meetings between industry and FDA officials, said they found a number of cases of "inappropriate contacts and communications between FDA officials and industry."

The Dorsen panel said it made no attempt "to pass on the scientific merits of drug approvals" but found FDA officials inclined to approve drugs "on a minimal showing of efficacy, which *may not be compelled* [emphasis added]" by the Food, Drug and Cosmetic Act as amended in 1962.

To an admittedly biased observer, the Dorsen report's conclusions in individual instances establish, in their cumulative effect, proof of a pro-drug or pro-industry bias. But in its overall assessment of the FDA, the Dorsen committee exaggerates the charge to validate a claim of innocence. "The FDA is not a tool of industry, and does not deserve to be called one," the Dorsen committee states.

The charge against the FDA is not that it is a "tool of industry" but that it is strongly biased in favor of drug companies and drug therapy to the disadvantage of the consumer of prescription or nonprescription drugs. The agency's pro-drug bias clearly is substantiated by the Dorsen committee's 800-page document on the allegations that arose from the 1974 Senate hearings. The report does not ascribe evil, malicious, or self-serving motives to this bias toward the industry and drugs—nor do we—but rather describes it as a deliberate, sincere, and reasoned decision to cooperate with the drug industry and to interpret the law in a manner that gives maximum advantage to the industry. The FDA's management has taken a deliberate course of being "reasonable," "cooperative," and nonadversarial in its dealings with the industry. Within this context and with the rise of the consumer health movement, the consumer becomes the FDA's adversary and the drug industry its ally.

The medical science, academic, research, regulatory, promotion, marketing, and prescribing aspects of medicine have become so entwined with the drug industry that none of the parts can survive without drug company support. In an assessment more true today than it was when written for *Esquire* magazine in 1969, Dr. James Goddard, FDA commissioner from 1965 to 1968, said: "The Drug Establishment is a close-knit, self-perpetuating power structure consisting of drug manufacturers, government agencies and select members of the medical profession. There are connecting links between all of the Establishment's flanks, which keep it thriving and well-protected. And a yawning gulf of ignorance separates the whole Establishment from the public at large."

Many consider Goddard, who came to the FDA as a career administrator from the Public Health Service, the last consumer advocate to run the agency. Goddard had succeeded George P. Larrick, who was considered a "pal" of the drug industry by the *Wall Street Journal*. *Drug Trade News*, an industry journal, characterized Larrick's tenure at the FDA as "one of sweetness and light, togetherness, loving one's neighbor [industry] as one's self." Goddard very quickly changed that perception of the FDA with an abrupt and strong tilt toward the public. Goddard was openly hostile toward the drug industry, accusing drug companies of obscuring "the prime mission of their industry to help people get well," using long-dormant legal authority to seize drugs and threatening to restrict the use of drugs to specialists. Some say, however, he was soft on the food industry.

Goddard, an appointee under the Democratic administration of Lyndon Johnson, was succeeded in 1968 by Dr. Herbert Ley, Goddard's like-minded director of the Bureau of Medicine. With the election of Republican Richard M. Nixon, a close friend of Elmert Bobst, the president of Warner-Lambert, Ley's days were numbered. The drug industry *Pink Sheet,* which described Nixon as "a man of integrity," cheerfully predicted shortly after Nixon's election that "Goddard types won't last long in the Nixon administration." Dr. Ley's downfall was hastened by his effort to remove Panalba, an antibiotic combination of tetracycline and novobiocin, from the market after thousands of adverse reaction reports, including fatalities, and a condemning evaluation by the National Academy of Science. The manufacturer, Upjohn of Kalamazoo, Michigan, had known of these highly toxic reactions but had declined to reveal them to the FDA. The drug had been highly profitable for the Michigan company. When Dr. Ley told Upjohn he was withdrawing Panalba's certification as safe and effective and thus forcing immediate withdrawal of the drug from the market, company executives appealed to Ley's HEW superiors in the new Nixon administration. Ley was overruled and ordered to hold hearings before taking action. Ley also was told not to tell anyone about Upjohn's intervention, engineered by Republican Representative Garry Brown of Michigan, but the matter was leaked to a congressional committee, which demanded the files in the case. Afraid of political embarrassment so early in Nixon's first term, HEW officials reversed themselves, and Ley proceeded with decisive action against Upjohn. During Ley's brief tenure at the top of the FDA, he also incurred the wrath of the Nixon administration by the controversial ban on cyclamates on the basis of a study linking the sugar substitute to cancer.

By the end of 1969 Dr. Ley had been forced out of office and he would tell the *New York Times* of the "constant, tremendous, sometimes unmerciful pressure" he was subjected to by the drug industry. Ley subsequently made Nixon's White House enemies list.

The Nixon administration, with its close ties to the drug industry, now had a chance to change direction at the FDA. The agency's short-lived pro-consumer era had come to a close after only four years. Named to succeed Ley was Dr. Charles Edwards, a bona fide member of what Goddard might call the Drug Establishment. He had served for five years in an administrative post with the AMA and four years with the powerful hospital and medical consulting firm of Booz, Allen & Hamilton. Edwards made it clear that he would lead the FDA "more in a direction of working with industry," and he picked agreeable assistants who shared this philosophy. Peter Hutt, a partner in the drug industry law firm of Covington & Burling, was named chief counsel, and Dr. Henry Simmons, who also had been with Booz, Allen & Hamilton, was appointed director of the Bureau of Drugs. Dr. Marion Finkel, who had worked for Merck, a major drug company, before joining the FDA in 1963, was appointed Simmons's assistant. Dr. George Leong, a radiologist who was recruited for HEW by a stockbroker active in GOP politics, transferred to the FDA as a special assistant to Simmons to study the drug application process. Dr. J. Richard Crout, who had been in academic medicine, joined the Edwards team at the FDA in 1971, eventually succeeded Simmons as director of the Bureau of Drugs in 1973, and continued in the position through 1978. The Dorsen report describes Dr. Crout as holding "a philosophy or a view of the law and the drug review process which is substantially more permissive vis-à-vis the medical profession and the pharmaceutical industry than the view held by Congressional and other critics."

But it was Dr. Leong's evaluation of the new drug application process that set the tone for the new FDA administration, although the Dorsen panel believes that "it is a reasonable inference that what he wrote was what his superiors [Simmons and Edwards] told him." What Leong did was turn the agency's legal mandate around, saying: "The *primary role* of the bureau of drugs in the Food and Drug Administration is to *assure the American public of the availability of safe and efficacious* new drugs without undue time delays." The Food, Drug and Cosmetic Act puts the emphasis quite differently, mandating the FDA to "the *protection of the public* from products *not proven to be safe and effective* for their alleged uses . . . [emphasis added]."

To those within the FDA who felt their responsibility was first and foremost the protection of the public against dangerous and ineffective drugs, Leong's new definition of responsibility, putting primary emphasis on approval of new drugs, smacked of a sellout to the drug industry and confirmed their worst fears about the new FDA administration. However Leong was viewed by the small but vocal cadre of public advocates with the agency, he was respected, praised, and promoted by his superior, Henry Simmons.

The Dorsen investigation confirms—but its report does not condemn—this pro-drug, pro-industry bias on the part of the FDA. The investigation also substantiates the allegations that the FDA's pro-industry hierarchy, having once set its course, deliberately and with sinister, underhanded methods removed and dispersed the medical officers within the FDA who disagreed and were in positions to block drug approvals.

In its characteristically schizoid manner, the Dorsen committee said it was not able to substantiate the "charge of industry domination" but then went on in the next sentences to supply support for the allegation. The report states: "The evidence does show, however, that FDA has been managed, during the period in question, by individuals who have made a conscious determination that the agency shall be cooperative with, rather than adversarial towards, the pharmaceutical industry. With that decision firmly made, management asserted control over a group of medical officers whose approach to industry was more adversarial in a manner which could aptly be described as 'political hardball.' The dissenters were effectively suppressed, primarily by resort to involuntary transfers. Moreover, management's execution of this policy was often untruthful, usually unkind, sometimes unlawful, and consistently unprofessional."

In every instance the investigators found that medical officers, all of whom were career civil servants with modest to excellent job performance ratings, who took a meticulous or "guarded" approach to the approval of new drugs and the monitoring of ones already on the market were removed from their responsibilities when they clashed with management's "cooperative" approach to the drug industry. Basically, the dissidents believed that in the approval of drugs the risks should be weighed heavily against benefits and that the emphasis given one or the other should depend on the seriousness of the malady for which the drug is intended.

One of the medical officers banished from a key drug review position and involuntarily placed in a position with no duties was Dr. John O. Nestor, who had joined the FDA in 1961. He had come to the FDA from private practice and with a personal experience that helped form his "inherently adversary" philosophy toward drug companies. In 1960 Nestor had suffered swellings and burns from an antibiotic; he learned later that the drug's toxicity was known to the manufacturer and the FDA but that no warning had been required on the drug's label. Dr. Nestor is direct, outspoken, and candid in expressing his distrust of the drug industry and the FDA's subservience to it. He has "never found an honest drug company" and believes the industry "has controlled the agency from the beginning up to this day [early 1979]" because the drug companies and the medical establishment have been able "to block anybody as commissioner or [division or bureau] director they don't want." He includes Goddard and Ley, considered anti-industry by the industry, in this indictment. In the view of FDA management, Nestor is a "troublemaker," a "nit-picker," "anti-industry," and, as one superior put it, "obstreperous, obstructive, and disruptive." This latter description came from Dr. George Leong, who came to the FDA as a result of the backing of a Nixon campaign contributor. Nestor, although considered highly competent as a drug reviewer, was constantly in conflict with his superiors, who disagreed with his more adversarial philosophy toward the industry and new drug applications. He was constantly being shuffled around the agency, presumably to get him to resign. One day in 1963 he returned to his office from grand jury duty to find "my office empty, my furniture gone. I found out that I had been transferred to a completely different branch of the division, without being informed or consulted."

Dr. Nestor's views clashed immediately with the new FDA management team of Edwards, Simmons, and Leong, who wanted to be more cooperative with industry. The drug companies were complaining about Nestor, then a drug reviewer in the Cardiorenal Division. In 1972, in violation of Civil Service procedures, Nestor was given a no-duty job in compliance. The Dorsen investigation vindicated Dr. Nestor's view of events and recommended that he be given a formal letter of apology and an opportunity to return to the Cardiorenal Division or be allowed to negotiate an alternative solution. Six months after the Dorsen report was issued in April 1977, Nestor still had not received the apology or the transfer back to his old job, and his efforts to meet with the new FDA commissioner, Donald Kennedy, were ignored. Finally, Nestor threatened Dr. Kennedy with legal action, and Nestor was put back into his drug-reviewing job after six years in a position with no duties.

During the period of banishment, Nestor had the last laugh. "I was put in an empty job. The only medical stuff I got was trivial 'Here, Dr. Nestor, return this man's Band-Aids. They're dirty.' They thought they had gotten me out of the way, but they made a serious mistake. I kept myself busy searching files, using duplicating machines. I was busier than hell supplying information as to what was going on to consumer groups, reporters, the investigators. The public got its money's worth out of me because of the skulduggery I was involved in."

In his interview with the authors, Dr. Nestor said the Dorsen investigation was better than he expected but less than he hoped for. Although the final report and the three volumes of information it is based on vindicate Nestor and the other medical officers who testified before the Senate committee about the strong industry bias of the FDA, Nestor feels the authors of the final conclusions "bent over backwards to say there was no undue influence of industry, when that is what the whole thing screams. I think it was the establishment protecting itself again."

Many critics believe the FDA takes a soft approach with the drug industry because many of its senior administrators eventually hope to win jobs in the industry. There is, in fact, a revolving-door practice between the agency and the industry. When Dr. Edwards, who came to the FDA from the AMA and the medical think tank of Booz, Allen & Hamilton, left the FDA as commissioner, he went over to HEW for a brief time and then joined a major surgical supply house as a vice-president. When he left HEW, he declared that he saw no conflict of interest in the fact that as FDA commissioner he had established and directed a review panel on surgical devices, to which Nestor commented: "That was as phony as a three-dollar bill. Jesus Christ, he set it up. How could he say there was no conflict of interest?"

Dr. Simmons, who also came to the FDA from Booz, Allen & Hamilton, joined the medical advertising department of J. Walter Thompson when he left the FDA. The Dorsen panel accused

Simmons of perjury in connection with its investigation and recommended that the Justice Department consider criminal proceedings.

When Dr. Leong left the agency, he became a consultant to
several drug companies. Chief Counsel Peter Hutt returned to
his drug industry law firm. Dr. Theodore Cooper, who was undersecretary for health at HEW, became dean of the Cornell Medical
School and in 1978 directed a consumer and doctor educational
campaign for Hoffmann-La Roche on the "Consequences of
Stress," which many viewed as more promotional than educational. The director of public affairs, James T. Walden, left the
FDA in 1978 to become director of public affairs for the Proprietary Association, which is the Washington lobby for the
over-the-counter industry. These are just a few of the more recent
high-level FDA officers who accepted industry jobs. It also must
be noted that Joseph A. Califano, Jr., appointed HEW secretary
by President Carter, was Hoffmann-La Roche's lobbyist and
lawyer during a sensitive period of proposed legislative and regulatory tightening of controls on Valium and other drugs. Califano,
who had served in the Johnson administration, played a major
role in keeping Valium and Librium out of tighter drug controls.

The Dorsen panel also waffled on this issue, saying it draws
"no sinister inference from the fact alone that officials came from
or went to regulated industry (or even both)" and then adds:
"It is worth noting, however, that while a significant number of
FDA officials have been exposed to the concerns of regulated
industry by working for it, few, if any, have been involved with
consumer groups or perceived the issues from their perspective."

Washington, D.C., is occupationally incestuous, and regulated
industries have a way of silencing their critics by putting them
on the payroll. One of those who had no difficulty resisting the
temptations of big money was Ben Gordon, an economist who
retired in 1978 after twenty years as a thorn in the drug industry's
side as a special assistant to the Senate Subcommittee on Monopoly and Anticompetitive Practices. Working the first ten years
with Senator Russell Long and the last ten with Senator Gaylord
Nelson, Gordon organized and directed many of the congressional hearings that revealed abuses not only by the drug industry but also by the FDA and the medical profession. When word

got out that he was retiring, Gordon received an invitation to lunch from a major Madison Avenue public relations firm specializing in medical and drug company sales and promotion. "They hired a separate room," Gordon recalls. "There were six guys. They said they represented a lot of drug companies, and a lot of drug company executives don't know how to deal with government. I asked them what they would expect from me. They said to prepare their testimony, brief them, support them. I said, 'You've got the wrong guy.'"

Gordon joined the consumer health movement, going to work for Ralph Nader's Health Research Group for a lot less money but more satisfaction. He does not hide his loathing for the drug industry. "If I was working for government, I wouldn't be able to call these guys son of a bitches and bastards, as I do now. Once I found out what I was dealing with, it was impossible not to be biased. I *am* biased for the public," Gordon says. Asked what he had learned in twenty years of investigating the industry, Gordon said, "They have done some good work but they exaggerate, and they are about the sleaziest industry that I've come across, and you can quote me on that."

Gordon believes one reason the FDA "takes so damn long" to take an ineffective or unsafe drug off the market is that there "is so damn much money involved" and the public does not have a counterbalancing economic tool. "Not too long ago I met a guy on the street who works for one of the pharmaceutical companies, and he told me one of the tactics used to keep the FDA helpless is simply by going into court at the slightest provocation and suing the hell out of them," Gordon said. The FDA with only about forty-three lawyers on its staff knows this and, in order to husband its legal resources, prefers to take a more cautious regulatory approach, thus delaying action that might be in the public interest but avoiding another court battle.

This approach is backfiring on the FDA today. With the rise of the consumer movement, the FDA now gets it from both sides. It knows that if it moves too fast, the agency will be sued by the drug industry, but if it moves too slowly, it sometimes will be sued by a consumer group. That's exactly what happened when the FDA decided to avoid litigation with OTC manufacturers by giving them more time under a study category to prove their drugs safe and effective under the 1962 law. The Health Research Group felt that fifteen years was long enough and took the FDA to court. But once again it is an unequal battle that pits the zealous but impoverished consumer groups against one of the richest industries in the world.

According to *Fortune* magazine, the pharmaceutical industry ranks as the second most profitable industry in the country with a median return of 8.5 percent on sales, slightly less than oil and mining companies. The drug companies rank second highest (behind broadcast and motion-picture companies) in stockholders' equity, showing a whopping return of 16.7 percent. By comparison, General Motors showed only a 6.1 percent return on sales of $55 billion in 1977, a return easily eclipsed by most drug houses. American Home Products, which markets both prescription and nonprescription drugs, had a 29.5 percent return on stockholders' equity and an 11.4 percent return on sales of $2.3 billion in 1977. Standard and Poors Corporation, an investment research and reporting firm, calls the drug industry "one of the most profitable in the United States despite its high degree of regulation." The key to this profitability, according to Standard and Poors and most other financial analysts, "lies in the development of patent-protected drugs."

Under the law, drug companies are given a seventeen-year patent on new drugs, meaning they have an open field to market without competition for seventeen years. This is the reason why Librium and Valium have been so profitable for Hoffmann-La Roche, a privately held Swiss company, that its privately traded stock goes for $40,000 a share. "How profitable are Valium and Librium?" asks Ronald Nordmann, vice-president for investment research at Blyth Eastman Dillon. "Well, how would you like twenty-five cents from every man, woman, and child in this country this year? That's what Roche's profits come out to on a per capita basis." He estimates that Roche's overlapping franchises on Valium and Librium earned Roche more than half a billion dollars from 1963 to 1977. To give some indication of how profitable the market is in psychoactive drugs, drugs acting on the central nervous system accounted for 28.6 percent of all prescriptions—or $2 billion out of $8 billion—in 1976, and this ratio has been maintained for several years. Because these drugs are so profitable and because the market is so large, most of the research dollar goes back into finding new psychoactive drugs.

The hottest new drug on the U.S. market in the late 1970s is Inderal, a new class of drug called a beta blocker, approved for use by the FDA for hypertension but used in Europe as a tranquilizer. The drug is marketed by Ayerst Labs, a division of American Home, and the company is anxious to get approval from the FDA to promote it for its antianxiety effects, although it already is being prescribed by some doctors as a tranquilizer. While the FDA will not allow Ayerst to promote the drug as a tranquilizer until it approves the drug for this indication, it has interpreted the law in such a way so that it permits doctors so to prescribe it without interference. Dr. Daniel Crane, the chief clinical investigator for Ayerst on Inderal, says it is a better tranquilizer than Valium because it does not produce a euphoric effect and thus is not prone to abuse. With considerable overstatement, he calls Inderal the "greatest thing since sliced bread."

The "greatest thing since sliced bread" has a long list of serious adverse reactions, including (to name just one) congestive heart failure.

Dollar sales curves for Inderal have been stunning in Wall Street's eyes. The drug brought in $46 million in 1976 and jumped 63 percent in 1977 to sales of $75 million. Analyst Nordmann expects the drug to have a minimum growth rate of 20 percent over the next five years on its hypertension indication alone. If the FDA approves it as a tranquilizer, the sales are expected to soar even higher.

The drug industry acknowledges its profits are high but says they are in a high-risk business and pour large sums back into research. The companies claim it takes about $50 million and seven to ten years to bring a new drug to market. Their assertion that most of the revenue goes back into research is disputed by most authorities, who claim that most of the receipts are used for advertising, promotion, and sales. The estimates for advertising and promotion, when expenditures for underwriting physician education are included, range from 20 to 25 percent. By contrast, the research budgets are estimated at between 10 and 20 percent of sales.

In 1977 the FDA submitted for congressional consideration a

sweeping change in the Food, Drug and Cosmetic Act that would cut the patent life of drugs from seventeen years to five and make a drug company's research data available for public inspection. Under the old law, the studies are considered trade secrets and are held confidential until a patent expires. FDA Commissioner Kennedy believes the shorter patent life will cut costs, spur research, and benefit both consumers and drug companies. The bill is vigorously opposed by the industry, got little consideration in Congress in 1978, and was expected to get the same treatment in 1979 and beyond.

Considering the past history, one cannot be encouraged that the FDA, or for that matter Congress, will take a more consumer-oriented approach to drug therapy. There are, however, a few simple things the FDA could do: educate the public directly with television and print commercials about the dangers inherent in drugs; use enforcement powers in the act to take drugs off the market immediately when they are determined to be unsafe or ineffective; and, most important, decide that its first and primary responsibility is to protect the public health, not, as it is today, to cooperate with the industry.

We believe that cooperation with the drug industry, to put it softly, has served not the public health but rather the vested interest of the drug industry and organized medicine.

We would like to see the FDA establish, alongside its bureaus of drugs and food, a bureau of people to represent the public as a counterweight to the vested interests of drug companies, organized medicine, professional grantsmen, academic scientists, and professional bureaucrats. The doctor-caused health problem of this nation is serious, and so is the suggestion.

Over-the-Counter Relief | 10

In drugstores and supermarkets row upon row of colorful bottles and boxes emblazoned with enticing names and slogans promise quick and long-lasting relief from colds, coughs, sore throats, stuffy noses, drippy noses, indigestion, constipation, diarrhea, insomnia, drowsiness, tension, muscular aches, and headache pain.

Radio and television airwaves and the pages of newspapers and magazines are filled with splashy advertising pushing these remedies with which you can treat yourself without a doctor's prescription. Can't sleep? Can't stay awake? Have a splitting headache? Suffer from lower back pain? Screaming kids have you on edge? Nervousness interfering with your work, your bowling, your relationships? Cold getting you down? Allergic to pollen? Sinus passages blocked? Suffering from irregularity? Feeling out of sorts? Take an OTC pill or potion; inhale sprays or fumes. For whatever ails or bothers you, there is a chemical solution on the counter.

According to the Proprietary Association, the trade and lobby organization of the over-the-counter drug industry, there are roughly 350,000 different nonprescription products from which to choose. The FDA thinks the number may be as high as 500,000. Whatever the number, Americans spend billions of dollars each year on self-medication. In 1977 consumers purchased $3.4 billion for OTC medications to treat everything from headaches to hemorrhoids and from nervous tension to postnasal drip. Self-medication is, in fact, the dominant method of health care in the United States. The Proprietary Association says only one-third to one-fourth of the cases of illness or injury are seen and treated by physicians. The majority of the cases are handled by the individual primarily with the assistance of drugs purchased without a prescription. Physicians also often recommend nonprescription drugs. According to a 1976 survey by the World Health Organization of the United Nations, the most common result of a patient-physician consultation is medication, with nonprescription drugs the choice 20 percent of the time. *Medical Economics*, a physicians' trade journal, found in a survey in which 600 American doctors responded that doctors "are frequent users and 'verbal prescribers' of OTC drugs and that those doctors who are 'high prescribers' of prescription products are also the highest level 'verbal prescribers' of OTC products."

Many OTC drugs are harmless, and many are ineffective; but some are dangerous in and by themselves and can be fatal when taken in combination with alcohol and other drugs. All OTC drugs should be considered potentially dangerous. Even aspirin or caffeine, generally considered safe drugs, can be fatal for individuals allergic to them.

The largest single chunk of the $3.4 billion spent by Americans for OTC drugs in 1977 was for psychoactive substances to relieve physical or psychic pain. *Product Marketing* magazine estimated that consumers spent $832.5 million on these painkillers. Each year Americans swallow nearly 19 billion aspirin tablets, and aspirin has been the most common method of treating mild to moderate pain since it was introduced into the U.S. market at the turn of the century. In addition to the millions spent on painkillers, or analgesics, Americans spend more than $30 million annually on sleeping pills or potions and $262.5 million on cold or cough formulations, most of which contain painkillers and/or sedative hypnotic chemicals of the psychoactive class.

These drugs are sold under a variety of names, in a variety of packages, and in a variety of slightly different formulations. They have soporific-sounding names like Cope, Compoz, Quiet World, Vanquish, Nytol, Sleep-Eze, Sominex, Allerest, and Nervine. The brand names are selected to create the impression of tranquillity.

With thousands of different brand names for each class of remedy, competition between manufacturers for the consumer's dollar is stiff, and the battle is fought with excessive, distorted, and often false claims in television commercials as well as in newspaper and magazine advertisements. The drug companies compete by promising bonus relief—extra strength, less strength, more sedation, less sedation, longer-lasting relief, more safety, timed-release action. Often the OTC drugs are promoted as the most powerful substances you can buy without a doctor's prescription. Often we're told this is what a doctor would give you if you asked.

What we are not told in these advertisements and commercials is that many of the chemicals in these drugs are unsafe and can even be fatal. Most people assume that since OTC drugs are sold without a prescription, they must be safe. It also generally is assumed that since the drugs are on the market, they have been checked by the FDA for safety and effectiveness. These common assumptions are false. They are myths perpetrated by lavish and deceptive advertising campaigns of the drug companies and by the blind trust most people place in the FDA and other state and federal health agencies. In fact, the FDA has examined only about one-third of the OTC products on the shelves to determine whether they are either safe or effective in the treatment of the targeted indication. As we shall show, many of the drugs that have been investigated by the FDA were found to be either unsafe or ineffective, and some of them remain on the market despite the finding.

Since 1962 drug manufacturers have had fair warning that they must be able to prove their OTC products—as well as their prescription products—are safe, as required by law in 1938, and effective, as required in 1962. Since 1962 the FDA has had a mandate to require such proof of safety and efficacy, yet the agency has been unable or unwilling to act with reasonable dispatch to carry out that mandate. Further, many of the common drugs, such as the bromides, that were thought to be safe in the early 1930s subsequently have been found to be highly dangerous. Despite this, the FDA has been slow to remove them from the market.

To illustrate the ignorance of the public about OTC drugs and deep-seated myths we hold about their safety and effectiveness, we offer this exchange from a Senate hearing held by Senator Gaylord Nelson of Wisconsin in October 1975. Nelson has been one of the more effective lawmakers in protecting the drug-buying public. There were two new members present that day— Senator Floyd Haskell of Colorado and Senator Robert Packwood of Oregon—when Dr. David J. Greenblatt of the pharmacology unit of Massachusetts General Hospital began the hearing with a statement saying in part: "Nonprescription psychotropic drugs are a multimillion-dollar industry. Some 5 to 10 percent of American adults take over-the-counter drugs as a means of coping with tension, anxiety or insomnia. The extensive use of such drugs is encouraged and perpetuated by an inescapable barrage of advertising in the popular media. One might conclude from this situation that nonprescription tranquilizers and hypnotics provide a safe and effective pharmacologic solution to the stresses of life. Examination of the scientific evidence, however, indicates exactly the opposite."

Dr. Greenblatt elaborated, noting that "cases of intentional overdosage, either for suicidal or hallucinogenic purposes, are being seen at emergency medical treatment facilities with increasing frequency." The doctor called for stricter control and requirements that the drug companies prove their drugs are safe and effective. Senator Nelson interrupted to point out that the 1962 law does require such scientific proof.

Senator Haskell was shocked and asked the obvious question: ". . . assuming the accuracy of the testimony that these drugs do not do what they are supposed to do and they do have side effects, how do they get on the market? . . . This is pretty shocking to have these things advertised in the public magazines and on television and people buying them, and then having them have a bad side effect. I had assumed before you market a drug, it had to go through the Food and Drug Administration, but I guess I am wrong."

Like millions of Americans, Haskell had been lulled and conditioned by Madison Avenue artistry into a belief that if a drug is sold over the counter, it must, first of all, be safe and, secondly, do what its promoters promise. He also assumed falsely that the FDA had checked and approved the OTC drugs in the marketplace. The FDA is in the process of doing this, but progress has been painfully slow, and the manufacturers successfully exploit the regulatory process by delaying for years carrying out orders to remove products found to be dangerous or useless.

The best advice one can give to the consumer, on the basis of the record, is to take the advertising claims with a grain of salt, if not with a healthy assumption that they are exaggerated at the least and false at the worst. A quick look at some recent advertising campaigns demonstrates the wisdom of this advice.

As the winter cold season of 1978 approached, the makers of Dristan promised users a "better winter with Dristan" because it has more decongestant strength, a stronger dose of antihistamine, and more painkillers than popular competitors. Bristol-Myers introduced its new all-purpose cold remedy, Comtrex, promising relief from no less than ten symptoms: nasal and sinus congestion, sneezing, runny nose, coughing, fever, postnasal drip, watery eyes, minor sore throat pain, headache, and body aches and pain. Datril 500 was claimed to be more effective than the potent and dangerous prescription Darvon compounds. Nyquil offered a better night's sleep, not a surprising claim since it is 25 percent alcohol. Ornex was promoted by Smith Kline & French as avoiding "antihistamine drowsiness." In the fine print on the label it was noted that Ornex contains acetaminophen, a common aspirin substitute that in overdose can lead "to liver toxicity and death." Comtrex also contains acetaminophen as a major ingredient, plus antihistamine, but the Comtrex label is not as forthright as the one on Ornex and warns only of drowsiness from the antihistamine.

The popular cold remedies typically contain a painkiller, a decongestant such as an antihistamine, and a throat soother or cough suppressant. The state of the medical art in the treatment and prevention of the common cold remains much as it was in 1961, when the editors of *Consumer Reports* wrote: "There is not the slightest doubt that wonderful new 'scientific' remedies for the common cold will continue to be hailed from time to time—and will fade away like their many predecessors." In advice as sound today as it was then, the editors said the best thing to do was to rest in bed for a day to avoid spreading the virus and to avert complications.

With nearly 1,000 different cold preparations on the market today and with Americans spending up to a billion dollars a year on them, the major area of competition between manufacturers is in promotional expertise. This is true of all OTC drugs. Although there are between 350,000 and 500,000 OTC products on the market, fewer than 1,000 active chemical ingredients are being used in all of them. Often OTC drugs in a particular class vary somewhat in their formulations and combinations, but basically all drugs in the class are made up of the same ingredients. The real competition comes not in the research laboratory but rather on Madison Avenue, with advertising making up the biggest single item in an OTC manufacturer's budget. According to Senate testimony, 64 percent of the gross income of Sominex was devoted to advertising; for Nytol it was 60 percent, and for Sleep-Eze it was 70 percent. This means that for every dollar the consumer spends on one of these sleep aids, all of which the FDA found to be ineffective and in some instances unsafe, a large percentage goes back into promotion to induce more sales.

As a group, the OTC manufacturers are, along with packaged food manufacturers, one of the major television advertisers. The primary target of this barrage of commercial messages is the female population. According to *Broadcast Advertisers Reports*, the heaviest period of commercials for psychoactive and analgesic drugs is during daytime quiz and soap opera programming periods, and they are aimed primarily at women, who are the biggest buyers of OTC products. During a six-month period in 1975 a total of 3,617 commercials for headache remedies, sedatives, and sleep aids were aired on network television, and 1,957 of these were shown during the day. Of 3,296 network commercials for cough, cold, and sinus remedies, 2,081 were shown during daytime hours.

During the six-month period in 1975 the drug manufacturers spent a total of $53.1 million on network and spot TV commercials for headache remedies, sedatives, and sleeping potions. Another $41.1 million was spent on cough, cold, and sinus remedies. In a year's time, the OTC makers will spend $350 million to $500 million by conservative estimates pushing their products, and most of the money is directed at the television audience. In 1977, Bristol-Myers spent $114,425,600 for network TV commercials, according to the Television Bureau of Advertising Research, and ranked third in TV expenditures behind Procter & Gamble and General Foods. American Home Products, another major OTC drug company, spent $108,428,700 to rank number four. By contrast, General Motors, the world's largest automobile company, spent $90,699,500.

As in the case of the sleeping aids and daytime sedatives, the products which are the least effective and, in some cases, the most dangerous are the most advertised. Senator Nelson describes the situation: "While panels of experts are deploring the use of these products, the drug firms are exerting huge efforts to induce the public to use them—and the contest is truly unequal." Nelson notes that the annual expenditures to advertise psychoactive OTC drugs of questionable safety and usefulness annually exceed the federal government's allocations to combat drug abuse. "In addition to the lack of efficacy and the potential dangers of these drugs, the tremendous wave of advertising over the media, especially TV, is designed to persuade us that a pill will solve almost every problem—real or imagined. Is it any wonder we have a drug abuse problem! The federal government, as of three years ago, spent over $229 million annually enforcing laws designed to limit the abuse of drugs, while at the same time manufacturers spent over $350 million annually pushing the use of over-the-counter drugs alone," Nelson said in opening hearings on OTC drugs in 1975. By 1976 the government's drug abuse allocation had increased to $300 million and the OTC advertising expenditure to about $500 million.

In a rare government action against false and misleading advertising claims, the Federal Trade Commission in 1973 began a legal challenge of the claims made by American Home Products for Anacin. The case was still dragging on six years later. Testimony in the action dramatically documents how OTC drug companies mislead the public with exaggerated claims based on pseudoscientific puffery. The case also illustrates how painfully slowly the regulatory process moves and how skillfully the drug companies are able to delay any meaningful remedial action.

For many years, American Home touted Anacin in an advertising campaign costing about $24 million a year as a more effective pain reliever than "plain" aspirin and other analgesics. American Home also said Anacin went to work faster than other drugs, that it starts to relieve pain within twenty-two seconds after being ingested. In an even more scientifically repudiated claim, American Home promoted Anacin as an effective tension reliever. On September 1, 1978, more than five years after the case began, FTC administrative law judge K. Hyun found American Home guilty of "false, misleading, and unsubstantiated claims" and ordered a remedial advertising campaign to correct false impressions of Anacin. After taking volumes of testimony, the judge concluded that the advertising claims for Anacin were "without scientific establishment." Anacin, after all, is simply a combination of plain aspirin and caffeine.

American Home was ordered to devote $24 million to an advertising campaign to state that Anacin "is not a tension-reliever" to counter the incorrect image of the drug. American Home appealed the decision, claiming in its answer filed on December 8, 1978, that the judge had made several errors in reaching his decision. Years of litigation could stall any action by the company to correct the false advertising message. To demonstrate how effective the Anacin ads were in convincing the public that this simple combination of aspirin and caffeine was useful in treating tension, a survey conducted by a competing drug company was cited in the court case showing that 73 percent of those persons who believe you can treat tension with a painkiller usually used Anacin to treat that symptom. "The overall impact of these advertisements upon a viewer is clearly that Anacin is not only a pain-reliever but is also good for tension, nerves, stress, fatigue and depression and helps one to cope with the ordinary stresses of everyday life," the judge said in his decision. The overwhelming scientific evidence presented at the trial proved that Anacin does not relieve tension, nervousness, stress, or any physical condition other than pain, and even the president and medical director of American Home admitted they knew this.

One of the more interesting sidelights brought out in the testimony was American Home's ability to buy research from a university in an attempt to prove its claim that Anacin was more effective than aspirin. American relied on a study done at the Tulane University School of Medicine, and one of the company's major witnesses was Dr. Gilbert McMahon, chairman of the school's therapeutics section. He was among several witnesses called by American Home to support the claim that Anacin was more effective than aspirin. The studies at Tulane were conducted under McMahon's direction under a grant made by American Home in 1974. McMahon, under cross-examination during the FTC proceedings, said he became aware that the studies would be used by American Home as part of its case in the FTC litigation, and he said he was uncomfortable at first about going ahead with the study. According to the judge's summary of this disclosure, "Dr. McMahon admitted that his initial reluctance to even consider such a study was overcome in large part by American Home's promise to increase the amount of grant money to Tulane University, which in part was used to support his research group. As Dr. McMahon stated: '. . . American Home was willing to pay Tulane University an awful lot of money and we are a poor school and the school needed the money. So, when they raised the grant, to tell the truth, we just—needed the money to support our group and to support the school.'"

McMahon, it should be noted, has long had close ties to the drug industry. Before joining the medical faculty at Tulane, he was clinical research director for Upjohn, vice-president for medical research at Ciba, and executive director for clinical research for Merck, Sharp & Dohme.

The crux of American Home's claim of greater effectiveness for Anacin than plain aspirin was that each Anacin tablet contained 400 milligrams of aspirin while a tablet of common aspirin is 325 milligrams. But the higher dosage of the aspirin content of two Anacin tablets, the recommended adult dosage, could not be proved more effective in relieving pain than two tablets of the generic version at a slightly lower dosage.

To illustrate another example of misleading advertising claims, Senator Nelson played a tape of a TV commercial for Nytol for Dr. David Greenblatt of Harvard and others attending a Senate hearing. The advertising script went like this: "On those occasional nights you cannot fall asleep by yourself, fall asleep with the help of Nytol. Nytol contains a tested ingredient; it helps you feel drowsy, so you can fall asleep. Nytol. Take as directed for safe, restful sleep. Sleep to beautiful feeling. Nytol."

Greenblatt, an expert in psychoactive drugs, called the Nytol commercial "misleading to the point of almost being a fraud. It suggests that the preparation has a tested ingredient which will make you feel drowsy. It might do this, but an inactive placebo might also make you feel drowsy. The suggestion that this medication has anything to offer humanity, other than an empty capsule, is entirely misleading and inappropriate to appear in the public media."

What the Block Drug Company, which markets Nytol and spends about $3 million a year advertising it, did not disclose was that the "tested ingredient" was methapyrilene hydrochloride, an antihistamine, which has been found by the FDA to be ineffective as a sleeping aid at the dosage level contained in Nytol and, furthermore, a potential cancer-causing agent. Nor did Block disclose that the other active ingredient in Nytol was plain aspirin. Like most drug companies, Block does not disclose contents in its commercial advertisements, referring instead to "tested ingredients" and other meaningless phrases.

The contents of all OTC drugs are listed by law on the box or bottle or in a package insert. The OTC manufacturers are also required to list the possible adverse reactions. These are invariably in the finest print possible and placed in a lower corner someplace where they are likely to escape notice unless one deliberately is looking for them. The cautions and adverse reactions are never advertised on television and radio or in print, except for the perfunctory notice to use as directed. Surveys done in New York indicate that only about 15 percent of the buyers of OTC drugs ever read the warning labels. That is the very first thing one should do before using any OTC or prescription drug. Another problem with the labeling of directions for use and adverse reactions is that millions of people are functionally illiterate because of visual handicaps, reading deficiencies, or intellectual shortcomings. One of the leading causes of accidental death among children is the overdosing on such common medicine-cabinet drugs as aspirin. Robert B. Choate, chairman of the Council on Children, Media, and Merchandising, estimates that there are 30 million children and 40 million adults who are functionally illiterate and vulnerable to accidental misuse of OTC drugs. In a petition to the FTC, Choate requested that the drug companies be required to provide audio and visual disclosure of drug contents, usage instructions, and possible adverse reactions. What he hopes to do is require the companies to include their "sins of omission." As an example, Choate notes that almost all OTC drugs labels say the drug should be kept out of reach of children, "but I don't think I've ever seen that warning repeated on television." Considering the power of the drug lobby in Washington, Choate is not optimistic about his proposal. "We never win victories. We only win compromises, and the compromises only come as a result of the threat of government action. Without that threat, they tell us to kiss off and get lost," Choate said of his long-running battle with the television networks and their advertisers.

Beyond the misinformation, lack of information, deception, and fraud surrounding the promotion of the OTC drugs themselves, there is another problem of serious concern created by the constant barrage of advertising messages that encourage the public to use drugs for every conceivable ailment and to make life free of petty stress. There is a growing body of evidence that indicates the OTC advertising helps condition society to dependency on drugs. Choate likes to use this quote from author Alistair Cooke: "The thing that bothers me most about commercials is the medical brainwashing that the family gets on television. It seems to me that it easily outweighs any lessons in chemistry or biology that the child picks up in school. The body of our knowledge about medicine is fed to us from a very early age by commercials—and it's idiotic medicine. Mostly, it's either harmful or useless."

Many persons working in the drug abuse field are convinced that the quick-relief TV commercial is contributing to the nation's drug abuse problem by conditioning children, as well as adults, to expect as a matter of right that drugs will relieve them of some of the painful experiences of living and eliminate or diminish the stress from everyday pressure. Dr. Anthony Kales, chairman of the Department of Psychiatry at Pennsylvania State University, believes this type of advertising "has tremendous impact and consequences" on the young. "I believe it encourages the widespread use of drugs for what usually are responses to normal frustrations of life," he told a Senate hearing in 1975. Youngsters, he said, need to develop a proper frustration tolerance through role modeling of adults who demonstrate that they "can withstand the stresses and anxieties in everyday life. But in these advertisements, the adults are depicted as very quickly taking medication to relieve even the most minimal level of daytime anxiety or nighttime sleepiness, and in so doing, the youngster is provided an extremely negative role model of how to handle frustrations, i.e., immediate self-medication." Kales believes for the young it is a "very small step to extend this concept of immediate self-medication of nonprescription drugs to immediate mood alteration with drugs of abuse."

Since 1954 Karst Besteman has been working in the drug abuse field. A social scientist by training, Besteman was an early member of the pioneer detoxification and rehabilitation center run by the federal government in Lexington, Kentucky. At the time of the interview Besteman was acting director of the National Institute on Drug Abuse. As a professional in the field and a parent, Besteman is frightened by the persistence of the drug culture in our society and by the fact that drug abusers are getting younger and younger with each passing year. "It's very scary," Besteman said. "Before World War Two the average heroin or morphine addict—mostly morphine addicts—coming in for treatment was forty years old. The average patient today is about twenty-two, and I understand AA is reporting a much younger age." He thinks part of the reason is the drug conditioning picked up from television commercials: "The message is 'Don't be uncomfortable. Don't struggle with your problems.' You know, it is 'Plop, plop, fizz, fizz, oh, what a relief it is.' It's right here. Take Nytol. Take Sominex. Take Super Excedrin. The theme is that if you are uncomfortable, don't be a dummy, be comfortable. Plunk something into your gullet. You have to feel better immediately. We not only have the major tranquilizers and the minor tranquilizers, but if you go into your drugstore, we have a lot of stuff on the shelf that alleges to be calming, soothing. We get to the kind of attitude that the human animal should never experience distress, and God forbid, if he does, he should plunk something into his mouth and feel immediately better."

It's not just the commercial but the program as well. "Take the thirty-minute television shows which set the theatrical premise, the tension, and always come to a solution," says Besteman. "What kind of perception do you somehow plug into your head if you grow up on that? I'm not saying television is evil or anything like that, but what is the implied or underlying message? Meantime, you're being hit with all kinds of commercials. Enjoy, have a beer. Get more prestige, drive a Buick turbocharger. Plop, plop, fizz, fizz, oh, what a relief it is. You come away with the most powerful mass media we've got telling people that people are only in stress for twenty minutes, and they solved it! 'Why, I've been miserable for a week, and I deserve to do something for me.'"

Maeline Amile, an assistant professor of clinical psychiatry at Mount Sinai Hospital in New York, is another expert in drug abuse who believes advertising for OTC drugs plays an "important role in creation of a climate where pill taking is accepted. These ads tell people that drugs are a way to escape, and there is nothing wrong with doing it because the people in the ads are very ordinary people, and if they are doing it, why shouldn't I?"

Dr. Nicholas Pace, chief medical officer of the General Motors Corporation, a member of the New York Commission on Alcohol and Drug Abuse, and a director of the National Council on Alcoholism, feels so strongly about the dangers of psychoactive drugs that he has prohibited their use by his medical staff. In his years of experience working with alcoholics and other drug addicts, Dr. Pace has seen society's attitude grow increasingly benign about using drugs to change reality. "We are all victims of a massive PR campaign," says Pace. "All phases of the media and advertising seem to say that in this country it is okay to take a pill, to get high, to escape. The public is bombarded daily with ads urging it to take one kind of pill or another, which is all part of the trading-up process that can lead to abuse or addiction."

Pace, Amile, and Besteman, along with many others working in the drug abuse field, are convinced that children learn drug-taking behavior at home from their parents and older siblings. Often this conditioning begins with OTC drugs. Says Amile: "Take a family that does not use drugs. You probably will not have much of a drug problem in a drug-free climate. But if you have a family that casually uses drugs, then the risk of addiction in that family's children is much greater."

One of the findings of the 1977 National Survey on Drug Abuse conducted for the National Institute on Drug Abuse identified the drug-taking habits of mothers as being more significant than the attitudes or habits of fathers in forming the habits of children. As we have shown, women use 70 percent of all prescription mood-changing drugs and a corresponding percentage of non-prescription psychoactive substances.

The survey showed that "teens were more likely to use both alcohol and illegal drugs if their mothers smoked cigarettes, were even moderate drinkers, and/or had ever used psychotherapeutic drugs under a doctor's prescription." On the other hand, "minimal levels of teenage use were observed in families where the mother did not meet any of these three rather moderate licit-substance-use criteria." The role of the father curiously was found to be less influential. In fact, the survey's authors noted that "little, if any, evidence of a similar correspondence between fathers' substance use and their sons' or daughters'." This was not explained, and one can only speculate on the reasons. The answer could be as simple as the facts that mothers traditionally play a bigger role in child rearing and that a mother's use of mood-changing drugs of all kinds stamps such use as being acceptable, leading to imitative behavior by offspring. The study suggests that "one possibility is that if mothers hold and transmit certain moral values to their children these values may to some extent inhibit the mother's use of legal substances, as well as her child's illicit drug use."

The survey also found that as drug use, whether licit or illicit, increasingly is "perceived as a commonplace event," the reaction of nonusers will become one of resignation to "reality" rather than one of shock upon encountering "the phenomenon of drug use." The survey confirms the impression that attitudes toward all drugs with the exception of alcohol and tobacco are growing softer or more lenient among young people. As the accompanying table shows, there has been a sharp reduction since 1972 in the percentage of youths who consider barbiturates and amphetamines to be addictive, while the percentage considering street drugs such as heroin and marijuana addictive has declined at a substantially lower rate. The percentage of adults considering the

Substances Regarded as Addictive, 1972–1977: All Youth and All Adults

	All youth: ages 12–17				All adults: ages 18+			
	1972	1974	1976	1977	1972	1974	1976	1977
Substances								
Heroin	88%	87%	86.7%	78.0%	89%	90%	87.3%	87.2%
Alcohol	71	78	83.3	80.9	75	78	85.1	86.9
Marijuana	50	54	54.3	47.3	59	68	61.7	59.5
Tobacco	58	62	61.8	62.4	67	72	79.5	82.1
Barbiturates	72	70	59.3	49.0	68	72	69.1	68.4
Amphetamines	67	61	51.9	40.0	64	65	60.4	59.4
Cocaine	66	74	72.4	65.4	75	78	74.2	71.8
Methadone	No data	59	43.0	27.7	No data	62	56.0	51.2

Source: National Survey on Drug Abuse, 1977 (NIDA)

surveyed drugs addictive also declined but at a lesser rate than for youth.

The national survey also found that while nonmedical—in other words, illicit—use of tranquilizers among young people has remained at about 3.8 percent of the population between the ages of twelve and seventeen, there has been a significant increase in nonmedical use of tranquilizers in the eighteen to twenty-five age bracket. In 1972 only 7 percent of the persons in this age bracket reported using minor tranquilizers for nonmedical purposes, but by 1977 the percentage had jumped to 13.4. This appears to confirm the impression that abuse of prescription mood changers for nonmedical purposes is spreading.

Authorities at the local level are also seeing an increasing amount of drug use of all kinds by children as young as the middle- and elementary-grade levels. This trend is explained, in part, by the commonplace acceptance of drugs in our culture. In commenting on the spread of illicit drug use in the affluent New York City suburbs of Long Island, Dr. Raymond J. Condren told the *New York Times*: "My own impression is that people have become so accustomed to using legal medicines that they tend to misuse other substances. They see their parents use Valium. It is our culture." Mrs. Joan Ayer, director of a youth center, agreed. "The ages of the youngsters involved are getting lower and lower," she said. "The problem here—and probably in most other areas on Long Island—is not due to a lack of cultural or recreational activities for these kids. It's a reflection of the times and any solution to the problem must take that into consideration."

According to a statewide survey of high school students in New York taken in March 1978, one out of every four high school juniors and seniors smokes marijuana ten or more times a month. Fifteen percent of the students surveyed also admitted to at least one use a month of inhalants; PCP, or "angel dust"; amphetamines; and other stimulants. Amphetamines ranked number three in preference among the students surveyed, and tranquilizers were number four. Cough medicine with codeine was number five, and depressants were number eight. When the so-called prescription or OTC drugs are lumped together, they are second in use ten or more times a month behind marijuana. The results of the New York State survey are not unique, and similar trends are being reported in other geographic areas.

No reasonable person blames OTC or prescription drugs for creating the drug culture all by themselves. There are many complex social, cultural, and economic forces at work, but their widespread use and the advertising hoopla that surrounds OTC drugs in the public media and the prescription drugs in the medical media contribute substantially to creating an atmosphere that says taking drugs not only is okay but is necessary for a happy, healthy, and productive life. Deeply concerned about the messages delivered to young people, the attorneys general from eighteen states in 1975 petitioned the Federal Communications Commission to ban advertising of OTC drugs from TV during the viewing hours of children. This includes daytime quiz and soap opera periods and evening "family viewing" times. Robert Choate, the children's TV and product advocate, notes that contrary to popular belief, the heaviest children's television-viewing time is not Saturday morning, when tighter codes on programming and commercials apply, but rather during the daytime and early evening of weekdays. Only 8 percent of the total children's viewing time is on Saturday morning.

After receiving the petition from the attorneys general, the FCC and the Federal Trade Commission held a joint hearing on the request and quickly dismissed the proposed ban. Choate said the hearing was "curiously managed" to divert the issue from the subtle conditioning messages relayed to children by OTC manufacturers to illicit street abuse of drugs. The hearing examiners came to the "shallow conclusion" that the OTC commercials had no impact, Choate says.

Choate cites a study by the Rand Corporation, a research organization, that demonstrates the obvious:

1. Children learn from television and imitate behavior viewed on television;
2. Children are more likely to imitate adult behavior than peer behavior viewed on television, and imitative behavior is even more likely "when children see an immediate reward situation such as exists when drug ads solve a person's distress in 30 seconds";
3. Children are influenced by commercials, and their ability to make discriminating choices decreases as their exposure to commercials increases;
4. Exposure to drug advertisements is positively correlated in young boys with use of over-the-counter drugs; and
5. Parents may be only marginally influential in countering the impact of television in child behavior.

Many experts in the field believe that OTC drug advertising should be regulated not by the FTC, as it is today, but rather by the FDA, which monitors—not too effectively—prescription drug advertising in medical journals and on closed-circuit TV and radio programming for physicians. Except for an occasional foray against a manufacturer, as in the case against American Home Products' Anacin, the OTC drug companies pretty much get by with a free rein on what they say and how they say it. The FTC is reluctant to pursue false or misleading advertising cases unless the FDA, which is reluctant to challenge the manufacturers legally out of fear of prompting legal action, has moved definitively on the medical and scientific claims. As we have seen, the FDA is either unable or unwilling to move with dispatch out of fear of litigation. In a classic Catch-22 situation, the FTC waits for the FDA, but the FDA delays or fails to act in order to avoid costly litigation and blames Congress for not giving it more authority to act promptly. Congress, meanwhile, either responds to drug industry pressure to prevent tighter regulations or declares that the FDA has the authority it needs under present law to act quickly and forcefully if it chooses to do so.

The best example of this bureaucratic snarl that catches the consumer in the middle is the case of the over-the-counter day- and nighttime sedatives. In 1975 an FDA panel of experts concluded after a three-year study that most of the ingredients in these sedatives are unsafe, ineffective, or both. Most of the evidence of their dangers and uselessness was available well before the panel began its study, and Senate testimony clearly established this in 1971. On October 30, 1975, Senator Gaylord Nelson summoned Joan Z. Bernstein, acting director of consumer protection for the FTC; David O. Bickart, deputy assistant director for national advertising; and other FTC officials to explain why the FTC had not taken action on the OTC drug commercials. Nelson cited the scientific evidence against OTC drugs commonly promoted and noted that "every single one of them makes a claim that is not supported by the scientific evidence, or withholds important information from the consumer." Since the final order of the FDA had not been issued against the daytime sedatives and nighttime sleep aids, the FTC decided cases against the companies for false or deceptive advertising would not be warranted, Ms. Bernstein testified. She said the FTC would "await the outcome of FDA's very thorough review of each drug category." Three years later, after the FDA had issued a "tentative" final order, the FTC still was waiting.

It also was revealed at that 1975 hearing by the FTC's Bickart that the FDA had asked the FTC to take no action against sleep aid advertisements and commercials pending further study of some of the ingredients. At the time the FDA staff was trying to get these drugs placed in a category that would allow further study rather than in a prohibitive category, which a majority of the panel of experts on the drugs favored. Asked in a hearing conducted by Nelson in June 1977 about Bickart's assertion, Donald Kennedy, then the new FDA commissioner, said he tried "to run that down . . . and I guess my attempt to test our institutional memory failed."

The first change that needs to be made to protect the public is to require OTC drug makers to prove that their products are both safe and effective before they are marketed and promoted in the media. As the situation is today, the government must prove that they are unsafe and ineffective before they can be removed from the shelves, and this process is long and ineffective. As we have seen, the drug companies have had since 1962 to prove that their products are safe and effective. Most have not done so, and drugs the government has found to be dangerous and ineffective are still on the market. The drug companies also should be required to make full disclosure of the contents of their drugs and their side effects in their mass media advertising. If this were the case, a Contac advertisement would have to tell us something like this: "Not for frequent or prolonged use. Do not exceed recommended dosage. If symptoms persist or are unusually severe, see a physician. If excessive dryness of the mouth occurs, decrease dosage. Discontinue use if rapid pulse, dizziness, skin rash, or blurring of vision occurs. Do not drive or operate machinery because this preparation may cause drowsiness. Individuals with high blood pressure, heart disease, diabetes, thyroid disease, glaucoma, or excessive pressure within the eye, and elderly persons . . . should use only as directed by a physician. Persons with undiagnosed glaucoma may experience eye pain; if so, discontinue use and see a physician immediately. May cause urinary retention in males with enlarged prostate. Keep Contac out of the reach of children. In case of accidental overdose, contact a physician or a poison control center immediately."

In addition to stating the warnings associated with the use of Contac, the ad would be required to reveal what's in the popular cold pills and, in language we can understand, what each chemical does. It might go like this: "Each capsule of Contac contains belladonna alkaloids, including atropine sulfate, scopolamine hydrobromide, and hyoscyamine sulfate. Belladonna is a poisonous substance often referred to as deadly nightshade. These belladonna substances can make you sleepy, and the Food and Drug

Administration says they are ineffective at the dosages in Contac and would possibly be toxic at higher dosages. Each Contac also contains chlorpheniramine maleate, an antihistamine to help dry your runny nose and stop your sneezing. You should know, however, that antihistamines are a depressant and can make you sleepy and dizzy and can cause headaches. That's why you shouldn't drive or operate machinery if you use Contac. The FDA has not yet decided whether this particular antihistamine is safe; it has determined that some are not. Phenylpropanolamine hydrochloride is also included in each Contac capsule to help clear phlegm from your lungs and respiratory passages. It is not known whether this substance is effective."

The chance is remote that Menley & James Laboratories, a division of Smith Kline & French, would make such disclosure in its advertising unless it was forced to do so, in which case it probably would choose not to advertise. During the hotly competitive winter of 1978, when the OTC makers openly attacked competing brands in advertising campaigns, it was easier to find out what was not in a particular brand of cold medicine than to find out what was in it. For example, Contac was promoted as not containing aspirin or an aspirin substitute or alcohol, but there was no mention of the ingredients it does contain.

The point of this exercise is that many popular and heavily promoted OTC drugs contain substances that are unsafe or ineffective or both and that the consumer has little opportunity to become fully knowledgeable of the drugs' content and side effects.

We have mentioned several times the 1962 amendments to the original 1938 Food, Drug and Cosmetic Act which required manufacturers to prove that their products were not only safe, as required in 1938, but also effective for their intended purpose. To back up the 1962 amendments, a drug efficacy study was undertaken by the National Academy of Sciences. But since the academy reviewed only 512 OTC drugs and found more than 300 of them ineffective, the FDA decided to conduct a separate review. Since there are an estimated 350,000 to 500,000 OTC drugs on the market, it has been an overwhelming project fraught with delays. Furthermore, the FDA decided to concentrate its resources first on prescription drug reviews, thus delaying the evaluation of nonprescription drugs. In 1972, ten years after the 1962 amendments, the FDA finally began its OTC study, creating seventeen panels of outside experts to study the drugs by therapeutic class—sleep aids and daytime sedatives, cough and cold medicines, skin bleaches, antiperspirants, analgesics, laxatives, antacids, and so on. By 1979 the FDA's panels had reviewed more than 14,000 volumes of scientific information and had only scratched the surface. Fewer than half the seventeen panels had completed their work. The first six panels to finish had classified fewer than a third of the 1,000 active chemicals making up all OTC drugs. For its part, the FDA, seven years after it began the active review and seventeen years after it was mandated to do so by the 1962 law, had issued final orders on only one of the seventeen drug classifications—the antacids. The rest were bogged down in regulatory bureaucracy. Even those drugs that panels had found to be hazardous or useless or both were months and years from being taken off the market by the agency. The regulations for conducting the review and implementing the panel conclusions were written to provide every possible advantage to the drug industry.

Under the 1962 Food, Drug and Cosmetic Act amendments, it was envisioned that the prescription and OTC drug manufacturers would have to prove that their products were safe and effective. Thus, it was anticipated that the OTC advisory panels would put drug ingredients into one of two categories:

Category I: Generally recognized as safe and effective and not misbranded. Can stay on the market.

Category II: Not generally recognized as safe and/or ineffective and misbranded. Must be removed from the market.

But in setting up the OTC review, the FDA added a third category. Category III was created to classify drugs that could not be determined as safe and effective or could not be determined unsafe or ineffective. Drugs placed in this category would be allowed to stay on the market pending further study. Of the first 271 ingredients evaluated by the panels, 30 percent were put in Category III for further study; 20 percent were found to be unsafe and/or ineffective, requiring removal from the market; and 50 percent were determined to be safe and effective for their intended use.

Put another way, only half the OTC drugs on the market could be established as safe and effective by experts in pharmacology who examined all available medical and scientific literature on the various drugs. The other half either definitely were unsafe or ineffective or could not be proved to be safe and effective.

Critics of the FDA argue that Category III was added to permit the agency to avoid confrontation with the powerful drug industry and build into the regulations opportunities for long delays. Their point—a convincing one, we think—is that a drug either is or is not effective and either is or is not safe; if there is doubt, the public safety should be the first priority, and the drug should be removed from the market until a final determination can be made. The critics of the FDA note that the regulations for the OTC review were written under the direction of Peter B. Hutt, who was chief counsel of the FDA from September 1971 until May 1975. Prior to joining the FDA, Hutt was a partner in the powerful law firm of Covington & Burling, which specializes in representing drug and food companies in legal battles with the FDA. When he resigned from the FDA, Hutt returned to his law practice at Covington & Burling as a specialist in food and drug law.

Borrowing a tactic long favored by the drug industry, the Health Research Group, a public interest organization established by Ralph Nader, filed suit in the U.S. district court in Washington charging the FDA with defying the 1962 law and catering to the interests of the drug industry rather than protecting the public health. The lawsuit, which was heard by U.S. District Judge John Sirica, asked that Category III be declared illegal. In a significant setback for consumers, Judge Sirica ruled the Nader organization had no right to file lawsuits on behalf of the public and threw the case out of court on March 14, 1979. The suit was still being heard with individual complainants.

The FDA argued that Category III at least provides the mechanism to get unsafe or ineffective drugs off the market at some future date. Under questioning by a Senate committee in 1977, Richard Merrill, then chief counsel for the FDA, said the category was created to prevent costly and numerous battles with the litigation-minded drug companies. He conceded, however, that he felt the FDA could win these cases, given enough time and resources. He told of one manufacturer, which he did not name, which the FDA had engaged in "eleven different lawsuits, and each time we have won a lawsuit he has changed the drug a little bit, changed the labeling a little bit, and said, 'Aha, it is not the same one you condemned before.'"

The FDA panel report particularly relevant to this book is the one on daytime sedatives and nighttime sleep aids. These drugs contain tranquilizing and other psychoactive ingredients that can be dangerous not only by themselves but in combination with other drugs, particularly alcohol. They also are an early step in the trade-up process that often leads to misuse and abuse of more powerful drugs of abuse such as Valium.

The FDA's panel on OTC sedatives, sleep aids, tranquilizers, and stimulants met seventeen times between November 1972 and September 1975. The panel quickly and unanimously concluded that all the sleep aids and daytime sedatives containing bromides and scopolamine were unsafe, ineffective, or both and should be removed from the marketplace.

The risks from bromides, FDA Commissioner Kennedy said, "are too great to permit general availability in OTC markets." These side effects include depression of the central nervous system, difficulty in speaking and thinking, and impaired memory. Bromides can also produce diarrhea and in large doses can lower body temperature, depress sexual drive, and cause somnolence, loss of coordination, and sluggish reflexes. There also are numerous cases in the medical literature of infant poisoning from bromides as well as strong evidence of bromide intoxication in newborns. In an article in the British medical journal *Lancet*, Dr. E. Rossiter reported on a child who showed "retarded mental and motor development and was below the norm in height, weight and circumference at the age of 2½ years." This retardation was traced to the bromides the child's mother had taken during pregnancy to relieve headaches. Among other cases reported was that of a seven-day-old girl who "entered a children's hospital with lethargy, poor sucking reflex," and an excessively high level of bromides in her blood. The girl's mother, a nurse, had taken a quart of an OTC bromide preparation the day before delivery.

The bromides, which were discovered in 1826, were widely used as over-the-counter sedatives and hypnotics prior to World War II. They also were heavily prescribed as a tranquilizer, but with the introduction of the first mass tranquilizer, Miltown, in the 1950s, bromides fell out of favor as a prescription drug for that use. However, they continued to be widely sold as an OTC preparation for nervous tension, headaches, and insomnia. Miles Laboratories' Nervine was one of the most popular of these preparations. Miles called Nervine a "calmative" and claimed it "effectively eases the nervous tension and irritability that can ruin your day, and a good night's sleep." Ignoring more than a century of toxicity reports, Miles said the bromide in Nervine was safe, well balanced with vitamins, and palatable to the taste. Following condemnation of bromide by the FDA, Miles took the bromide out of Nervine and substituted the antihistamine methapyrilene, a substance the FDA also said was ineffective and dangerous. The risks from the "improved formula" Nervine can be as dangerous as those from the old. In addition, there is evidence that methapyrilene can cause cancer, a finding we'll examine in the pages to follow.

The advisory panel and the FDA also did not hesitate to condemn scopolamine, the common substance found in Sominex and other sleep aids. The FDA said the usual side effects of scopolamine include dryness of the mouth, blurred vision, sensitivity to light, and cardiac effects. The FDA said these side effects can "rarely be avoided with doses required to obtain significant therapeutic benefit." In other words, scopolamine can induce sleep, but in the dose needed to do that, it produces problems far more severe than the lack of sleep.

The FDA also listed these "sometime" side effects of the drug: acute glaucoma, constipation, urinary retention, lack of sweating, skin rashes, ataxia, hallucinations, belligerence, and violence. Scopolamine also can impair the thinking process, as Dr. M. M. Ghoneim of the Department of Anesthesia at the University of Iowa points out in an article in *Psychopharmacology*. He believes scopolamine "in the therapeutic dose range impairs memory function . . . recall of material learned . . . with deficit in memory more pronounced and prolonged with scopolamine than with diazepam [Valium]."

Scopolamine is a derivative of the belladonna plant, the "deadly nightshade" commonly used by obstetricians of a century ago and to lesser degree today. It has lived on in OTC preparations.

Sleep-Eze, which is manufactured by American Home Products' Whitehall Laboratories, is an example of a sleeping pill that contained scopolamine. In addition, Sleep-Eze contained methapyrilene, an antihistamine also considered unsafe because of its potential for toxicity and the possibility that it causes cancer either by itself or in combination with certain normal body substances, notably saliva.

American Home, the king of the OTC market, promoted the combination of scopolamine and methapyrilene as "brilliant" because each "would reinforce and increase the effectiveness of the other." The package insert for this combination of drugs is one of the most misleading and distorted statements ever made on behalf of a product. "For years," the statement says, "men of science sought a *safe* answer to this age-old problem [of insomnia]. And after persistent research, their efforts have been rewarded with this remarkable, new, *non-narcotic* sleeping tablet called—Sleep-Eze." The company cited "clinical tests" of chronic insomniacs that proved Sleep-Eze was as effective as barbiturates and safer. Not mentioned was the fact that most drugs on the market are safer than barbiturates.

What the FDA's advisory panel found out about scopolamine and methapyrilene was entirely different.

As the result of the panel's finding that both drugs are either not safe or ineffective, American Home changed the formula, offering a "new" Sleep-Eze made up only of pyrilamine, another antihistamine. Although it provided a more detailed and honest statement of warnings, American Home did not mention that the FDA panel was unable to determine pyrilamine's safety and effectiveness as a sleep aid and placed it in Category III for further study.

As was the case with the "improved formula" Miles Nervine, the old formula Sleep-Eze could be found alongside the new on pharmacy shelves years after the panel's report and the FDA's "tentative" acceptance of it. Although the FDA has the authority —and the responsibility—to order these dangerous and ineffective drugs off the market immediately, it rarely has used this power out of either fear of drug company wrath or lack of zeal on behalf of the public consumer.

The FDA advisory panel quickly and with little disagreement decided that scopolamine and bromide should not be used in OTC preparations. Such was not the case with methapyrilene, the antihistamine used in daytime sedatives and some sleeping potions and pills. In general, the panel could not find any justifiable reason for using the daytime sedatives. All they really do is make you sleepy, and they have no tranquilizing or sedative effect beyond that. The panel was split, however, on whether to ban them by placing them in Category II or to give the drug companies three more years to prove their safety and effectiveness by placing them in Category III. In addition to the well-known side effects of dizziness and sleepiness caused by antihistamines, new evidence linking the antihistamine methapyrilene to cancer was presented to the panel by William Lijinsky, director of the Frederick Cancer Research Center in Maryland. Dr. Lijinsky had discovered that methapyrilene created cancerous tumors in rats when it came in contact with nitrite. This combination of methapyrilene and nitrite is a potential cancer hazard for humans because everyone is exposed to nitrites, which are commonly used in cured meats and are present in normal saliva.

Dr. Lijinsky came upon the link quite by accident. He had become interested in the study of over-the-counter sleep aids toward the end of a fifteen-year study on nitrites. He had been testing antihistamines in combination with nitrites. The combination forms a nitrosamine which he describes as "one of the most potent carcinogens known." In his research Dr. Lijinsky found a high incidence—30 percent—of liver tumors in rats as a result of the combination. What particularly surprised him was his inability to find any studies in the medical literature on methapyrilene as a possible cancer-causing agent. He had assumed "at the time these tests were carried out that long-term testing of all substances approved as over-the-counter drugs had been carried out prior to approval. How wrong I was! To my dismay, I found recently that this was not so and that many widely used drugs on the market have never been subjected to testing for all adverse biological effects, including carcinogenesis."

As a result of his findings, Dr. Lijinsky recommended to the FDA that methapyrilene be banned and other antihistamine substances found in cold and sedative drugs be tested for their cancer-causing effect. He had made such a recommendation for testing of all drugs that react with nitrites to a congressional panel in 1971, and the committee had forwarded the recommendation to the FDA. Six years after that initial proposal, Dr. Lijinsky reported back to a Senate committee that "nothing was ever done" about the testing, despite growing evidence that nitrites found in human saliva and cured meats such as bacon do, in fact, form cancer-causing combinations.

Dr. Lijinsky's finding threw the FDA panel for a loop, adding yet another controversy to the debate over daytime sedatives, most of which relied on antihistamines for their sedative effect. A majority of the panel wanted to ban the daytime sedatives with antihistamines, but Dr. Karl Rickles, the panel chairman who ruled the group's deliberations "with an iron fist," and the FDA staff wanted them placed in Category III for further testing. Several times the panel voted to ban the substances, and each time a new vote was ordered. Finally, the FDA sent its lawyers to the panel in an effort to use legal argument to win its point of view, which the FDA was unable to win on medical or scientific evidence. The panel's members had grown divided, and one person who was present at most of the meetings said there was a "lot of yelling and screaming." Dr. Frances Norris, medical director of the Division of Licensing for the Maryland Department of Health, was one of the panelists who wanted antihistamines taken off the market immediately. Although she was threatened with dismissal from the panel if she made public disclosure of its activities and disagreements, Dr. Norris nevertheless told the Nelson Senate committee in late 1977 about the FDA's interference in the panel's scientific deliberations and the manipulation of its conclusions for legal or procedural reasons rather than for public health reasons. The fifth and final vote reversing the majority decision to ban the antihistamines came after the panel had been enclosed in a room on a "very hot and stuffy day," she said. The FDA sent two lawyers to "harangue" the panel for hours, and one of them pleaded with the panel not to ban antihistamines from the OTC market because of "his own need for antihistamines" for an allergy. "They talked to us for at least two-thirds of our day, with legal legerdemain, saying it is better for the people if you put it in Category Three than Category Two and so on."

Another member of the panel, Dr. Sumner Kalman, a Stanford University pharmacologist, supported Dr. Norris's version. "I believe what they said, in effect, is that we are going to have a hard time proving your claim that this drug is not efficacious. I really do not believe it is proper for the in-house staff [of the FDA] to tell an advisory group, which should make its judgment on the basis of evidence, that its determination about a drug's status should be based on a procedural maneuver."

The FDA prevailed, and the daytime sedatives were put in Category III, giving the drug industry three more years to prove their safety and effectiveness. However, two years later, in June 1977, there was a sudden reversal.

At the same Senate hearing where Dr. Norris made her revelations about being pressured by the FDA staff and by panel chairman Rickles, Rickles suddenly changed his vote, telling Senator Nelson he had been "too generous" with the drug industry and now "strongly" recommended banning the substances immediately. He also expressed impatience with the FDA for failing after two years to take any final action to remove the other substances found to be ineffective or unsafe from OTC shelves.

One week later, on June 21, 1977, FDA Commissioner Donald Kennedy, who had been on the job for only about a year, issued what the FDA calls "tentative final orders" to remove not only the nighttime sleep aids containing bromides and scopolamine but also the daytime sedatives containing methapyrilene.

But the FDA did not order manufacturers to remove or recall these products. Instead, the agency gave the drug companies yet another opportunity to submit comments and request hearings. Given another invitation to delay implementing the FDA's order, the Proprietary Association, which represents OTC manufacturers, and several OTC drug houses, including Bristol-Myers, Block Drug, and the J. P. Williams Company, asked for more hearings, and in early 1979 the FDA said it didn't expect even to schedule the hearings for at least another six months. Once again the drug industry had lost on the issues but won the battle. The public lost.

In May 1979, however, the National Cancer Institute confirmed the link between methapyrilene and cancer, and HEW Secretary Joseph Califano ordered the FDA to act swiftly to remove OTC products containing the substance from the market.

Although many of the clearly established dangerous and ineffective OTC drugs had been reconstituted with other substances, most of which were of questionable safety and effectiveness, the old formulas could still be found on drugstore and supermarket shelves four years after the panel issued its report.

Even more disheartening and frightening is the fact that since 1962 the drug industry has had warning under federal law that it must provide controlled scientific studies proving the safety and efficacy of OTC drugs. But except in rare instances, the industry has failed to do so, and the FDA, which has the authority if it wants to use it, has failed to require this proof with any reasonable dispatch. Further, the FDA has legal authority to order immediate recall of products found to be unsafe and ineffective but has elected not to use this power, preferring to coddle the powerful makers instead of protecting the unsuspecting takers.

Beyond
Brave New World | 11

The most recent developments in the field of psychotropic drugs suggest that science and medicine are on the verge of discovering a way to alter our moods, quiet our anxiety, and increase our intelligence without harmful side effects. Soon it might be possible to pinpoint and isolate the chemical switches in the brain that control mood and intelligence without affecting other parts of the central nervous system. There is, however, growing evidence that such a chemical world is not likely to be a safe one.

In the past fifteen years there have been significant advances in unlocking the mysterious workings of the brain. Perhaps the most significant discovery is that the brain is a chemical organ consisting of several billion nerve cells that send signals back and forth through chemical switches or neurotransmitters. This chemical storage and messenger system has been compared to a large computer which stores and retrieves information at a phenomenal rate. To explain how the chemical brain works, we have borrowed a simple illustration from the 1978 report of the President's Commission on Mental Health: "While you are reading this page you are only dimly aware of the hardness of the chair or the color of the table top because you are focusing your attention on the printed page. The act of looking at the page, transforming the black ink symbols into symbolic abstractions which provide language clues . . . represent[s] billions of neurons communicating through rapid chemical messages. These chemical messages not only allow you to receive the information contained in the printed text, they may also evoke from you emotional responses like excitement or confusion. Both the message and the emotion come about through the chemical communications between nerve cells."

Research that examines this chemical messenger system and that identifies and isolates the brain's messengers—the transmitters and the receivers—is leading to an understanding of how existing psychoactive drugs such as Valium and Thorazine work and to the development of new classes of drugs to treat and control—and perhaps to prevent—some of the more severe forms of mental illness. By pinpointing and isolating the right chemical switches, scientists believe they will be able to develop drugs that resemble the appropriate chemical messenger in the brain and thus intervene biochemically to compensate for deficiencies or correct malfunctions that cause the mental disorders. Many medical scientists believe, for example, that schizophrenia is caused by malfunction of the dopamine system of neurotransmitters. This theory holds that the phenothiazine drugs such as Thorazine calm hyperactive schizophrenics and activate withdrawn ones by blocking the dopamine chemical messengers in the brain. Another class of drugs presently in use, the monamine oxidase inhibitors such as Nardil, is believed to block the action of monamine oxidase, an enzyme that makes some of the neurotransmitters work, and to relieve symptoms of depression. New classes of painkillers that attach themselves to the brain's natural opiate chemicals called endorphins also are being developed.

`Hoffman-La Roche, the manufacturer of the two best-selling tranquilizers, Valium and Librium, is busily engaged in research to identify benzodiazepine receptors in the brain. Dr. Leo S. Hollister, a Stanford University psychopharmacologist, believes that "benzodiazepine-like material might regulate the so-called 'normal level of anxiety,' just as endorphins may modulate tolerable levels of pain. One could postulate that people with low-level trait anxiety may have adequate concentrations of this natural substance that may lower their anxiety response level.

If this should prove to be the case, it would suggest that people with high-level trait anxiety have been somehow cheated of an adequate supply of this natural substance." [1] Hollister acknowledges that this theory is still "blue-sky speculation," but researchers at Lederle Laboratories, a division of the American Cyanamid Company, say they have identified two benzodiazepine receptors in the brain and have developed a drug that zeroes in and locks onto these sites. Lederle asked the FDA for permission to test the drug on humans. The scramble to develop a better mass tranquilizer than Valium is fueled by the large potential market and by the new research findings that promise, at least vaguely, that there could be developed a drug that zeroes in like a "silver bullet" to the proper anxiety-controlling receptors without affecting other parts of the central nervous system in a scattershot approach. In other words, it is the eternal search for the perfect drug that does only what it is intended to do and does not produce negative side effects.

Drugs such as Valium and Thorazine attack the brain's neurotransmitters like a shotgun blast, which accounts for their harmful and unpleasant side effects—the irreversible disorder known as tardive dyskinesia, which afflicts 20 percent of mental patients being maintained on phenothiazines like Thorazine, and the drowsiness and confusion that sometimes accompany benzodiazepines like Valium. Often, as with the benzodiazepines, the drug companies capitalize on the side effects. The larger dose formulation of benzodiazepine in Dalmane permits Roche to use the drowsiness side effect, unwanted in the daytime tranquilizer, as a primary indication for a sleeping pill.

It also is true that the positive benefits—Valium's use as a temporary bridge over a life crisis—were accidental findings, and the discovery that there might indeed be Valium receptors in the brain came many years after the drug was found to relieve anxiety. In its scatter-gun approach to the brain's chemical system, Valium found the right receptors as well as the wrong ones, if such Valium-like chemical messengers exist at all.

With the new advances in the study of the brain coming "so quickly these days that one can hardly keep up with them," as

[1] Medical Writers Seminar, January 10, 1979, launching the consumer portion of Roche's promotion on the "Consequences of Stress." See Chapter 8.

Hollister put it, drug company researchers are stepping up their search for the magical and thus far elusive formulations that block or stimulate only the right receptors and leave the others alone, thus eliminating harmful or unpleasant side effects. Even such a notable drug researcher as Dr. Nathan Kline, director of the Rockland, New York, Research Institute, is skeptical. "You hope you find the kind of drug that is therapeutic and has no side effects, but the odds are probably about one hundred percent that if there are no side effects the drug is useless," Kline said in an interview, "so that whatever you do, there always is a risk-benefit ratio." This statement aside, Kline has been unabashed in his enthusiasm for a synthetic beta endorphin used experimentally to treat fourteen patients for anxiety and depression. The tests, conducted by Kline and his colleague Heinz Lehmann of Montreal, were not conducted in a double-blind control situation. Kline and Lehmann reported finding no bad side effects, although other researchers have reported finding addiction in animal tests using the same compound. The enthusiasm for the new receptor drugs is unrestrained, despite preliminary doubtful evidence that they are (1) safe and (2) effective. Dr. Mark Gold, a psychiatrist at Fair Oaks Hospital in Summit, New Jersey, told a television interviewer for NBC in October 1978 that clonidine, a drug approved by the FDA for use only to treat high blood pressure, was found to be effective in experiments in blocking narcotic withdrawal symptoms without itself producing dependency or euphoria. With enthusiastic overstatement, the finding was called the "apparently most significant finding in the field of chemical addiction in over 200 years." Gold's research was conducted on just eleven addicts being withdrawn from methadone maintenance.

One of the hottest new drugs on the U.S. market in the late 1970s was Inderal, a beta blocker approved by the FDA for hypertension in 1968 and for migraine headaches in early 1979. Ayerst Laboratories, a division of American Home Products, is anxious to market the drug as a tranquilizer, a use for which the drug is sold in Europe, and has been given permission by the FDA to test the drug for antianxiety properties on humans, a necessary step to seeking approval for marketing in the United States. Dr. Daniel Crane, chief clinical investigator for Ayerst on

Inderal, is confident Inderal will be approved as a tranquilizer and eventually supplant Valium as the nation's number one mass sedative. He contends that Inderal will replace other minor tranquilizers because its beta-blocking property reduces anxiety without producing the euphoric feeling that often leads to abuse and addiction. Among the possible adverse reactions the FDA requires Ayerst to list are congestive heart failure, mental depression leading to insomnia and perhaps catatonia, light-headedness, hallucinations, disorientation, memory loss, vomiting, abdominal cramping, fever, and rash. Clearly, Inderal misses the mark as a "silver bullet" wonder drug, indicating rather the primitive state of the art in developing "natural" drugs that do only what they are designed to do.

In today's home medicine chest, prescription and nonprescription drugs, whether the drug is Valium for anxiety, Ritalin for hyperactivity, or Contac for colds, fill the shelves. The rationale, whether diagnostically sound or not, is that these drugs are helpful in curing ailments or relieving their uncomfortable symptoms. The drugs we take for fun or to enhance or alter our mood for social reasons—to become the "life of the party," to match the beat of a rock concert, to relax from a hard day, or just to experiment—are placed elsewhere. The vodka is in the liquor cabinet, the beer in the refrigerator, the marijuana in a can, the cocaine in a plastic packet in a shoe. There is, in short, a separation, albeit sometimes blurred, between the drugs we take for medical reasons and those we take for social or recreational purposes. But with the development and widespread use of psychoactive medications for mood and mind control, the separation between the drugs we take to alleviate disease and those we take simply because we want to feel better or different is growing increasingly thin. The experimental drugs for medical use now on the laboratory drawing boards might eliminate the separation entirely, confusing medical with social purpose. The physician, as the dispenser of these pills and potions, could become not only the healer of the "sick" but the arbiter of what the "healthy" feel, think, and do.

The extensive research into the chemistry of how drugs interact within this complicated chemical system has put science on the cutting edge of producing new drugs not to treat illness or counter pain, for example, but to control and adjust the human development and experience of normally healthy people. These "life-enhancement drugs," as they are euphemistically called, put us on the frontier of what medical writer Gene Bylinsky calls a "choose-your-mood" society. These experimental drugs would take society well beyond anything envisioned by Aldous Huxley in *Brave New World* and into the "chemocratic" society of science fiction writer Stanislaw Lem's *The Futurological Congress*, where every human function is altered, controlled, repressed, stimulated, and monitored by specific drugs. In his book *Mood Control*, portions of which originated as *Fortune* magazine articles, Bylinsky describes the "coming psychem supermarket" in which drugs, in experimental testing stages, and certain foods will be used to "play the mood-and-emotion keyboard much as a pianist plays notes and chords." Dr. Arnold Mandell, a professor of psychiatry at the University of California, believes the new drugs will bring a new era of preciseness to psychiatry: "Here psychoanalytic observation will be used, if it is used at all, to measure the effects of drugs on the quality of transference relationship, on the patient's memories, and on dreams and fantasies. All of these will be viewed as data from the brain, testifying to its biological status. Blood tests or spinal taps will tell just what pills we need. We will learn to think of ourselves, our personalities, as an orchestra of chemical voices in our heads." [2]

In postulating on new uses for drugs, New York psychiatrist Nathan Kline sees potential for "opening vistas for enlarging man's creating and productive capacities." He foresees the application of drug technology to:

—prolong childhood and shorten adolescence to take advantage of "the period during which the acquisition of knowledge and skills comes most easily";

—reduce or "completely circumvent" the need for sleep to provide "constructive use of these additional billions of man hours every day";

—provide "rapidly-acting intoxicants that produce satisfactory dissociation and euphoria" without the unpleasant and sometimes

[2] Mandell is quoted by Toby Cohen in "Beyond Valium," an article in *New York* magazine (February 5, 1979). An assistant to Mandell said he has put aside drug research in favor of studying "other ways to achieve the same results."

harmful side effects that accompany alcohol, marijuana, opiates, and amphetamines;

—bank and stoke sexual responses "so that temperature and activity could match more closely the appropriate environmental circumstances [and] increase the sum total of pleasure and, at the same time, allow man to devote more of his time, intelligence, and energy to more exclusively human activities";

—control affect and aggression by putting lithium in the water supply, as we do chloride and fluoride, as a health measure—"if it is capable of preventing pathology without circumscribing normal human feelings";

—control the genetic code or chemical messenger functions "to eliminate most gross physical pathology so that deviations so extreme as to be regarded as ugly will no longer occur";

—increase or decrease activity by deferring fatigue or hyperalertness at appropriate times through "natural" products such as those synthesized from plants;

—prolong or shorten memory to enrich life by allowing us "to remember whatever we wished" and "forget those things we had seen or done which were unbearable";

—enhance positive and negative learning experiences that would improve performance and prevent "fatal flawing" by learning "that may well scar the organism for an indefinite period" (Kline adds: "The availability of such inducements to learning would likely alter the total educational process so that the time consumed to acquire any one segment would be greatly reduced and the scope greatly broadened to include character education as well");

—produce or discontinue transference to "turn off" the reaction of a second party much as we use deodorants, mouthwashes, and perfumes "in only slightly disguised form" for the same purpose;

—provoke guilt "relevant to a particular type of situation to prevent its repetition," thereby making punishment "truly rehabilitative and practically instantaneous," or to relieve "unwarranted and destructive guilt feelings" (Kline says it may be necessary for a board "consisting of a judge and a clergyman as well as a psychiatrist . . . to agree that such relief of guilt was justifiable before appropriate medication could be given");

—enhance or inhibit the "juices" which mediate the mothering behavior (says Kline: "There are cases where an increase of this function would be in order, but undoubtedly the greatest use would be in terminating such behavior once it had outlived its usefulness. The human female gets involved in more difficulties—and in turn involves others in problems—more because of excess inappropriate mothering behavior than because of untoward sexual passion or, for that matter, any other emotion");

—extend time for pleasurable experiences and shorten it for "certain experiences which one wishes to have done with as rapidly as possible";

—create conditions of "jamais vu" (novelty) to provide "fresh wonder" to old and continuing relationships and "déjà vu" (familiarity) "to deal more competently with problems that are made more difficult simply because they are new";

—deepen "our appreciation of the beauty which surrounds us and allow us to experience afresh the awe of human existence [so that] we can perhaps better discover—both emotionally and intellectually—the nature of the human venture." [3]

To Kline, an influential psychiatrist who serves on committees of the National Institute of Mental Health and the World Health Organization and was twice the recipient of the prized Mary Lasker Award for his work in psychopharmacology, the development and use of "medications" for the above purposes are an appropriate extension of technology and no more artificial or unnatural than most trappings of culture. "It is an attempt to alter the course of events, whether it's a disease or people who take drugs because they feel they can expand their consciousness. The yoga do it by exercises. I've never seen lions going around doing yoga breathing or standing on their heads. People do all kinds of things to expand their vistas and consciousness. In principle, I don't see that drugs are any more abnormal than reading, music, art, yoga, or twenty other things—if you take a broad point of view," Kline said in an interview. In terms of risks within this "broad" view, Kline feels drugs in and by themselves are less

---

[3] Kline first presented this scenario for drug use in a paper, "The Future of Drugs and Drugs of the Future," published in the *Journal of Social Issues* in 1971. He offered a reprint as a summary of his views for the purposes of this chapter and as background for an interview on the subject.

dangerous to society than the "artificial" capacity to write and read. "What has it done in the long run? It has caused wars. People get killed as a result of reading things. So I would say a habit like the use of books or education has much more actual potentially disastrous side effects. We still really don't know much about what people call advertising or propaganda. Here, I think, the abuse is much greater than it is in terms of medication because of the people who use it. Doctors at least operate within the framework where, in general, they apply whatever they are doing to relieve patients of pain or suffering. It is misapplied at times, and at times they apply substances which later turn out to have had side effects they didn't know about. But the application of something like propaganda or advertising is done without that framework at all. It is done in terms of selling products or getting people to conquer or kill their neighbors or to dominate women or to do all kinds of things of this sort. I don't see that, within this framework, the use of drugs is all that risky."

The day of the chemical society served by a "psychem supermarket" offering a drug for every human moment, mood, and function is no longer a wild sketch of a science fiction writer's vision. A drug that Kline says appears to "be quite good in extending memory and may be useful for it" is in the testing stage. There are no side effects "that we know of with this particular drug," Kline adds. Researchers at Wyeth Laboratories, a drug company, say their research into endorphin, believed to be the brain's natural opiate, indicates "these peptides are the actual source of all reward." Larry Stein, a Wyeth drug designer, believes that "by working with them we might come up with the greatest pleasure drug ever." [4] Researchers at the University of Texas are experimenting with a substance called luteinizing releasing hormone, which they believe may be the brain's natural aphrodisiac. In tests in rats and in humans, researchers at Texas and in Europe have found LRH effective in stimulating or, for that matter, inhibiting sexual response and have reported it can be administered by pill or by a nasal spray. Scientists at Tulane University were able to induce repeated orgasms in a woman by injecting neurotransmitters into her head.

Avram Goldstein, a pharmacologist and director of the Addic-

[4] *Wall Street Journal* (August 12, 1977).

tion Research Foundation in Palo Alto, California, worries about where this tinkering will lead: "The functions of our bodies, the regulation of our behavior by a complex interplay of nervous and hormonal effects, represents the perfection of millions of years of evolutionary adaptation. Whatever roles endorphins play, we can be sure they are regulated with exquisite precision in normal people—the right amount released at just the right places and for just the right length of time. To swamp the endorphin receptors everywhere in the body at once with a high concentration of exogenous opiate can only upset the natural system. As a pharmacologist, I have to reject the notion that by administering this or that drug we can harmlessly improve on Nature, to make us feel better or perform better, to make us smarter or less anxious—and all that without penalty." [5]

Medical science's preoccupation with discovering magical solutions to social problems through chemistry prompted Dr. Leon Eisenberg, chairman of the executive committee of the Harvard Medical School's Department of Psychiatry, to warn fellow scientists that history is replete with proof that there is, in fact, "no pharmacologic free lunch." Citing the experience with amphetamines, which Eisenberg finds useful in a limited way in treating narcolepsy and hyperkinesis but which are also drugs of serious abuse with harmful consequences, he said about the enthusiasm to find a new "smart pill": "I cite the example of the amphetamines as a prototype of what we are likely to discover—namely, effective drugs, useful in a limited range of circumstances, with a potential for misuse proportionate to their potency. If we permit ourselves the luxury of imagining magic substances that enable all takers to learn more rapidly, we enter the realm of science fiction. That may be a stimulating way of posing questions about the human condition, but it violates pharmacologic reality. It invokes visions of letting the genie out of the bottle when there is neither genie nor bottle before us, at a time when our fund of basic knowledge is rudimentary." [6]

Eisenberg's concern is shared by another prominent scientist,

[5] Jack Fincher, "Natural Opiates in the Brain," *Human Behavior* (January 1979).
[6] Paper presented at a conference on "The Future of Neurology and Pharmacology of Learning and Behavior," American Association for the Advancement of Science, Boston, February 20, 1976; reprinted in the *School Review*, University of Chicago (November 1976).

Dr. James L. McGaugh, vice-chancellor of academic affairs and professor of psychobiology at the University of California—Irvine. McGaugh has "few reservations" about developing effective treatments for clearly identifiable disorders of learning and memory but has "serious reservations about developing drugs and other treatments which are to be used as neurobiological aids to the education of people who do not have disorders of learning and memory. We have come to accept the use of drugs as aids to daily living. It would, I believe, be quite easy for us to accept the view that pills for improving learning and memory should be routinely taken along with vitamins, aspirin, and various patent medicines. The question that will be asked is: 'Why not?' There are several answers to this question. First, most of us—including most children—do not need such aids any more than we need the other drugs that we currently overuse. Most of the learning and remembering that we engage in does not need to be aided. Second, such treatments can readily become substitutes for other conditions which aid education. The laboratory studies indicate that animals can learn more readily when given certain drugs. But the same learning can be produced simply by giving animals more training. The drugs do not do anything that cannot be done by providing more experience."

What McGaugh says is true. There are other ways to facilitate learning, but in a society bent on finding and using the cheapest and quickest—the most cost-effective—route to a particular end or the solution of a complex problem, the use of drugs to teach and learn will be irresistibly tempting. Considering the enthusiasm with which educators, doctors, and some parents embraced stimulants such as Ritalin to manage behavioral problems at home but particularly in the classroom, it is not hard to envision the advent of the pharmacologic classroom of the future. In fact, some educators see it as inevitable, and soon. "Look at this little thing about hyperactive children" relative to schools and medication, says James Bosco, a professor of education at Western Michigan University. "You can say this is a foretaste of the future. How we use these devices in schools in 1978 may provide a prologue on how these things are going to be used in 2000." Drugs like Ritalin are crude and primitive compared to what is on the horizon, and Bosco believes teachers will learn sophisticated techniques for application of the new pharmacology in the classroom. "That sounds very Buck Rogers, but I don't think it is one hundred percent crazy that it might emerge," he said in an interview.

In a paper, "Teaching with Drugs," presented at a meeting of the Midwest Philosophy of Education Society in 1974, Bosco speculated on the "awesome potential" for using chemical and electronic techniques to teach and learn: "Future teachers will be trained in a school which is an amalgam of contemporary schools of education, medicine and pharmacy. A considerable portion of the teacher's training will be devoted to understanding physiology and psychopharmacology, which will equip the teacher to use substances which affect learning and learning-related behaviors. Medications will be used for a variety of reasons, such as for pupils who are having difficulty with perceptual discriminations, for pupils with attention malfunctions, for some who have difficulty remembering mathematics facts. The teacher's records will contain information about the types and dosages of medications which the teacher is administering. Each school building will contain a bio-monitor which screens basic physiological functions of children on drug regimes. When physiological processes fall outside of tolerance intervals, a consulting physician can advise the teacher; otherwise, the teacher will continue the drug therapy until the objective has been achieved."

To Bosco, who was interviewed four years after presenting that scenario, it is the "age-old problem of using technology sensibly—when to use psychopharmacology and when not to use it. How not to use it blindly." But referring to his own studies showing that stimulants for hyperactivity often are used blindly today, Bosco says he "kind of worries about Act Two when you see how Act One is going."

The blind side of drug technology is that if chemicals can be created and are economical—whether drugs to make a dullard a genius, to match sexual desire with opportunity, or to change a mood from sad to happy—they not only should be developed but should be used. Not to do so is considered scientific nihilism. To quote Nathan Kline: "I really think that we exist in an artificial world. Culture is artificial. Civilization is artificial. Oil is artificial, if you will, or the use of it. Nuclear power is. Why should we deprive ourselves of potential improvement through physical means as well as through social, psychological, and other means?" The "real problem in the field of psychopharmaceuticals," says Kline, is not the creation of the new classes of drugs but "determining who should make the decisions as to when they should be used, on whom and by whom." Not surprisingly, Kline votes for doctors. "I think they are relatively safe if they are in the hands of physicians. God knows, we are not a perfect profession; but we operate at least in general in a fairly moral framework, and there are enough correctives constantly being exercised that in the long run, I think the outcome is likely to be a favorable one."

As we have seen, teachers will want to play a role, controlling the testing and determining which child needs which drug. Most certainly, the politicians and the bureaucrats will demand a voice. So will the social scientists and the businessmen and the labor leaders, for if we can use drugs to mold mind and mood in a pharmacological cloning process, each special interest will want to clone to suit its purpose. The possibilities are frightening for the individual and for, if you will, the human spirit.

As we have followed the tranquilizing of America, we have seen the individual—the "me" in all of us—get swept aside in a heedless rush for the quick and easy chemical way out. We have seen how each generation of new psychoactive drugs—Valium replacing Miltown, Miltown replacing phenobarbital—is heralded as safer, faster, and more effective than its predecessor. Poorly trained in the content and effect of drugs and heavily dependent on acquiring knowledge about drugs from the manufacturers, doctors embrace the new psychoactive wonders with abandon, and patients welcome the promised relief and presumed safety. As a new drug replaces an old one, eliminating the apparent harmful effects, the broader questions of their use do not get asked or answered. If science can eliminate the addiction potential from tranquilizers, society does not need to confront the problems of stress. If science can give us a new and better "smart pill," society does not need to do anything about the social problems confronting a disadvantaged child at home, in his neighborhood, and in his world. If science can provide a powerful sedative that eliminates the Parkinson-like shakes, society does not have to worry about the ethical questions of warehousing the mentally ill. If science can bring us a pill that will happily sedate the elderly without making them sleep all day, we don't have to worry about our own immortality, and society does not have to concern itself with finding a productive use for senior citizens.

In simple terms, if drugs can do everything for us, we do not need to do anything for ourselves, and we need not take any responsibility for ourselves or our society.

As we approach the day of a drug for every mood, thought, feeling, and deed, we need to ask ourselves whether we want to take the risk of a continual dwarfing of the human spirit by making the "me" the drug in me.

Appendix 1

Prescription Drug Chart

The Twelve Most-Abused Prescription Drugs
(in order of degree of abuse)

Drug	Medical Use	Ill Effects
Valium (*diazepam*)	Minor tranquilizer used to relieve tension and anxiety, treat certain muscle spasms and convulsions, and counter the effects of acute alcohol withdrawal. Should not be used for longer than four months.	Tolerance leading to increased use; may cause psychological and physical dependence. May lessen sexual drive and cause disorientation, trembling. Overdose may produce low blood pressure, depressed respiration, coma, possibly death. Use with alcohol and other CNS drugs increases risks.
Dalmane (*flurazepam*)	Sleeping pill, sedative, and antianxiety drug. Should not be used for longer than two to four weeks as a sleep aid and should never be used as a daytime sedative.	Tolerance; psychological and physical dependence and addiction are possible. May cause confusion, drowsiness, faintness, unsteady walk. Overdose may result in breathing problems, coma, and death. Use with alcohol and other CNS drugs increases risks.
Darvon (*d-propoxyphene*)	Pain reliever.	Tolerance; may cause psychological and physical dependence and addiction. May cause drowsiness, insomnia, euphoria, confusion. Overdose may produce convulsions, depressed respiration, stupor, possibly death. Use with alcohol or other medications increases risks.
Librium (*chlordiazepoxide*)	Minor tranquilizer used to relieve anxiety, tension, and the withdrawal symptoms of acute alcoholism. Should not be used for longer than four months.	Tolerance; risk of psychological and physical dependence and addiction. Overdose may produce somnolence, confusion, diminished reflexes, coma, possibly death. Use with alcohol and other CNS drugs increases risks.

Drug	Medical Use	Ill Effects
Luminal (*phenobarbital*)	Barbiturate used as anesthetic, sedative, anticonvulsant, sleeping pill.	Tolerance; high risk of psychological dependence and addiction. May produce drunken behavior. Overdose may cause coma, fever, loss of reflexes, depressed respiration, possibly death.
Elavil (*amitriptyline*)	Antidepressant.	Serious side effects—especially if taken with other drugs or alcohol—may include high or low blood pressure, disorientation, hallucinations, anxiety, insomnia, tremors, seizures. Overdose may cause abnormal heartbeat, congestive heart failure, severe low blood pressure, stupor, coma, possibly death.
Seconal (*secobarbital*)	Barbiturate used as painkiller, sedative, and sleeping pill. Not recommended for continuous use.	Tolerance; high potential for psychological dependence and addiction. May produce excitement, symptoms of hangover, allergic reactions. Overdose may depress breathing and reflexes, lower body temperature, cause coma, possibly death.
Tuinal (*seco/amobarbital*)	Sleeping pill. Not recommended for continuous use.	Tolerance; high risk of psychological dependence and addiction. Overdose may depress respiration and reflexes and can cause rapid pulse, coma, possibly death.
Quaalude (*methaqualone*)	Sleeping pill and sedative. Should not be used for longer than three months.	High potential for psychological dependence and addiction. May cause headache, symptoms of hangover, fatigue, torpor. Overdose may result in delirium, convulsions, coma, accumulation of fluid in the lungs, possibly death.
Placidyl (*ethchlorvynol*)	Sleeping pill. Not recommended for continuous use.	Tolerance; psychological dependence and addiction are possible. May cause vomiting, nausea, gastric upset, dizziness, blurred vision, numbness. Overdose may result in low blood pressure, difficulty in breathing, abnormal heartbeat, coma, possibly death.

Drug	Medical Use	Ill Effects
Adapin Sinequan (*doxepin*)	Antidepressant.	May cause drowsiness, nausea, vomiting, low blood pressure. Overdose may produce stupor, blurred vision, depressed breathing, convulsions, heart problems, coma, possibly death. Use with alcohol increases danger.
Equanil Miltown (*meprobamate*)	Minor tranquilizer used as antianxiety drug and sedative. Should not be used for longer than four months.	Tolerance; psychological dependence and addiction are possible. May cause drowsiness, dizziness. May also result in slurred speech, excitement, euphoria. Overdose may produce coma, shock, respiratory failure, possibly death.

Other Prescription Drugs Subject to Abuse
(alphabetical)

Drug	Medical Use	Ill Effects
Benzedrine *see* Dexedrine		
Cylert (*pemoline*)	Adjunctive therapy for hyperactive children. For short-term use only; not proved safe and effective for prolonged use.	Tolerance and dependence are possible. May cause weight loss, insomnia, stomachache, irritability, mild depression, nausea, dizziness, headache, hallucinations, liver problems (including jaundice), convulsions. Overdose may cause restlessness and rapid heartbeat.
Demerol (*meperidine hydrochloride*)	Narcotic prescribed for relief of moderate to severe pain. Not for continuous use.	Tolerance; psychological and physical dependence and addiction. May cause respiratory or circulatory depression, respiratory arrest and heart failure, dizziness, sedation, nausea, sweating, fatigue, headache, euphoria, dry mouth, constipation, flushing, fluttering of heart, fainting, inability to urinate, rashes and hives. Overdose may cause stupor, coma, circulatory collapse, cardiac arrest, and death. Should not be used with alcohol and other CNS drugs.

Drug	Medical Use	Ill Effects
Dexedrine (*dextroamphetamine sulfate*) Benzedrine (*amphetamine sulfate*)	For narcolepsy; as adjunctive therapy for hyperactive children (high risk for minimal gain); for obesity (use as a diet pill involves high risks for doubtful gains; some states have prohibited use of amphetamines for treatment of obesity).	Highly addictive. Tolerance leads to psychological and physical dependence. May cause insomnia, hyperactivity (speeding), personality changes, psychosis often clinically similar to schizophrenia, high blood pressure, dizziness, euphoria, tremors, headache, dry mouth, diarrhea, constipation, upset stomach, weight loss, impotence and other changes in libido. Overdose may cause rapid respiration, confusion, combativeness, hallucinations, panic, convulsions, coma, death.
Haldol (*haloperidol*)	Major tranquilizer used for management of symptoms of psychotic disorders; used also for control of tics and uncontrollable vocal utterances.	May cause drowsiness, dizziness, fatigue, insomnia, confusion, inability to perform routine tasks, irreversible tardive dyskinesia (uncontrollable movements of tongue, face, and jaw), bronchial pneumonia, dehydration, tremors and shakes. Use with alcohol and other CNS drugs substantially increases risks.
Limbitrol (*chlordiazepoxide and amitriptyline*)	Fixed combination minor tranquilizer (Librium) and antidepressant.	Tolerance leading to increased use and psychological and physical dependence. May cause drowsiness, blurred vision, dizziness, dehydration, constipation, impotence, tremors, confusion, loss of appetite, fatigue, high and low blood pressure, skin rashes, jaundice, headaches. Overdose may cause congestive heart failure, stupor, coma, and death. Use with alcohol and other CNS drugs increases risks.
Lithium carbonate (*a natural salt compound*)	For control of manic episodes of manic-depressive psychosis.	Blood poisoning can occur at doses close to therapeutic levels. Toxicity risk high in persons using diuretics. May cause tremors, dry mouth, upset stomach, fatigue, No known antidote for toxic overdose.

Drug	Medical Use	Ill Effects
Mellaril (thioridazine hydrochloride)	Major tranquilizer used for management of psychotic disorders, such as schizophrenia, and management of symptoms of senility. Widely used to control aggressiveness in disturbed and retarded children, but has not been proved effective for this use. Not recommended for anxiety.	May cause drowsiness, blurred vision, dry mouth, constipation, nausea, vomiting, sexual dysfunction, breast enlargement, loss of appetite, jaundice, sensitivity to sunlight, agitation, heart failure, irreversible tardive dyskinesia. Use with alcohol and other CNS drugs increases risks.
Prolixin (fluphenazine hydrochloride)	See Thorazine.	See Thorazine.
Ritalin (methylphenidate hydrochloride)	Amphetamine used as adjunctive therapy to other remedial measures (psychological, educational, and social) for hyperkinesis in children; also for narcolepsy.	Tolerance; psychological and physical dependence possible. In children, may cause loss of appetite and weight, abdominal pain, insomnia, abnormal heart rate, nervousness, rashes, pain in joints, nausea, anemia, hair loss, agitation, tremors, dizziness, blood pressure changes (up or down). Overdose may cause overstimulation of CNS, resulting in convulsions and coma, euphoria, confusion, hallucinations, delirium, palpitations, cardiac arrhythmia, hypertension.
Serax (oxazepam) Tranxene (clorazepate dipotassium) Verstran (prazepam)	Minor tranquilizers similar to Valium and other benzodiazepines, used to relieve anxiety. Should not be used for longer than four months.	Tolerance; may cause psychological and physical dependence. May lessen sexual drive, cause drowsiness, dizziness, headaches, disorientation. Overdose may result in breathing problems, weak and rapid pulse, coma, possibly death. Use with alcohol increases risks.

Drug	Medical Use	Ill Effects
Stelazine *(trifluoperazine hydrochloride)* Chemically similar to Thorazine	*See* Thorazine.	*See* Thorazine.
Talwin *(pentazocine hydrochloride)*	Potent analgesic for moderate to severe pain. Not for prolonged use.	Tolerance, psychological and physical dependence and addiction. May cause nausea, diarrhea or constipation, abdominal distress, loss of appetite, dizziness, drowsiness, euphoria, headache, nightmares, insomnia, fainting, blurred vision, hallucinations, sweating, chills, flushing, hives, difficult urination, low blood pressure, rapid heartbeat. Overdose may cause difficult breathing, coma, and death. Use with alcohol and other CNS drugs, including methadone, increases risks.
Thorazine *(chlorpromazine)*	Major tranquilizer used for management of severe psychotic disorders. Sometimes used but not proved effective for hyperactive children, for alcohol withdrawal, for mild to severe cases of anxiety, or to reduce pain.	May cause drowsiness, fainting, jaundice, breast enlargement, dry mouth, constipation, convulsive seizures, irreversible tardive dyskinesia, cardiac arrest, immobilization of cough reflex causing death by aspiration. Use with alcohol and other CNS drugs substantially increases risks.
Tofranil *(imipramine hydrochloride)*	For symptoms of depression; sometimes prescribed but not proved effective for treatment of bedwetting in children.	May cause high or low blood pressure, rapid heartbeat, heart attack, stroke, fainting, confusion, hallucinations, delusions, anxiety, agitation, insomnia, nightmares, numbness or tingling, loss of balance, tremors, ringing in ears, dry mouth. Use with alcohol and other CNS drugs increases risks.
Tranxene *see* Serax		

Drug	Medical Use	Ill Effects
Triavil *(perphenazine and amitriptyline)*	Fixed combination major tranquilizer (a phenothiazine) and an antidepressant used for symptoms of depression and anxiety in severe forms.	Serious side effects possible, including tremors, shakes, irreversible tardive dyskinesia, skin rashes, jaundice, low and high blood pressure, dehydration, headaches, vomiting, constipation, blurred vision, eye damage, palpitations, myocardial infarction, stroke, confusion, hallucinations, anxiety, delusions, nightmares, tingling, dizziness. Overdose may cause congestive heart failure, stupor, coma, and death. Use with alcohol and other CNS drugs increases risks.

Verstran
see Serax

Appendix 2

Where to Get Help

For Pill and Alcohol Addiction

Alcoholics Anonymous
General Services
468 Park Avenue South
New York, N.Y. 10016

The general services office will send information on alcoholism upon request. There are AA chapters everywhere, usually listed in the white pages of the telephone book.

National Council on Alcoholism
733 Third Avenue, 14th Floor
New York, N.Y. 10017

The council is a good source of information on alcoholism and treatment programs, and local county chapters can be found in most areas. The council, however, provides no information on dual addiction, taking a head-in-the-sand position on pills.

Women for Sobriety
P.O. Box 618
Quakertown, Pa. 18951

This is a new self-help group for women only.

Pills Anonymous
P.O. Box 473, Ansonia Station
New York, N.Y. 10023

Modeled after AA, PA is just beginning to spread outside New York.

Association of Halfway House Alcoholism Programs of North America
786 East 7th Street
St. Paul, Minn. 55106

A guide to day or residential rehabilitation programs.

Information on Childbirth, Maternal and Paternal Care

American Foundation for Maternal and Child Health
30 Beekman Place
New York, N.Y. 10022

The International Childbirth Education Association
P.O. Box 10852
Milwaukee, Wis. 53220

National Association of Parents & Professions for
  Safe Alternatives in Childbirth
P.O. Box 267
Marble Hill, Mo. 63764

American Academy of Husband-Coached Childbirth
P.O. Box 5224
Sherman Oaks, Calif. 91413

American Society for Psychoprophylaxis in Obstetrics
1411 K Street NW, Suite 200
Washington, D.C. 20005

For Children

Closer Look
P.O. Box 1492
Washington, D.C. 20013

An HEW clearinghouse for information on childhood ailments, resources, legal rights, and special programs.

Council for Exceptional Children
1920 Association Drive
Reston, Va. 22090

Association for Children with Learning Disabilities
4165 Library Road
Pittsburgh, Pa. 15234

Feingold Association of the United States
759 National Press Building
Washington, D.C. 20045
    or
Vickie Giraldi
56 Winston Drive
Smithtown, N.Y. 11787

National Coalition for Children's Justice
66 Witherspoon Street
Princeton, N.J. 08540

National Association for Down's Syndrome
P.O. Box 63
Oak Park, Ill. 60305

National Association of Retarded Citizens
2709 Avenue E East
Arlington, Tex. 76011

For the Elderly

National Council on the Aging
1828 L Street NW
Washington, D.C. 20036
Research, resources, and services.

National Council of Senior Citizens
1511 K Street NW
Washington, D.C. 20005
Primarily a lobbying organization.

Retired Professional Action Group
200 P Street NW, Suite 711
Washington, D.C. 20005
A Ralph Nader activist group.

Gray Panthers
3700 Chestnut Street
Philadelphia, Pa. 19104
A rapidly growing organization of senior citizens with local affiliates in
most states.

American Association of Homes for the Aging
1050 17th Street NW
Washington, D.C. 20036
Represents nonprofit nursing homes.

General Health Information

Boston Women's Health Book Collective
332 Charles River Road
Watertown, Mass. 02172

National Women's Health Network
Parklane Building
2025 I Street NW
Washington, D.C. 20006

Health Research Group
2000 P Street NW, Suite 708
Washington, D.C. 20036

The Ralph Nader health watchdog; the public's best advocate on health matters in Washington.

Appendix 3

Suggested Reading

Prescription and Nonprescription Drugs

Physicians' Desk Reference
Medical Economics Book Division
Box 554, Oradell, N.J. 07649

The *PDR* is the standard reference book used by doctors for information on prescription drugs, which are indexed by brand, generic, and product classifications. The company discourages sales to the public but copies are available in most libraries. Be aware that the drug descriptions in the *PDR* are supplied by the drug manufacturers, who pay for the listings; and in some cases, the labeling information does not conform to FDA requirements.

Prescription Drugs and Their Side Effects
by Edward L. Stern
Grosset & Dunlap ($3.95, paperback)

An analysis of the 150 most frequently prescribed drugs as tabulated by the New York State Pharmacy Board.

The New Handbook of Prescription Drugs
by Richard Burack, M.D., with Dr. Fred J. Fox
Ballantine ($2.50, paperback)

First published in 1967, this handy reference book was revised in 1975. In addition to providing basic information on drugs, including negative scientific findings not found in books relying on manufacturers for information, this handbook provides generic and brand price comparisons, a good index, and an introductory course on the drug industry's control over the flow of information to the medical profession.

√ *The People's Pharmacy*
by Joe Graedon
Avon ($3.95, paperback)

A good guide to both prescription and nonprescription drugs, common-sense self-treatment programs, and easy-to-understand explanations of common ailments.

The Medicine Show
by the Editors of *Consumer Reports*
Pantheon ($.95, paperback)

Another excellent home reference book on prescription and OTC drugs, home remedies, and pricing information. Originally compiled in 1961, *The Medicine Show* was updated in 1976.

Nonprescription Drugs and Their Side Effects
by Robert J. Benowicz
Grosset & Dunlap ($3.95, paperback)

Includes a guide to the 500 most commonly used OTC drugs.

A Doctor's Guide to Non-Prescription Drugs
by Dr. Morton K. Rubinstein
Signet ($1.95, paperback)

Describes how to identify symptoms of common ailments and what to do about them. Provides ample warnings of the dangers of drugs and debunks the misleading claims of manufacturers.

Handbook of Non-Prescription Drugs
American Pharmaceutical Association
2215 Constitution Avenue NW
Washington, D.C. 20037
Available from the APA ($7.50)

A good reference book on what's in OTC drugs but not very strong on adverse reactions.

OTC Handbook
Medical Economics Book Division
Box 554, Oradell, N.J. 07649 ($8.95)

This new OTC drug handbook by the company that produces the *Physicians' Desk Reference* will be available in bookstores in 1980.

Prescriber's Guide to Drug Interactions
Medical Economics Book Division
Box 554, Oradell, N.J. 07649 ($8.95)

This pocket-size guide to drug interactions covers twenty-three categories of drugs and their interactions, including alcohol, tranquilizers, barbiturates, and vitamins. It is available by writing the publisher.

Women

Our Bodies, Ourselves
by the Boston Women's Health Book Collective
Simon and Schuster ($4.95, paperback)

One of the most important books a woman can have in her home reference library. It is written by women for women.

The Hidden Malpractice
by Gena Corea
Jove ($1.95, paperback)

Documents discrimination against women by doctors, hospitals, and medical schools.

Women & Madness
by Phyllis Chesler
Avon ($2.25, paperback)

A well-documented and sensitive account of how women are victimized by the mental health establishment.

I'm Dancing as Fast as I Can
by Barbara Gordon
Harper & Row ($8.95, hardcover)

One woman's personal account of getting hooked on Valium, her agonizing and painful cold-turkey withdrawal, and her victimization by the mental health system.

Turnabout: Help for a New Life
by Jean Kirkpatrick
Doubleday ($6.95, hardcover)

Dr. Kirkpatrick tells how she achieved sobriety after twenty-seven years of drinking and offers a program for other women, Women for Sobriety, as an alternate to Alcoholics Anonymous.

Women and Drugs
Special Bibliographies No. 4
National Clearinghouse for Drug Abuse Information
National Institute on Drug Abuse
P.O. Box 1908
Rockville, Md. 20850 (free)

A good source of available literature on women and drugs, including brief abstracts.

Children

The Myth of the Hyperactive Child
by Peter Schrag and Diane Divoky
Dell ($2.25, paperback)

Exposes the propensity of educators and doctors to label children as sick and then drug them to keep them under control. An excellent source of information with an extensive appendix.

Why Your Child Is Hyperactive
by Dr. Ben F. Feingold
Random House ($7.95, hardcover)

Feingold outlines his belief that hyperactivity can be caused by artificial food flavorings and colorings, and provides an additive-free diet and practical advice on how to follow it.

A Sigh of Relief
produced by Martin I. Green
Bantam ($6.95, paperback)

An illustrated first-aid handbook for childhood illnesses and injuries.

Something's Wrong with My Child
by Milton Brutten, Sylvia O. Richardson, and Charles Mangel
Harcourt Brace Jovanovich ($7.50, hardcover)

Contains useful information on hyperactivity, learning disabilities, and other childhood problems, but, in our view, the authors are much too enthusiastic about the use of drugs for treatment.

Learning Disabilities: A Family Affair
by Betty B. Osman
Random House ($8.95, hardcover)

Written primarily for parents, this book includes a valuable appendix, including resource guides, dos and don'ts on diagnostic testing, legal rights, and income tax deductions.

The Elderly

Why Survive? Being Old in America
by Dr. Robert N. Butler
Harper & Row ($5.95, paperback)

The most informative book available on the elderly and their mistreatment by the medical profession, nursing homes, and government agencies. Includes an excellent appendix of resources.

The End of Senility
by Arthur S. Freese
Arbor House ($8.95, hardcover)

Exposes the myths of senility and tells how the elderly can deal with anxiety, hypertension, and other common problems without excessive reliance on drugs.

Over 55 Is Not Illegal
by Frances Tenenbaum
Houghton Mifflin Co. ($7.95, paperback)

A good source book for the elderly.

General

Mind Control
by Peter Schrag
Pantheon ($10, hardcover; paperback also available)

An exposé of methods, including drugs and surgery, being used to control thought and feeling.

Suffer the Children: The Story of Thalidomide
by the Insight Team of the *Sunday Times* of London
Viking ($12.95, hardcover)

The untold story of how an "ideal" sleeping pill came to the market, only to be found in fact a killer and crippler of children.

✓ *200,000,000 Guinea Pigs*
by John G. Fuller
G. P. Putnam's Sons (available in most libraries)

This sequel to the book that was instrumental in the enactment of the original Food and Drug Act describes how the public is the loser as a result of the powerful control the drug industry has over the medical profession, Congress, and the FDA.

Index

Division of Health Facilities Standards and Surveillance, 185
Mental Hygiene Medical Review Board, 159
nursing homes in, 174
New York State Association for Brain Damaged Children, 93
New York Times, 219, 223, 245, 270
Nixon, Richard M., 245, 248
Nonprescription drugs. *See* Over-the-counter drugs
Nordmann, Ronald, 252, 253
Norris, Dr. Frances, 229, 281, 282
Nursing homes, 174–79, 180, 181–82, 184–85, 188, 211–12
Nutrition Foundation, 138–39
Nyquil, 52, 259
Nytol, 52, 256, 260, 263–64

Oakley, Dr. Godfrey, 109
Opium, 12
Ornex, 259
Ortho Pharmaceuticals, 202, 224
Ostrower, Roland, 135–36
Our Bodies, Ourselves (Boston Women's Health Book Collective), 92
Over-the-counter drugs, 12, 52, 229, 255–83
alcohol and, 52
elderly's use of, 164, 169
for pregnant women, 82
statistics on abuse of, 11–12
See also names of drugs
Oxazepam. *See* Serax
Oxytocin, 87, 88, 92–95

Pace, Dr. Nicholas, 267
Packwood, Robert, 258
Page, Milton, 223
Painkillers, 11, 19, 21, 164, 173, 256, 260, 285, 299–304 *passim. See also names of drugs*
Panalba, 245
Parke, Davis, 92, 207, 224
PCP, 270
Pennsylvania State University, 265
Pentobarbital. *See* Nembutal
Percodan, 173
Percy, Charles, 179
Pfizer Laboratories, 79, 204–5, 224, 225
Pharmaceutical Manufacturers Association, 191*n.*, 209, 229

Phenobarbital. *See* Luminal
Phenothiazines, 19, 82, 143, 153, 154, 156, 217, 285, 286. *See also names of drugs*
Phenylpropanolamine hydrochloride, 274
Physicians' Desk Reference (PDR), 38, 92, 98, 218–19, 240
Physicians Radio Network (PRN), 203–4
Pills Anonymous, 8, 29, 30
Pines, Wayne, 38
Pink Sheet, 232, 245
Pitocin. *See* Oxytocin
Placidyl, 300
statistics on use and abuse of, 10
Plotkin, Robert, 160, 161
Pommerenck, Kenneth, 188–89
Pondimin, 233
Pregnancy and childbirth, drugs used during, 19, 82–111, 115–16, 141, 241–42
"Prescribing Valium and Other Drugs" (Waldron), 14
President's Commission on Mental Health, 284–85
President's Committee on Mental Retardation, 151, 152, 153
Prevost, Dr. James A., 159
Procter & Gamble, 138, 261
Product Marketing magazine, 256
Prolixin, 157, 303
Promethazine, 88
Proprietary Association, 250, 255, 256, 282
Psychiatric News, 199, 221–22
Psychopharmacology, 278
Psychotropic drugs, 9, 12, 101, 258
alcohol and, 56. *See also* Sedativism
elderly's use of, 164–89 *passim*
new developments in, 284–97 *passim*
See also names of drugs
Public School 205, Manhattan, 135–36
Pursch, Dr. Joseph A., 8, 12, 28, 30, 31–34, 42, 49–50
Purvis, William, 216
"Put Her Down on Drugs: Prescribed Drug Use in Women" (Fidell), 67
Pyrilamine, 279

Quaalude, 10, 300
Quarzan, 213
Quiet World, 256
Quinlan, Karen Ann, 42–43